# A World Turned l

## *A Spiritual Pilgrimage*

### *by Rosemary E. Radley*

*"Friends and family are captivated by Rosemary's laughter"*

Published by
Erlanger Press
4 Beechwood Road
South Croydon
Surrey
CR2 0AA

Copyright @ 2015 Rosemary E. Radley.

The author has asserted her right to be identified as the author of this work in accordance with the Copyright, Designs and Patents Act 1988

All rights reserved. No part of this publication may be reproduced, stored in a retrieval system, or transmitted, in any form or by any means, electronic, mechanical, photocopying, recording or otherwise, without the prior permission of the author.

All Scripture quotations, unless otherwise indicated, are taken from the Holy Bible, Revised Standard Version, copyright @ 1946, 1952, and 1971. National Council of the Churches of Christ in the United States of America. Used by permission. All rights reserved.

ISBN No. 978-0-9933170-0-2

# ACKNOWLEDGEMENTS

I take this opportunity to thank most sincerely the Rt Revd Christopher Chessun, Bishop of Southwark, for his Foreword to my autobiography.

Thanks are due, in no small measure, to the labours of Gordon Drayson, my computer buff, as I call him. He has laboriously prepared the manuscript and the photos for their inclusion, and much else in readiness for the book's publication.

I thank Robert, my husband, for all the help he has given me by reading through the manuscript and making useful suggestions.

I thank Fr Michael and Daphne Brotherton, also Fr Patrick Phelan for kindly reading my manuscript and making helpful suggestions.

I thank the many friends who have encouraged me in the writing of the book.

# FOREWORD

The autobiography of Rosemary Radley offers a fascinating insight into her life and especially her journey of faith. Every Christian has a story to tell, usually of joys and sorrows in this life and the way in which these impact on their spiritual life. Rosemary's story is especially interesting because it reflects an exploration that covers a number of different experiences within the established denominations and later with a profound awareness of the blessing of the Holy Spirit.

The bigger picture of Rosemary's life is described from her birth just after the start of the Second World War in inner South-East London through to the present day. It is a story that is a mix of pain and struggle and at times great adversity. The honesty with which she describes her life is central to the story as it unfolds. There is humour and a lightness of touch, which characterises every page as a rich narrative emerges.

Running through the text is a vivid description of the parts of South-East London that Rosemary has lived in and the rapid changes in successive decades. The reader is able to enter into the reality of the picture that is painted and almost to taste and see what life was like in the different periods that are covered.

Rosemary describes a life that has been far from easy due to serious illness and the death of two husbands after short marriages. With great honesty, the narrative is nevertheless firmly rooted in hope and the abiding importance of the Christian faith throughout.

An important part of the story is the support that is given by different clergy. Rosemary describes turning to them for spiritual support and guidance, which are central to the making of a good life.

Alongside spiritual support they are able to see the whole person and to understand the medical challenges – which Rosemary has met with courage and determination.

# Foreword

We all have a story to tell and in this autobiography we are given insights that will resonate with many readers. We are reminded that it is our lives and varied experiences that make us the people we are. At the heart of this book is the life of one person who has lived through times of good and ill, yet Christian faith has sustained her in every circumstance, something for which we can all rejoice and give heartfelt thanks.

*The Rt Revd Christopher Chessun*
**Bishop of Southwark**


The Rt Revd Christopher Chessun, Bishop of Southwark, was introduced to the House of Lords in December 2014. He will sit on the bench of the Lords Spiritual.

# INDEX

Acknowledgements .................................................................... 3
Foreword ..................................................................................... 4
Index ........................................................................................... 6
Preface ....................................................................................... 9
A World Turned Upside Down ................................................ 11
1 - A Hole In The Head ........................................................... 13
2 - Hatcham, Here I Come! .................................................... 15
3 - Wartime Blackheath I ........................................................ 23
4 - Wartime Blackheath II ....................................................... 35
5 - Wartime Blackheath III ...................................................... 45
6 - Evacuations, Here, There And Everywhere ..................... 55
7 - Now The War's Over ......................................................... 61
8 - Boxing Day At Denmark Hill ............................................. 73
9 - Genuine Victoriana ............................................................ 79
10 - Blackheath High School .................................................. 87
11 - On The Move Again! ....................................................... 91
12 - Disaster Strikes Again ................................................... 101
13 - Beautiful Thoughts To Horrible Thoughts .................... 105
14 - On Pilgrimage To Ethiopia ............................................ 117
15 - An Affirming Visit To France ........................................ 123
16 - St Giles' Church, Farnborough, Kent ........................... 127
17 - We Seek Medical Help .................................................. 131
18 - A Dark Night .................................................................. 137
19 - A Heart Of Stone Into A Heart Of Flesh ...................... 143
20 - Ward 2 At The Maudsley .............................................. 147
21 - The Czech Connection .................................................. 151
22 - Almost Back To Square One! ....................................... 157
23 - Second Conversion Experience ................................... 159
24 - Preparations For Holy Matrimony ................................ 169
25 - The Swinging Sixties? Never! ....................................... 173
26 - Derek And I Are Wedded At St Joseph's ..................... 175
27 - Under The Surgeon's Drill And Knife .......................... 185
28 - Overwhelmed By The Spirit And Problems Galore .... 191

29 - Grand Mal Seizures Strike Me Down ........................................... 201
30 - Holy Spirit Renewal (1) ................................................................. 207
31 - Holy Spirit Renewal (2) ................................................................. 211
32 - A Most Fulfilling Post ................................................................... 221
33 - First Widowhood ......................................................................... 225
34 - Widow Meets Widower ............................................................... 231
35 - Shattered! .................................................................................... 239
36 - My Third Marriage ...................................................................... 243
37 - The Years Restored ..................................................................... 245
38 - Wanted Yet Not Wanted ............................................................. 251
39 - In The Womb Of The Conference .............................................. 253
40 - A Conversation With Father X ................................................... 255
41 - The New Millennium .................................................................. 259
Finale .................................................................................................. 263

## Addenda
1 - Unexpected Encounter At The Old Bailey ................................... 265
2 - Coffee At The Grand Hotel, Fraserburgh .................................... 269
3 - The Nursing Sisters Of St John The Divine ................................. 273
4 - Adventures In Language .............................................................. 277
5 - Saint Teresa of Avila .................................................................... 281
6 - Pope John XXIII And The Second Vatican Council ................... 285
7 - Wartime Rationing ....................................................................... 287

A World Turned Upside Down

# PREFACE

Everyone has a book inside them, so we are told. This is Rosemary Radley's book.

Rosemary was born in 1939 at the start of the Second World War, in Hatcham, an area of New Cross in South-East London, The chosen title of her memoirs, *A World Turned Upside Down*, is the name of a public house about a mile up the road from where she was born, not that she nor her immediate family patronised the establishment! But the name was familiar and it occurred to her that it was an apt description of her life and so, for her autobiography.

She visited the public house for the first time, fairly recently, in the hope of finding out something of its history and the origin of the name.

At times, Rosemary has been given the impression that some assume she has swanned through life without a care - far from a life that has forever been turned upside down. She trusts her autobiography, relating occasions of sorrow and joy, darkness and light, will set the record straight.

It transpires that there is a family connection - nothing disreputable, she assures us!

"The vicissitudes of the Second World War have set the seal on my life," Rosemary declares. "I was born into war and it's been battle ever since!"

She tells of some of the battles she has had to face and, by the grace of God, the victories achieved.

Rosemary was too young to remember the London Blitz of 1940, but she lived through it and has included entries from her mother's diary relating what the family went through in the Blitz. However, from 1942 onwards she has many memories of the War, vivid and varied.

There was much that Rosemary witnessed in wartime Blackheath and she looked to her mother for help. As the barrage balloons were raised up into the sky, the sirens started to wail, a bomb exploded round the corner, and later, the doodlebugs were flying overhead, Rosemary blithely plagued her with many a question, expecting 'instant' explanation.

Rosemary is a Londoner born and bred – she has been called a London sparrow! From both sides of the family, she has Scots blood in her: Rosemary was a Sutherland before she married, and still is a Sutherland, of course. Her mother was an Anderson. Rosemary's grandparents and Great-grandparents have made contributions: from Wantage in Berkshire, Warminster in Wiltshire, Guildford in Surrey etc.

Epilepsy has blighted Rosemary's life. The Sutherland motto, *'Sans Peur'* (*'Without Fear'*) helped her as she ploughed her often lonely furrow, especially when she entered the Dark Night of the soul, feeling utterly abandoned by God.

Rosemary realises that most people have their ups and downs. Generally, it is two steps forward and one step back, but in Rosemary's life her experience has sometimes been the other way round - one forward and two back! Just when everything seemed to be going well a great chasm has opened up, which entailed climbing down, and then climbing up the other side - which proved to be even steeper. Everything seemed to be going fine, only for disaster to strike again. Time and again, her world was turned upside down, and her faith sorely tested.

Rosemary relates how, through failure and later inner healing, she has known transformation in her spiritual life, which she trusts has made her a better witness to Jesus Christ.

She would like to take this opportunity to extend her gratitude to the many people who have helped and encouraged her, in ways great and small, on her pilgrimage through life, so far - too many to mention by name.

## A WORLD TURNED UPSIDE DOWN

The public house called 'The World Turned Upside Down' lies at the North-West end of the Old Kent Road. The pub was almost destroyed in June 1995 when fire ripped through it. It was later restored.

The unusual name was familiar to Rosemary, though neither she nor any member of her family had previously darkened the portals of the establishment, that is, until Rosemary made her way there fairly recently, when she met the licensee, who was serving behind the bar. Before posing her questions Rosemary thought it *politique* to order a drink:

"A gin and bitter lemon, please."

The licensee duly obliged, and her enquiries commenced:

"I'd be grateful if you could tell me the history of this pub and the origin of its unusual name?"

The licensee gathered up his thoughts and wistfully replied as best he could:

"I'm afraid little is known of the pub's history. I took it on after the fire and had it refurbished. The paintwork was green before the fire, but I've had it painted red because the locals consider green unlucky!"

"Can you tell me how the pub got its name?" Rosemary enquired again.

"I'm told this is the site of the last point before victims embarked for deportation from the docks. Here they could take their last drink before departing for Australia, the place where the world is turned upside down!"

This was all he could say on the matter.

Rosemary finished her drink, thanked the licensee and said Goodbye, just a little disappointed that he hadn't been able to furnish her with more history of 'The World Turned Upside Down' before the fire.

The public library opposite gave Rosemary a print out of the insertion of the pub in the 'Dictionary of Pub Names'. There are two others with the same name, but an especial mention is made of "The World Turned Upside Down in London, SE1." It states that the origin of the name is biblical, taken from Chapter 17 of the Book of Acts, written by St Luke, where he relates the preaching of Paul and Silas in Thessalonica. When Paul said, "This Jesus, whom I proclaim to you, is the Christ" (v.3) some Thessalonians believed, but others reacted angrily saying, these Christians "have turned the world upside down" (v.6).

The Dictionary entry also states that, "This London pub had a sign showing a man walking to the South Pole!"

"So what?" you might ask!

On Rosemary's visit to 'The World Turned Upside Down' when she had hoped to learn more of the pub's history, she had been unaware that the pub sign held personal significance.

**Rosemary relates what she was to learn later:**
"Not far from 'The World Turned Upside Down' pub, a certain Walter How was born on Christmas Day 1884, in Drummond Road, London, SE1.

"I was already aware that Walter How was my Grandmother Anderson's first cousin; and that Walter had accompanied Ernest Shackleton, the explorer, on his last expedition to the Antarctic, 1914-16. Walter was Shackleton's trusted right hand man on *s.y. Endurance*. He was the people's local man!

"Initially, it hadn't occurred to me that 'the man shown walking to the South Pole' was a depiction of Walter How, my first cousin twice removed."

Rosemary returned to the 'World Turned Upside Down' to have another look at it and to study the pub sign. She was too late. The pub had been closed down and the pub sign had gone, too!

N.B. The name of the pub is certainly of Christian origin. There was a ballad called 'The world turned upside down', originating in the 1640s, as a protest against the Puritans of the time. They tried to reverse tradition and turn Christmas from a time of celebration into a time of dour solemnity, which was against what seemed to be the natural order of things. With the restoration of the monarchy, Christmas was once again a time of joyful celebration.

As you read Rosemary's story, you'll understand why this theme of a world turned upside down is significant for her. So many times has her personal world been turned upside down by events beyond her control.

# Chapter 1

# A HOLE IN THE HEAD

## *Into the Operating Theatre*

The long-awaited day drew nigh: the date of my brain surgery.

This, surely, was the answer to my prayer to end my suffering. For years, my life had been blighted by epilepsy, and an operation seemed the only answer.

I also looked forward to the possibility of a long past memory being recalled.

Down in the pre-med room, I lay on my left side and watched the 'cruel barber' mercilessly shearing off my hair from the right side of my head in readiness for the operation. Jokingly, I castigated him,

"Look what you're doing, cutting off all my beautiful locks!"

A local anaesthetic was administered and Rosemary, the 'shorn lamb', was duly wheeled into the operating theatre 'alive' (well almost!) to what was about to take place. You see, I had agreed to be awake for this operation, so I could respond to the surgeon's questions.

Mr Falconer and his theatre team were standing round the operating table to welcome me. Still lying on my left hand side, a nurse covered my eyes by firmly tying a bandage from one side of the operating table to the other side. Next, she tied both my hands together at the wrists, in front of me, and securely fastened them to the side of the table. A wise precaution, I suppose, to prevent the possibility of a hand instinctively reaching up to my head and jolting the surgeon's hands!

As preparations continued, a doctor was sitting close by my head, ready to give an encouraging word, as and when necessary, at critical moments in the procedure going on above me. I was glad he was there, not just for his presence and for his calming words, but because I lacked a free hand to deal with a quite unexpected problem: a tantalising itch on my cheek in need of a scratch!

Have you ever had an itch on your face needing to be scratched, but had neither hand free to deal with it? Well, that was my predicament! I had to ask this kindly doctor to scratch the itch for me, which he graciously did! Much easier said than done, trying to direct another's finger to the exact spot. I had to give him directions:

"Up a bit, down a bit, a bit to the left, down a bit further." I felt a little stupid.

Before the operation proper, there was quite a long session of drilling holes in my skull, interspersed with sawing between the holes, then came more drilling and more sawing, more drilling and more sawing, till the moment came for the surgeon to give me a word of warning:

"You will hear a crack in a moment!"

I waited.......

C-R-A-C-K!

A tremendous crack rang out in the rafters of my head, almost deafening me in the right ear! I'm glad I'm not squeamish.

The piece of skull was duly removed, revealing the scar on the brain, that had to be cleaned up."

There were a few further but smaller cracks - presumably because there hadn't been a clean break! I forgot to ask afterwards.

The surgeon then began work on my brain.

That was 1961. I'll return to this later. But it's time now to turn back the clock to the beginning.

## Chapter 2

# HATCHAM, HERE I COME!

### *Mummy's perfect Poppaloo – me!*

I was born at the start of the Second World War - a time when the world really was turned upside down by turmoil and conflict - at No. 100 Erlanger Road, Hatcham. What an appropriate name, for the place to be born!

Hatcham is the original name of the whole area in South-East London, known today as New Cross. When asked for my place of birth, it's simpler to say New Cross, the name by which it's better known today. However, Hatcham is the older name, derived from the Anglo-Saxon, meaning 'Hacci's village'.

Whenever my mother told someone that "we'd moved to New Cross before the War", she liked to add, "when it was respectable!" She recalled the area when practically every household had a live-in maid. A friend's father told me recently that "Pre-World War Two, Erlanger Road was considered classy!"

With the start of the Second World War my parents had to make a difficult decision: whether or not to be permanently evacuated from London for the course of the War. They were advised that were they to stay, the possibility of being killed by a bomb was fairly remote (no one knew the Blitz was coming!). However, the prospect of finding themselves in some unknown part of the country held no appeal - they decided to stay.

I can well believe that the Sutherland motto, *'Sans Peur'* ('Without fear') and the Anderson motto, *'Stand Sure',* were subtle influences on my parents' decision to remain in London.

I am exceedingly grateful for their decision. It means I can truly say, "I'm a Londoner, born and bred" - no disrespect to Scottish forebears and the many others that have contributed to my being, from up and down the country!

My parents were married in 1936 (not that that is a memoir!) in St Catherine's Church, Hatcham, near the top of Erlanger Road. They'd had a house especially built for them in Blackheath. They didn't move in straightaway:

they let Peg, my father's sister, and Pat, her fiancé, live there instead; they hadn't been able to find anywhere to live, because of the War, This meant, much to my mother's sorrow, that after their marriage, they had to live at No. 100 Erlanger Road the home of my mother's parents and grandparents, for much longer than originally envisaged, that is, until Peg and Pat had found a place.

My mother told me much later of the frustration her exile had caused her:

"After Daddy and I had got married I was so looking forward to living in my lovely new house in Blackheath. Whilst I quite understood that Peg and Pat needed somewhere to live, I was fed up that *we* weren't able to live there. We had worked hard saving up to buy the house. Also, I was hoping that you'd be born in Blackheath."

In the event, I was hatched in Hatcham!

My mother experienced further frustration. Much later, of course, she told me quite openly, how she had deferred having a baby in 1938 because there were rumours of war at the time. Her frankness surprised me, for generally she found mention of intimate things difficult. Come 1939, she found herself faced with the very situation she'd hoped to avoid: the country on the brink of war and she on the brink of giving birth - to me, her first born.

Before that, my dear Mama had yet another crisis to face - no mid-wife! This must have struck another fearful chord in her worrisome heart, to add to the existing unknowns of the situation. The local authority informed her,

"All nurses have been called up for immediate duty because of the War, so none is available. It was suggested that she "Try contacting the Nursing Sisters of St John the Divine. Their House is in Watson Street in nearby Deptford." She duly did.

(See Addendum 3 for more on the Sisters.)

Providentially, the nuns of this Anglican Community were all trained midwives, and came to my mother's rescue - and mine! Thanks to the Sisters, I was safely delivered, on the 25th September 1939, at No.100 Erlanger Road, three weeks after the start of World War Two. My contact with an Anglican Religious Community couldn't have come much earlier! I can say again, this time with wry amusement, that "nun was available".

There were four generations residing in that Hatcham house: my Stevens

Hatcham, Here I Come!

Great-grandparents, my Anderson grandparents, my Sutherland parents and me!

## Fear and frustration!

For seven months of the nine since conception, at this crucial time, all my mother's fears and frustrations were being communicated to me – fear of the War, frustration at being a new mother at such a terrible time, frustration at not living and having me in her own house etc. This would have consequences for me fifty years later. (See Chapter 37: Wanted Yet Not Wanted.)

Thanks to the Sisters, I saw 'the light of day'. My mother told me I was born at the unsociable hour of 4.15 a.m. so it must have been 'the dark of night' I saw! I don't mean that jokingly – so much of my life has been enrobed in darkness. There have been moments of light – at times, intense spiritual light – yet, more often than not, darkness has prevailed.

*Four generations on the female side of the family.*

The following quote from Psalm 139 has a certain prophetic ring about it!

"If I say, Peradventure the darkness shall cover me: then shall my night be turned to day. Yea, the darkness is no darkness with thee, but the night is as clear as the day: the darkness and light to thee are both alike.

For my reins are thine; thou hast covered me in my mother's womb."
(Psalm. 139. vv.10 -12)

That year, the 25th September fell on a Monday. I don't put much confidence in the ancient rhyme, but in the doubtful possibility that it holds a grain of truth I can claim to be Fair of Face! That *is* said jokingly!

*Mummy holding me in the garden of No. 100 Erlanger Road*

## Baptism at St Catherine's Church

My Baptism took place at St Catherine's Church, Hatcham. Rosemary Elisabeth (with an 's') were the names chosen.

Mummy told me later:
"It was Nana's suggestion that you should be called Rosemary."
"Why did Nana want to call me Rosemary?" I asked.
"Because she liked the name!" came the swift reply.
(A silly question, really.)

## The Rosemary tendency

Presumably, the herb rosemary grew in profusion in days of yore: 'The Rosemary Branch' is a public house, still extant, in nearby Lewisham Way; and there used to be 'The Rosemary Branch Tavern' in Rosemary Road, just over the border into Peckham; neither of which remains.

*Champagne and cake after my Baptism – my Father holding me, Grandmother Anderson, and Great-grandmother Stevens (far right)*

My grandmother liked the name, no doubt. I do wonder if she was aware of the rosemary tendency in the area, subtly prompting her to suggest the name for me.

I was duly baptised, 15th October 1939, Rosemary Elisabeth in the Name of the Father, the Son, and the Holy Ghost. I still have my Certificate of Baptism, so don't remember the event, I was only twenty days old.

My mother recalls it in her diary:

**15th October,** Today is Rosemary's christening day. She cried all morning.

After lunch she was put in her christening robe and looked most angelic. She wore my christening robe and didn't murmur all the time in church, even when the Revd Fenton poured holy water over her head three times. Rosemary remained good for the rest of the afternoon, while we had champagne and christening cake."

The day of my Baptism, 15th October, happens to be the Feast Day of St Teresa of Avila, the Spanish Carmelite nun, not that my parents were aware of that nicety. I have a certain affinity with St Teresa and my baptismal date seems providential.

My mother continued to keep a diary, of my progress during the War, relating facts, printable and unprintable, relating my eating, sleeping, crawling activities, etc. etc.

She also gives interesting wartime events that inconvenienced our life during the Blitz and the bombs that fell nearby.

## The trek from Hatcham to Blackheath

Peg and Pat moved out of our Blackheath house, 61 Langton Way, having finally found a flat. My parents, with me in tow, could now move into my mother's "lovely new house".

Heavy furniture must have been already *in situ* but many personal effects had still to be transferred. They walked, assisted by my mother's parents, with all their belongings and all 10lbs of me, from Hatcham to Blackheath – quite a distance!

Being only five months old, obviously I don't recall that day either, but my mother relates the trek in her diary:

**Feb. 4th 1940** Sunday afternoon saw the great trek to Blackheath. Mummy and Daddy helped us carry bags. I carried Poppaloo [*me!*] and my arms nearly broke.

She slept in her own room for the first time. Rosemary is a happy baby. She laughs a lot."

It is with some amusement, I read that when various aunts and uncles and others called to inspect the latest member of the Sutherland clan,

"the audience was captivated by Rosemary's laughter!

"When the nurse visited us at Blackheath, my mother continues:

"Rosemary laughed at her from the Karri-cot, but objected to being picked up.

"Nurse says, 'She's perfect'. Of course, we think she is.' "

Little did my mother know how sadly disillusioned she was to be with her "perfect" Poppaloo!

## The marriage of Auntie Peg and Uncle Pat

Peg and Pat had found a flat, and were unable to have a church wedding, again because of the War. Instead, they were married at Camberwell Registry Office. My mother's diary shares a vignette of the ceremony:

**14th June 1941** Went to London for Peg & Pat's wedding.

Rosemary is nineteen-months old and is just beginning to walk.

She was dressed in her new pink coat and bonnet.

Rosemary disgraced herself in church [sic] saying, "Cuckoo" in the middle of the "I will" part!

Lots of kisses for Rosemary at the reception!"

As the bride's only niece, I was commissioned to make a formal contribution to the day. (You've just read my informal contribution!) The bride and groom were just leaving the building and I was at the door, waiting to give the bride a posy. Unaccustomed, though I was, to standing on ceremony, I think I fulfilled my duty with a certain aplomb. The photo of the event shows a gracious Auntie Peg receiving my formal contribution to her day, with other members of the family looking on appreciatively. Unfortunately, any aplomb I might have had looks doubtful, seeing Mummy so close behind, ready to give me a steadying hand!

Understandable, I suppose, considering I'd only just started to walk!

*Making my formal contribution to the bride*

# Chapter 3

# WARTIME BLACKHEATH I

## *"You can't possibly remember the War!"*

The prospect of a second world war with Germany was doubly dreadful to the people of Great Britain, for when the Declaration of War was made, it was only 20 years after the end of the First World War with Germany, described then as "the war to end all wars". Memories of the dreadful *debacle* of the trenches and the terrible slaughter of millions of our courageous young men were still fresh in people's minds. Also, the destitute women left behind, having lost husbands and *fiancés*, brothers and fathers.

During the Second World War I recall the grown-ups discussing the disbelief they felt when they heard the formal announcement, 'We are at war with Germany!' - "How dreadful – another war, so soon, so close? I could hardly believe my ears. But, here we are - war it was, and is!" Such were the understandable woeful sentiments of nigh disbelief.

Wartime Blackheath, wartime London, wartime Great Britain was a world of wailing sirens, exploding bombs, barrage balloons and doodlebugs, interminable queues and ration books. These and much else governed our everyday life. This was the only world I knew, after life in the womb – and even that had been disconcerting!

### Historic Telegraph Hill Park

Opposite No 100, on the other side of Erlanger Road lay, and still lies, Telegraph Hill Park: so-called because it was the last of a long line of semaphore stations linking the South Coast with the Admiralty. It conveyed the news of Nelson's victory at the Battle of Trafalgar.

Recently, the Park was refurbished for the Queen's Jubilee.

On one of our visits back to No. 100 to see the grandparents and Great-grandparents, a photo was taken of me outside the house, wearing a pair of not very *chic* green dungarees. I was about three years old.

*Outside No. 100 Erlanger Road in my green dungarees.*

## My memories of the War

This book was started, as a result of a woman chatting with three others, not *that* much older than me, who, on learning that I was born at the start of World War Two, informed me, in patronising tones:

"Oh! You were born in 1939? You can't *possibly* remember the War!"

I gave my mildly indignant reply:

"Well, I do! Of course I remember the War. My wartime memories are vivid and varied!"

If I'm honest, I think I felt *very* indignant by this sweeping assertion that I couldn't possibly...!

It decided me to put pen to paper to recall my many memories, hence this book was unwittingly commenced!

Wartime Blackheath I

My first ever memory of the War was in April 1942. I was 2½ years old I was walking up the Royal Arcade in Norwich with Mummy. That was my *very* first memory - more of that later.

I can identify my first memory in wartime Blackheath as the day my sister, Alison, was born, 28th September 1942 - three years and three days after I was born. That is only the start – there's much more to come of this, too.

What follows are my memories as a little girl, who was 5½ years old when the War ended, in May 1945. My memories give the background to my formative years and how the events of World War Two influenced my subsequent life and thinking. They are totally personal, unless mentioned otherwise, such as the relevant events recorded by my mother in her 1939/1941 diary. Whilst I have tried to be historically and chronologically accurate, I don't pretend to have related memories as an historical and chronological record.

I would add, I have never read a book on WW2 and there is no one around now to prompt me.

As is well known, central London and the London docks on the River Thames took the worst of the bombing. New Cross was not exactly central London, but The Surrey Docks, now re-designated Surrey Quays, were not far away. The bombing in South-East London was unremitting.

I don't pretend to remember the London Blitz, I was only one! My mother describes in her diary something of how life was for us in the Blitz and how a bomb fell at the end of the garden adjoining the garden of the house in Erlanger Road; and that we were assailed by an air raid, even on a visit to far-off Westerham!

I set out below, my mother's jottings in her diary, relating her memories of what we lived through in the Blitz:

In 1940 London went through the Blitz and suffered greatly. A bomb had fallen in the garden of the house in Waller Road, adjoining the end of the garden of No. 100 – literally, a bit too close to home!

During the Blitz and after, there was bombing night and day.

**August 18th** A warning went off while I was shopping with Rosemary. I ran home as hard as I could, bumping her over the unmade stony length of Langton Way [the eastern end].

**August 28th** Early Friday morning, bombs and gunfire before the siren sounded.

Picnic on Hosey Common, Westerham, with an air raid thrown in.

Terrific gunfire. Lay under the trees with Rosemary.

Two more warnings on Sunday with some gunfire. We sat in the passage on the floor and ate our dinner, with Rosemary crawling on the floor.

**Sept. 1st** In and out of shelter all the week with air raids.

*The family with baby sister Alison*

**Sept. 9th** Air raids getting worse and worse. Bombs in Charlton, Eltham and Welling.

All-night raids. Noise wakens Rosemary. Wonderful hot weather but too good for air raids.

**Sept. 22nd** Rosemary sleeps comfortably under the stairs, while we are in the passage on mattresses. She enjoyed her first steamed pudding."

## Comings-and-goings at No. 61 Langton Way, Blackheath

September 1942, three days after my third birthday, something different was happening in the house: there were many mystifying comings-and-goings.

The doorbell rang and I was told it was Dr Mizen, who left after a short visit. And later, I was told that Nurse Alison had just been and gone. I knew something was happening upstairs in the little front bedroom. I had no idea what.

Then baby Alison, so-named after the mid-wife, was brought down and introduced.

## The sunshine didn't last long

Alison and I had a song, popular at the time of our respective arrivals.

Mine was 'Run, Rabbit, Run'; Alison's was 'You Are My Sunshine!'

Alison became grisly because, unknown to us at the time, she was feeling unwell. We were always singing *her* song, but the sunshine didn't last long, for when Alison was 2½ she caught Pink Disease. She was very ill and became even more grisly. Her hands and feet went bright pink, and her hair fell out in clumps. She would curl a lock of hair round her fore finger and without even a tug, out came the hair! We tried to stop her, but we couldn't always be around. She would pull her hair out in bed at night when, obviously, no one was present to take her hand away from her head.

Whenever we sang the 'You are my Sunshine' song to her sitting in her high chair or playing in the playpen with our meagre toys, her grisly face lit up with a sunny smile in recognition,

As a result of the Pink Disease, Alison's lungs and bronchial tubes were badly damaged. She was left with a dreadful, unstoppable cough, which has never left her – even to the present day!

Much, much later, it transpired that the pills prescribed for her illness contained mercury, and the pills had caused the Pink Disease.

## Further memories of the War years

We, in Blackheath, had more than our fair share of bombing because Blackheath was in the direct flight path from Germany to London. My poor mother had to cope with my constant questioning.

## Our Morrison/Sutherland shelter

At the start of the War, every household was issued with an air raid shelter for protection from air raids; each had the choice of either a Morrison shelter to be erected indoors, or an Anderson shelter to be erected out-of-doors. We had a Morrison shelter.

Because the Anderson Grandparents had an Anderson shelter, I wanted to know, "Why don't we call ours a Sutherland shelter?"

"No,! such was Mummy's firm response. "The Morrison shelter is named after Herbert Morrison, the Government Minister in charge of issuing both kinds of shelter." I felt obliged to forget my novel idea

The Anderson shelter was made of corrugated iron, and had a rounded roof. If air raids were forecast for the day when we'd intended going to see the grandparents, our visit was usually postponed. So, I never went into an Anderson shelter and have no expertise on the subject.

A friend has since told me that half the Anderson shelter was above ground, and that the floor was about four feet below ground. Fitted benches were installed but were very uncomfortable.

The Anderson shelter possibly offered greater protection than the Morrison, but when the air raid siren went off on a cold winter's night and the occupants of the house had to make a stumbling sortie into the cold dark night, perhaps in pouring rain, no lights permitted, because of the blackout - its distinct disadvantage must have made them wonder if they had made the right choice!

Whatever its name, our Morrison shelter was erected in our front room. It was a metal 'cage-like'- structure: 6ft 6ins long, from back to front, 4ft wide; and about 2ft 9ins high, surrounded from top to base by mesh squares of about 2" x 2", giving it the cage-like appearance. (Exact measurements given to me by Robert, my husband!) It had a flat, flimsy metal roof, and I had strict instructions:

"Now you must *not* walk on the flat roof, and it's *not* for playing games on!" The temptation was always there and, suitable though it looked for both possibilities, I managed to resist.

When the siren sounded, we dived into our Morrison shelter. It gave a sense of security but the protection afforded was limited. I recall my parents' discussion on the matter, from which I learnt that if the house received a direct hit there would be little chance of survival; and if a nearby house received a direct hit, the Morrison would only help to stave off shrapnel and smaller *debris*. In the event, neither happened!

We grew accustomed to that ominous wail of the siren, during the day and the night, and the sound of bombs exploding, bringing destruction to someone or something somewhere. Apart from a barrage balloon being raised skyward, giving us a long-term warning sign, we never knew for sure about a possible air raid until the siren sounded.

## Quite a scary moment

My father was called up and he joined the RAF. He was employed as a maintenance fitter and was stationed, wherever needed, at various aerodromes around the country. He had certain weekends off, when he would come home. Mummy, Nana, Alison (in the pram) and I stood at the top of the slope at Blackheath Station, waiting to meet him off the train.

Usually this was uneventful, but on one occasion the siren started to wail, and suddenly there was a tremendous bang! A bomb had fallen near to the Blackheath Post Office, under 200 yards from where we were standing. A profusion of *debris* showered down upon us: Mummy bent over baby Alison, and Nana bent over me, to save us from getting hurt. The ground was thickly covered with *debris* of all kinds, as were Mummy and Nana! I think that was the nearest I'd been to a bomb when it actually went off. Quite a scary moment.

"Daddy will soon be here," Mummy reminded me, I suspect to take *her* mind as well as mine, off the bomb explosion. It wasn't long after the shock of the bomb exploding, that Daddy's familiar whistle, the 'Laurel and Hardy' signature tune, was heard as he walked up the slope. He'd been completely unaware of the bomb having just gone off, until he reached us at the top and beheld our predicament. He was not a little disconcerted to find us standing there in the aftermath of a bomb explosion, covered in and surrounded by *debris*, - not hurt, just a bit shaken.

## My AFIZ cross

I had a little gold cross and chain that I always wore round my neck, just in case I got separated from Mummy. The cross was inscribed, somewhat sacrilegiously, with my Identity Number, starting with AFIZ.

After the War was over, Mummy explained.

"It gave me great peace of mind to know that you could be easily identified and restored to me, were you to be found amongst bomb damage rubble by somebody else."

Fortunately, this never occurred and none of our family was "bombed out".

In general conversation, the cross was referred to, rather flippantly, as Rosemary's AFIZ cross – it sounded a bit too much like a fizzy drink!

AFIZ has remained with me ever since, as part of my National Health Number.

## German prisoners of war

Mummy delighted in going down to Blackheath Village, as did I. It had, and still has, atmosphere; historical and welcoming. The Village welcomed us two or three times a week, air raid warnings permitting.

Now and again, as we crossed the Heath, we would encounter a small contingent of dishevelled men being unceremoniously marched across the Heath on the other side of the road and in the opposite direction. To me, they appeared gruesome.

"They're *Germans! German* prisoners of war!" Mummy informed me in low, threatening tones. "They live in the Nissen huts on the Heath. But there's nothing to be frightened of. We're quite safe!" she quickly reassured me of this, to allay the concern shown in my face, on learning that the men were *Germans*. I found it hard to believe that these were the very men who'd been dropping bombs on us.

### Later on – the doodlebugs

Later on in the War the V-1 rockets, otherwise known as doodlebugs, were the bombs that Hitler sent over, to destroy and to kill. Their destination was indiscriminate - they would drop anywhere.

One night, we were woken up by the siren's ever-ominous wail in that awful "minor key", ascending and descending, ascending and descending, on and on it went, warning us of an imminent air raid. The doodlebug was soon droning above us, its deep chugging sound very recognisable.

"So long as we can *hear* it, we're safe! There's no need to worry. It's only if the doodlebug cuts out, that we need to worry!" Mummy gave me a word of assurance. "When the droning stops, the rocket falls on whatever is below."

Silence can be golden or it can be ominous. The silence of waiting under the doodlebug droning above, was an uneasy silence, not knowing if this doodlebug might be the one that would cut out and fall on *us*. Each time, we had to accept that "this could be it. Obviously, we were spared – I am here to tell the tale! Great was the relief when we were certain that the drone had passed over us and we knew the doodlebug wasn't for us. We could breathe again. But it was with mixed emotions when we knew it must have dropped to earth somewhere, leaving us wondering where? And what had been hit? And who, this time, might have lost their life, house and home?

Before clambering up the stairs and getting back into bed, it was always wise to wait in the air raid shelter for the high-pitched note of the official 'All Clear' to sound out through the dark of the night. And the nights were *very* dark with wartime blackout conditions prevailing - not a chink of light to be seen.

On another night, the wail of the warning siren started. Out of bed we scrambled, and down to the air raid shelter we went. Not long after our descent, the All Clear sounded – it must have been a false alarm. Back into bed we clambered, when suddenly the warning siren went off again, prompting urgent parental commands at my bedroom door:

"Come on, quick, wake up! The siren's going again." This time, there was greater urgency in Mummy's voice.

Out of bed I got - fast, dressing gown quickly donned again, and a quick flit down the stairs, for the second time that night, wondering,

"Why, so soon after the All Clear had sounded?" Again, we huddled together in our Sutherland, sorry, Morrison shelter, gripped with foreboding, helplessly clutching our gas masks for the second time that night.

We waited… and waited… and waited… with the growling drone of the doodlebug overhead getting closer and closer. Again, we were spared! And with the All Clear again ringing in our ears, back to bed we went. Twice in one night seemed a bit much, with such a short time between.

## Gas masks go with us everywhere

It was rumoured that Hitler might use gas, not that I understood at the time what that really signified. Each one of us was provided with our own gas mask, just in case.

I've been told since that mine was a Mickey Mouse gas mask. Truly, even though my gas mask went with me everywhere, I have no recollection of it being a Mickey Mouse one. Presumably, they considered it appropriate for a little girl, but this little girl was unimpressed. I don't recall it, in the least. My memory is of the grown-ups' masks, which I considered were more the real thing. I'd dismissed my Mickey Mouse one, as childish, not to be taken seriously.

## Doodlebug search gets Mummy scolded

A third memorable night was when we gathered in the shelter listening to the ominous growl of a doodlebug overhead. We sat there waiting on tenterhooks, again hoping that this wasn't to be the one that might cut out and drop on us. But, drop somewhere, it did, of course. Next morning, Mummy seemed more intrigued than usual to know where it had fallen. She had the idea that it was possibly in the New Cross area.

"Let's go and see if we can find out where the doodlebug fell and see what damage has been done," she suggested. Perhaps she was silently worried about the safety of her parents and grandparents.

Unexpectedly, on our way home from our venture out, we met Mr Shirley on the No. 53 bus, the father of my mother's best friend at Aske's school. Mummy greeted him and went on to explain the purpose of our outing that morning:

"We sat in the shelter last night as a doodlebug was going overhead. I've just taken Rosemary to see if we could find out where it landed."

With that, he gave Mummy an uncalled for scolding:

"You shouldn't take Rosemary to see that sort of thing!" he said angrily. "It's not good for her!"

He really did give Mummy such a ticking off, quite unnecessarily. When Mummy saw her mother next day, she complained bitterly about it. She didn't think she had done anything wrong. Nor did I! I felt really sorry for Mummy. Our outing didn't greatly distress me. I took it in my stride. I'd already seen many a bomb-damaged house lying in ruins, and I'd witnessed the dreadful plight of people who had been bombed out, made homeless and forced to become squatters. Terrible, yes, but it was all part of my everyday experience.

Ironically, Mummy's unjustified telling off has remained in my memory more than the damage caused by the previous night's doodlebug, that we'd gone out to find. I'm not sure that we did, in fact, discover for certain where it had fallen!

## Not all gloom and doom!

Amidst the doom and gloom of wartime Great Britain, there was a lighter side to life.

I was having fun playing in the garden. I sat innocently on the low red brick wall surrounding the circular pond at the end of our Langton Way garden. I was leaning over, trying to catch a goldfish in my hand, when I leant too far, lost my balance, and fell headfirst into the cold water. My dear Mama standing at the kitchen window witnessed my sudden departure from sight and rushed out to the rescue. The water wasn't that deep. The rescue was successful!

### The Garden of Stainton Lodge

The row of five new houses, of which ours was one, were built in 1936, on what had been the garden and stables of Stainton Lodge, a Grade II Listed building, still extant on the corner of Stratheden Road and Shooters Hill Road. Thanks to our house having been built on the Stainton Lodge garden, we had a mature pear tree on the left hand side and a mature apple tree on the right, both halfway down our garden.

With the burgeoning of spring, Mummy issued another stricture:

"The bulbs will soon be coming up between the pear tree and the apple tree, so you mustn't walk between the two trees. If you do, you'll spoil the bulbs and we'll have no flowers. Don't forget! Be sure you walk round the other side of the pear tree or the apple tree."

I did my best to remember because I didn't want to spoil the array of beautiful crocuses and daffodils that would soon burst forth; it was all too easy to run across, unthinkingly, the bulbs being invisible!

## Chapter 4

# WARTIME BLACKHEATH II

### *'Waste not, want not'* – *this motto I would teach*

### Wartime blackout

Another aspect of life in wartime Great Britain, that had to be adhered to by everyone, was what became known as 'the blackout'. Every household, office, factory, etc. was responsible for doing its bit to ensure that every light in the land after dark was extinguished or blacked-out. For this, the Government issued every establishment with black material, from which a set of blackout curtains was made-to-measure to fit every window. To maintain 'the blackout' the curtains had to be in place *every* evening to cover up *every* chink of light, so preventing the pilot of an enemy 'plane seeing the land below.

In late autumn and the winter months when the days were drawing in and darkness fell early, Mummy had to keep an eye on the time, and our enjoyment of Blackheath Village had to be curtailed. It was essential that we got home in time to put up the blackout curtains.

"Come on, we must be quick; it will soon be dark!" Mummy would exclaim, looking at her large antiquated wristwatch. "We *must* get home to put up the blackout curtains before it gets dark!"

In those days, if one small chink of light was visible, the tin-hatted air raid warden would be at the door to inform the occupants, with urgent instructions to cover up the offending chink.

I think we always managed to get back home before darkness fell. I don't believe we ever had the warden come to the door of No. 61, but the threat was there if we were lax in putting up our blackout curtains. Falling bombs were not the only invasions of the War – our lives were also invaded by austerity of life.

Shopping was a hit-and-miss affair, disrupting our lives in a different sort of way from falling bombs! Shortages were endemic: all basic food, clothes, fuel and even soap were in short supply and on ration. We listened to the news bulletins on the wireless to find out if there'd been some hoped for increases in our various rations - it was not beyond the realm of possibility that there would be decreases!

When air raids were always a possible threat, we would switch on the wireless to hear the air raid forecast for the day. If it sounded bad, we had to think seriously about the shopping expedition we'd intended to make.

On one particular day, the forecast was uncertain about air raids, so Mummy considered it was worth going out and hoping for the best:

"The wireless has suggested we *might* expect air-raids today; it wasn't certain. We've run out of several things, so I think we must chance it. We need vegetables and we're low on flour, sugar, butter and eggs; also, we're on our last loaf of bread. It's best to go shopping in the morning before the shelves get emptied." Hoping she had made the right decision, Mummy continued in a concerned voice.

"Let's get ready to go - the sooner we go, the better," she added, hastily.

So, off we went, to join the inevitable queues, with ration books: fawn for adults, green for children, and blue for babies, all predictably deposited in Mummy's shopping bag. Each book contained "points" for our food rations and coupons for our clothes ration, essential items to have with us whenever we went shopping. The "points" in each ration book were little squares of paper which determined the amount we were permitted to buy each week, and which had to be cut out on the purchase of the commodity they represented. How paltry were the amounts permitted then each week, compared with what we are accustomed to today! (See Addendum 6)

## Mummy forgets to phone the coal merchants

We were some way along Stratheden Road, on our shopping trip, when suddenly Mummy remembered that she hadn't phoned the coal merchants.

"I didn't phone Charrington's to order our coal for next winter. I completely forgot!" I promised Daddy I'd do it before the end of August. I'm afraid we must go back, to be sure that we get our winter coal delivery at the summer price." She couldn't afford not to, in more ways than one. "I'm sorry, we must go home. If I don't make that phone call Daddy will be cross! I must put in the order to-day," Mummy insisted.

Oh dear! We had to walk back to the house. As soon as we got home Mummy duly made the essential phone call to place our order for winter coal - the very day before the offer closed. Mummy could now relax!

Our food shopping expedition was postponed until the morrow when, we left to join the inevitable queues.

The first queue of the day was at Bason's, the greengrocers at the top of Westcombe Hill, run by the two elderly Bason brothers. When we got to the front of the queue, they greeted us cheerily; the elder brother always wore his shabby old cloth cap; the younger of the two wore a fairly respectable straw hat. Vegetables purchased, Mummy paid the bill to their sister, known as Miss Bason, her dark brown hair drawn back in a neat bun, sitting at the till near the door.

Next, we walked up the Old Dover Road, passing The Roxy on the left hand side, a small cinema of ill-repute which drew a disapproving "Tut, tut" from my mother. "It's a fleapit!" she told me, disparagingly. Later, the Roxy received a direct hit. Mummy shed no tears when she learnt it was not to be rebuilt.

It was in December 2013 that I learnt that a Marks & Spencer store had been built on the site of The Roxy. Mummy would have been glad to know that!

Our second queuing experience of the day was usually Parker's, the fishmongers, further up the Old Dover Road, also on the left. We had set out with the firm intention of buying fish at Parker's first, but there was *such* a long queue. Groan! We were faced with a decision of great consequence! Should we join the queue at Parker's now, or get our groceries and meat first and return for our fish later? A real dilemma!

"Look at that queue! Let's get our groceries first," Mummy suggested. "We'll go back later to get the fish, when the queue's shorter."

Both Ortons and Aylitts were a bit further on, in Dellacourt Road, as it was then, off to the right. We were registered with Ortons for our grocery rations and with Aylitts for our meat ration. Even so, we couldn't be sure that what we wanted would be available; it was often "Hobson's choice".

The queue at Ortons was not too daunting, so we joined it and quickly got to the front. Mummy handed over her order for bread, eggs, jam, cornflakes, a little sugar, and margarine this week instead of butter.

"It's your birthday in a few weeks' time," Mummy reminded me, as if I *needed* reminding! "I must consider *now* the ingredients I'll need for your cake. We'll have to go without certain items in the meantime, and save them up for later," she warned. "I'll order margarine today, instead of butter, and for the next three weeks."

With a special event coming up, such as my birthday, a long discussion ensued with the lady serving us, whose job it was to ensure that Mummy would have sufficient ingredients when the day of the cake-making session came.

As this crucial discussion went on, I looked behind us and saw the queue was getting longer and longer! But we couldn't leave until the lady behind the counter had performed the unenviable task of calculating the right number of "points" that Mummy would need, for the birthday cake ingredients, Calculation done, she then painstakingly cut out our "points" from each ration book, for *this* week's order.

"Well, Mrs Sutherland, I think we have calculated correctly, for you to have all the necessary ingredients for Rosemary's cake, in three weeks' time!"

What a palaver!

Groceries purchased, we crossed the road to Aylitts to buy our meagre meat ration – two scraggy lamb chops and some mediocre beef sausages, no disrespect intended to Mr Aylitt, the butcher, that's how things were in the War.

We made a speedy return to Parkers, which produced further abject groans! The queue had gone and so had all the fish!

"Oh dear, we were stupid!" said Mummy, crossly. "We should have bought the fish before getting our groceries." Even if we had joined in order to buy the fish first, so long had been the queue it was quite possible that Parkers might have run out of fish before we got to the front. One never knew. Dilemma and disappointment were part and parcel of life in wartime Britain!

Queuing, quite rightly, meant first come, first served – it was the only way of ensuring fair play in the sale of scarce goods. It was more than a person's life was worth if she or he dare jump the queue.

## Queuing is the order of the day

Queuing was a daily discipline for shoppers in the War, and an exercise

in patience. We had to queue for practically everything. People would see a queue when they had no idea what the queue was for - they joined it, all the same, just in case! Often, it only became apparent what the shop was selling that day when purchasers emerged with their goods and told the patient souls outside at the front of the queue. Even if the shop was selling something that patient souls were in need of, the shop could easily sell out before they reached the front. One had to be prepared for the shopkeeper's final announcement:
"Sorry, we've sold out! We're shutting up shop now."

So started the habit, the pastime, of queue forming, for which the English seem to be renowned: a habit that sadly, seems to be a fast disappearing today, especially when waiting for a bus! Surely, even in today's very different circumstances, it's only fair, that the person who has waited 25 minutes should be allowed on the bus before those who have waited only five minutes or, sometimes, just arrived!

At the end of our morning's shop, and assuming we had successfully shopped at the fishmonger's first, which was usually the case, we made for home along to the end of Dellacourt Road, turning right down the stonier eastern end of Langton Way, and then across Stratheden Road to our house.

## Waste not, want not!

'Waste not, want not' was the motto of the day, especially at mealtimes! The daily diet was monotonous and our meagre food rations had to be eked out for the coming week. *Everything* put in front of us had to be eaten up, almost till the enamel was scraped off the plate. In those days, children's plates and mugs were made of enamel - plastic had been invented but was yet to be used for making such things as children's plates, bowls, mugs, etc.

"Eat up all your food," we were instructed by our parents, who then added in threatening tones, "If you don't eat it all up, that's all there is!" And it wasn't an empty threat, either – it was true.

Corned beef was on the menu *ad nauseam*: my abiding memory was, corned beef for lunch, corned beef for tea, and next day, yet more corned beef." Mummy did her best to serve it up in different guises, trying to make the dish more acceptable, but it couldn't really be disguised: the fact remained – it was corned beef!

The 'waste not, want not' maxim applied to all aspects of life, not just food. Nothing was taken for granted. Nothing was thrown away. "We might not get any more!" This applied even to small remnants of soap. Mummy's instruction was:

"Don't throw away the end pieces of a bar of soap. Collect them up and put them in the jar on the kitchen windowsill, with all the other little pieces of soap. When we've collected enough we'll make a 'new' bar out of all the bits."

Below is the *'Waste Not, Want Not!'* rhyme, as I remember it:

> *Waste not, want not!*
> *This motto I would teach,*
> *Let your watchword be despatched*
> *And practise what you preach.*
> *Never let life's chances,*
> *Like sunbeams, pass you by*
> *And never waste the water*
> *Until the well runs dry.*
>
> *Dearly beloved brethren,*
> *Is it not a sin,*
> *If, when you peel potatoes,*
> *You throw away the skin?*
> *The skin feeds the pigs,*
> *And the pigs feed you.*
> *Dearly beloved brethren,*
> *Is it not true?*

## Family leisure pursuits on the Heath

The Heath was, and still is, a much-frequented place for informal leisure activities: fathers and sons kicking footballs or flying kites; girls playing rounders or doing handstands; mothers and families picnicking on the grass; others sailing boats on the Prince of Wales pond near the Princess of Wales public house in Pond Road; and yet others just enjoying a leisurely afternoon walk.

Much of this was in abeyance because of the War and would only return when the War ended. I loved riding my little blue bike across this vast expanse of grass surrounded by gracious Georgian residences, including The Paragon, widely admired for its unique architecture.

Now and again, a certain local young woman, by the name of Clare Cotton, could be seen cantering her horse across the Heath, her blonde hair streaming out behind. Clare Cotton on horseback was a well-known sight.

The New Argosy, halfway down Tranquil Vale, was Mummy's favourite haunt. She could never resist a bit of window-shopping as she looked at the limited array of china, glass, etc. She was always hoping to see pieces to add to her 'Pink Thistle' tea service, which she treasured, given to her for a wedding present; but she was never to find any further pieces, the War had abruptly stopped its manufacture. Sometimes, her eyes alighted on a piece of china that appealed. She looked longingly, yet hesitantly, - she cut short her gaze, and turned away, muttering,

"No, I mustn't!" Money was scarce, and was to be spent on essentials only.

A little further down, we stopped off at Henkels, and bought Chelsea buns for tea, food points permitting; next was Jobbins, opposite Blackheath Station, where they baked their own bread. We loved the smell of the bread being baked, and just sometimes we were permitted to indulge in a little refreshment.

## The mystery of the disappearing cylinder

Hinds, now long gone, was a family-owned department store up the hill on the other side of Blackheath Village. Just inside the last door of Hinds a little old gentleman was always there waiting to serve us. He gave me lots of pretty little square pieces of material. I had a bit of fun playing with them, but they were of limited use, a mere diversion in those bleak, toy-less times.

Mummy bought materials from Hinds, and the elderly gentleman meticulously cut out our material and our clothes coupons. When Mummy paid for the material, both money and coupons were placed in a small cylinder, which was sent away on a long wire. To where? I didn't know. It was a mystery. The cylinder completely disappeared. We had to wait, so I was told, for

Mummy's change to be sent back. The cylinder returned to the counter and, 'miraculously', there inside it was exactly the right amount of change! I was even more mystified!

This was the era of thick lisle stockings – that's all there was, that is, apart from silk stockings, which were expensive and kept for best only. . Nylon stockings were unheard of - nylon, like plastic, had been invented but were not yet available in the shops.

*Alison and I wearing our Fair Isle jumpers*

Buying clothes was hazardous: they were hard to find, and not exactly *chic*. In those straightened times, people mostly learnt to 'make do', cutting up and adapting pre-war garments they already had in the wardrobe.

Much new clothing was cheap and of poor quality. It was, therefore, always advisable before one made a purchase of a wartime-made garment to look for the Utility Mark introduced by the Government to show that the garment was of a basic reliable standard.

Alison and I were fortunate, we had a mother who was good with the needle. She used our clothes coupons to buy from Hinds, the limited materials available, to make our summer dresses. Daddy stoically gave up his beautiful Sutherland tartan kilt, which I know he prized, and Mummy had the task of cutting it up to make skirts for Alison and me to give us warmth in the cold winter months.

We were also fortunate to have both grandmothers as knitters. They knitted us beautiful cardigans and jumpers, following the most complicated patterns. The ones I recall most were the two very intricate multi-coloured Fair Isle jumpers, for which the grandmothers used up all the odd unused balls of wool from pre-war days. These jumpers were works of art and we treasured them, but the day came when we had to accept the sad fact that we had grown out of them.

A World Turned Upside Down

## Chapter 5

# WARTIME BLACKHEATH III

### *Anti-aircraft guns boom across Blackheath*

Children's books were hard to come by during the War. I had a few, one of which was an ancient specimen, known as a rag-book. As the description implies it was made of cloth and was of very poor quality. Another slender wartime volume, still in my possession, relates the antics of 'Bulgy the Barrage Balloon' as he faced the enemy in the sky. As already stated, barrage balloons were a familiar sight in the skies over South-East London during the War. Another slender volume I once possessed was 'The Story of the Paper Dolls', which showed how anti-German feelings spilled over, even into children's lives.

It told the tale of two little sisters who saw a china doll in a shop window. They implored their mother to buy it because china dolls were not being made in England during the War. Their mother readily agreed to buy it, but 'just in time', she saw where the doll had come from and immediately told the two little girls,

"No, no, you can't have that. It says 'Made in Germany'." Purchase was out of the question. The girls went home feeling so disappointed: they had to resort to cutting out paper dolls at home, instead – a very poor substitute.

I was not a very doll-orientated little girl, but I wished I'd had just one china doll. Angela Cole, the big girl who lived opposite us in Langton Way, very kindly gave me her china doll from the pre-war era.

"Oooooh! Thank you very much," I said. "I'll call her Angela."

---

I was about four or five near the end of the War. I wanted to know the whys and wherefores of everything to do with the War. I plagued my mother with questions, from the purpose of barrage balloons to the reason for the empty bandstand in Greenwich Park.

## Sunday walk in Royal Greenwich Park

I enjoyed our weekly walk in Greenwich Park after Sunday lunch.

The main imposing entrance to Greenwich Park led straight off the Heath and onto the grand avenue leading up to the statue, overlooking Greenwich, of General James Wolfe, renowned for having beaten the French at the Battle of Quebec.

The main entrance to the Park, wasn't the most convenient for us. Our usual way in was through the side gate, which took us through to the well kept lawns, the flowerbeds and the many beautiful ancient trees; also we passed the enclosure where the timid unsociable deer lived; they kept themselves to themselves; and then we made for the duck pond, where feeding the ducks was always on our itinerary.

From the duck pond we would turn towards the grand avenue, mentioned above, and walk along it to see General James Wolfe's statue on the horizon. Before we reached his statue I saw a forlorn-looking, circular, raised platform on our right, a little distance from the avenue.

"What's that?" I asked Mummy, as I pointed towards it.

"That's the bandstand," Mummy told me, "where the band used to play every Sunday afternoon, before the War."

"Why doesn't the band play now?" I wanted to know.

"Because of the War," she said sadly.

"What a lot of things the War seemed to have stopped!" I thought. When the War did come to an end, there remained disappointment, for the band *never* came to play in Greenwich Park, as I'd imagined it would.

Why not? There was no obvious reason. Possibly, finance. I suppose there were many more important things needing attention. Maybe the bands themselves had been disbanded (an apt word in this context) as a result of the War. I longed to hear the band play on that bandstand in Greenwich Park. I waited and waited, but, sad to say, it was not to be. I'd waited in vain.

[It was much, much later, long after we had left, that I heard the band had returned on Sunday afternoons. I made enquiries, but nobody seemed to know exactly when the tradition re-started.]

## The mystery of barrage balloons

Life in the War was full of mysteries, particularly, barrage balloons. To me, they were "tiny specks", I'd often seen, high up in the sky of South-East London.

When Mummy saw a barrage balloon she would comment ominously,

"There's a barrage balloon in the sky, it means a possible air raid is expected!"

"Why does a tiny barrage balloon's appearance in the sky mean that we might have an air raid?" I asked. "Why hasn't the siren gone off?" and "Why don't we get into the shelter?" I still didn't understand. So, on further enquiry, Mummy explained,

"If enemy planes are expected, barrage balloons help to keep them away."

That answer didn't satisfy me either. From my limited perspective, those 'little things' up there, attached to what appeared to be delicate silk-like threads, were significant, and they seemed to be doing nothing.

"Mummy, You said the barrage balloons in the sky meant an air raid might be expected. How can a barrage balloon stop German planes dropping bombs on us? It looks too far away and too small to do anything!"

This time, she gave a more detailed explanation:

"The barrage balloon is sent up, later to be lowered, when the heavy wires that attach the balloon to the ground will catch low-flying German 'planes in its wires. That will bring the German planes down and they crash. The German pilots know that there is every chance their 'planes will get entangled in the wires if they fly too low. In order to avoid this happening, they will try to fly their planes above the balloon to avoid crashing, but when a plane is flown so high it means that bombs can't be dropped accurately."

"Oh, I see!" said I.

One day, as we walked across Blackheath, we happened to pass a barrage balloon that had been lowered onto the Heath. I was intrigued to see it lying on the grass quite close to the side of the road. The balloon had been deflated and it lay there, a vast amorphous heap of strong, silvery material, disconcertingly ugly.

"Isn't it large!" I gasped silently.

The barrage balloon was simply enormous! Strange to think that not long before, this huge, lifeless silvery mass was that "tiny speck" in the sky; and what I'd naïvely described as "delicate threads of silk" were, in fact, thick, heavy wires, strong enough to fasten this voluminous mass of balloon material, when inflated, to the ground. I realised that these "little" things high in the sky were far from "little"!

Later, we saw the barrage balloon being re-inflated, as it was being prepared to ascend. I could hardly believe the enormity of the inflated balloon, as it gradually got larger and larger as more and more helium (a very light gas) was pumped into it. Slowly, it left the ground and ascended higher and higher, soon to become once more a "tiny speck" in the sky. Now, I understood.

---

## The boom of the anti-aircraft gun

Yet another mystery presented itself.

Now and again, we would hear gunfire booming across the Heath. I didn't understand, for, again, no one was showing any great concern. "Why was the siren not wailing?" and "Why was there no dash for the shelter?"

The sound of gunfire usually meant the enemy was shooting. The siren went off and we had to get into the shelter quickly. Evidently, not always! More questions for Mummy to deal with!

"We can hear guns shooting! Why aren't we getting into the shelter?" I asked fearfully.

"It's friendly gunfire," Mummy assured me, it's an anti-aircraft gun - one of our guns - so we don't need to get into the shelter, and there's no need to be frightened,."

"Strange!" I thought to myself, "I hadn't realised that the sound of gunfire could sometimes be friendly!"

This *anti*-aircraft gunfire, as it was called, was, evidently, the firing of an English gun stationed on the Heath, aimed at bringing down German 'planes as they approached London. The reason for my difficulty in understanding, dawned on me, later: the stumbling block was, of course, this word '*anti*' - at that point, I hadn't done Latin!

Until quite recently, I'd forgotten about searchlights during the War. At any one time, there could be one, possibly two or three, searchlights, each of which shone like a big arc, up and over the dark night sky, as a means of helping the British look out for enemy 'planes. In addition, the lights would dazzle the pilots, as they approached.

---

## A V-1 rocket destroys St German's Church

St German's Church, in St German's Place, was an elegant Georgian building overlooking the Heath, with white walls within and without, and a blue and gold colour scheme within. The church was built in the same period as the elegant houses on the other side of the Heath. Canon Reginald Vincent Galer was the Rector. My parents were not great churchgoers; however, they sent me to the St German's Sunday school, held in a house in Shooters Hill Road, not far from our house.

I don't mean to be wholly unappreciative of Sunday school, but for me, it wasn't the real thing, no substitute for what happened in church. People, young or old, cannot be taught to worship Almighty God; worship is done in response to the presence and grace of God, as an act of faith. Who is more equipped to respond to God's grace than the uncluttered mind of an unsophisticated, innocent child? "Unless you change and become like little children …" as Jesus said. (The Bible - Matthew 18:3).

I recall standing at the window of the Sunday school teacher's living room on the first floor. I looked longingly over the Heath, wishing I could be over there in St German's Church. I may have been young, but for me, the real thing went on in church.

Sadly, St German's Church was bombed and completely destroyed by a V-1 rocket, in June 1944. I may have been only 4¾ but I remember the incident well; the destruction of our church really upset me. Ironic, *nicht wahr*, that it was the Germans who bombed St German's Church?

To be fair, I have since learnt that the church was, in fact, dedicated to St Germanus of Auxerre in France. The church was built on land belonging to the Duke of St Germain's, Cornwall. There are other names in the locality associated with Cornwall, such as Liskeard Gardens.

It was the blast from this V-1 rocket that blew in our solid wooden front door. I have a vivid memory of coming downstairs to breakfast on the morning after the V-1 fell, only to behold our front door blasted off its hinges, blown inwards and lying in the hall, revealing an empty doorway open to the elements - broken glass was scattered everywhere. I had to step gingerly over the door and all the *debris* surrounding it, to get to the dining room for breakfast.

A man came round to partially reinstate the door; he nailed it back in place in a temporary/permanent fashion, and was so fixed, that it was back *in situ*, but unopenable.

"Now, you *must* remember, you can't use the front door – you can only get in and out of the house by the back door." Yet another of my mother's strict instructions - all too easy to forget when one is so accustomed to doing otherwise! I would cycle home from school and blithely knock on the front door, only to be reprimanded! It seemed an age before the men from the War Damage Commission came round to fix the front door properly so we could use it again.

Like our front door, the church was unusable. In the end, our front door was restored to us but, alas, not our church! What a travesty! It lay in ruins for a very long time after the War had come to an end, never to be rebuilt; the church was eventually replaced by a modern block of flats, an ugly edifice that stuck out like a sore thumb in a row of gracious Georgian houses.

## Another Enormity – a Lancaster bomber

I encountered yet another wartime enormity: a Lancaster bomber. It must have been when we visited one of the aerodromes where my father was working, that I saw this large, lumbering aeroplane taxi-ing towards us, awesomely close - seemingly too close for safety!

"Oh! Isn't it big!" I exclaimed.

"It's a Lancaster bomber," Daddy told me. "Don't worry, it's one of *our* 'planes."

The grown-ups were also in awe of its tremendous size, so you can imagine how it appeared to little me. I hear the plane being spoken of today. I'm very glad I actually saw a Lancaster Bomber for myself.

---

## A London sparrow

I love going up to London. I'm a Londoner! Going up West, as it was invariably described, is now taken for granted, but at the end of the War, such an expedition was considered an especial treat. There has hardly been a time when I didn't go up West, for something – shopping with Mummy, shopping alone, and later for events musical, historical or ecclesiastical.

More recently, I met my Radley mother-in-law in London. It was apparent to her that I "flexed my wings" when I came to London. She called me a London sparrow! It's true, on arrival in London, unwittingly, I seem to come alive!

My first venture up West was with Mummy and Nana, just after the War ended. I witnessed the severely bombed John Lewis store in Oxford Street - it had received a direct hit in the Blitz. The store was covered in scaffolding, its pane-less windows were patched up; and the entrance wasn't easy to find. So, when I first saw it, Lewis's looked uninviting, at least, to this little girl. I couldn't but feel sorry for the bombed John Lewis's, while D.H. Evans, next door, (now House of Fraser) had been spared and was far more inviting. Then, after its rebuilding, Lewis's appeared to be the nicer of the two stores. (That taught me a lesson, even then, and now it can be applied to the Christian life.)

Near the end of the War, we usually went to see my Anderson grandparents on a Thursday and, on occasion, we met my grandmother at Pynes, the respectable New Cross family department store, where she treated Mummy and me to lunch. Then, sad to say, Pynes was bombed. The bombing of Pynes prompted my grandmother to suggest,

"Let's go up West, now that we can't go to Pynes. We'll have lunch in D.H. Evans!"

"That's a good idea," Mummy agreed. "We'll meet you there. The No. 53 bus takes us all the way from The Royal Standard, Blackheath, via New Cross, to Oxford Circus."

This was a really exciting day out for me. I'd never been up West before.

We went into D.H. Evans, and by escalator up to the restaurant on the top floor, where we joined the queue waiting to be seated by the 'tic-tac' ladies, as I call them.

The lady at the entrance to the restaurant, communicated with arms, hands and fingers to colleagues posted at different corners of the restaurant, informing them by her 'tic-tac' gesticulations, that there were customers wanting a table for two or three or whatever; and, by return, her colleagues also using 'tic-tac' gestures somehow managed to convey an appropriate reply, that there was, or was not, a table available in her section of the restaurant, for that number of persons.

I was absolutely fascinated by this in-house mode of communication. I tried to understand their gesticulations - a few eluded me!

Lunch was exciting at our newly found meeting place, D.H. Evans - it was an extra special treat. Soon it was time to make for home - on the No. 53 bus again.

Just before we got to the bus stop, we were in for a surprise! A man, with a camera at the ready, suddenly jumped out in front of us and clicked his box, taking a photo of the four of us walking along Oxford Street: My grandmother and me to the fore, my mother and Alison behind. I'm ashamed of the dreadful face I'm making. I almost didn't include the photo because of my contorted face! Rightly or wrongly, I decided to include the photo here because it shows a corner of the bombed John Lewis' store on the left, and there's an old-fashioned double-decker bus making its way along Oxford Street towards Marble Arch.

The photographer pressed a ticket into my grandmother's hand, in the hope that she would order a copy.

We got back to my grandparents' house and we told my grand-father about this unexpected incident. My grandmother gave him the ticket that the photographer had given to her, and asked if he would get the photo. It would cost 7s 6d (12½p) - a lot of money then. My mother quailed at the thought of expending so much on a mere photo. She was adamant, she would not entertain any idea of ordering it at that price – "Waste of money," she opined. We can't afford it.

The ticket was left with my grandfather, who kept his silence. Evidently, he was not deterred, and he went ahead and ordered the photo! My mother was cross when she heard what her father had done!

I am grateful to my grandfather: the photo gives a little insight into war-torn London. It may have been deemed "waste of money", but the photo has been of interest and amusement, ever since.

(I expect my dear grandfather was mindful that his order would help the finances of the photographer, doing his best to earn a £ or two.)

"Oxford Street just after the War - "A good thing the wind didn't change!"

A World Turned Upside Down

## Chapter 6

# EVACUATIONS, HERE, THERE AND EVERYWHERE

### *Norwich - a City of significance*

### Evacuations, here, there and everywhere

We were evacuated all over the place. Daddy went ahead of us to work at the aerodrome to which he had been assigned, and when he had settled in he would look for a suitable farm willing to accommodate the three of us. When that had been found, Mummy and I would join Daddy.

Many were the kindly people who opened their homes to welcome us evacuees from London.

I heard Gloucester being discussed. I don't recall our time in Gloucester, but I believe, I was present - *incognito*!

### My earliest memory - the Royal Arcade, Norwich

Norwich was our next destination. My father was stationed at Horsham St Faith aerodrome, near Norwich. He found us accommodation in a farmhouse in the village of Old Catton, also near Norwich.

Norwich is a City of some significance to me: it is the place of my first memory. I was 2½ years old, dressed in my little brown coat and brown bobble hat. I was holding Mummy's hand, as we walked up the Royal Arcade, when suddenly, I decided to slip my hand from hers, and I strode out in front of her, declaring in no uncertain terms: "I want to be another lady!"

Where *did* I get the idea from? I know not! I can only assume that, on some previous occasion, Mummy had pointed out a lady to me, referring to her as "another lady". Presumably, the lady's status appealed and I wanted to join the ranks! So here I was, in the Royal Arcade that day, wishing to inform people that there was, in fact, "another lady" around. However I got the idea, it was *very* early in life, was it not?

Unhappily, my audacity was not looked upon favourably. Mummy strongly disapproved of the antics of her little darling. Later, she told me sternly, "You wouldn't do what you were told. You refused to walk with me. You screamed and you wouldn't stop screaming!"

Oh dear! I was an embarrassment. But, I couldn't see that my little bit of drama was *wrong*! Truly, I don't recall the screaming! Screaming apart, I *do* recall resisting Mummy's endeavour to make me "behave". I was only demonstrating my independence of spirit, and, as such, I felt more a little person than a naughty child!

I don't remember Old Catton itself, nor the farm where we stayed, but I do have a vague impression of trees, lining the far side of a field we passed, as Daddy drove us to our 'digs' in Old Catton. And I associate this car journey with a certain song: 'Merrily, merrily off we go…' Daddy must have been singing it as we went along. He was a great singer of well known popular songs. I can still sing the tune with a smattering of the words.

After every sortie Mummy and I returned to Blackheath. We would use our time back at home to live life as normally as possible, if anything during the War could be described as normal. It was normal to me - I knew no different.

We listened to the wireless every morning to see if air raids were forecast. If the news was good we did shopping up the Old Dover Road in the morning and went down to Blackheath Village in the afternoon. Crossing the Heath gave me the supreme opportunity, to state again my declaration of independence on two or three further occasions. As before, I strode out ahead of Mummy and again informed her, "I want to be another lady!"

Unfortunately, Mummy was still cross with me for not walking with her, but she didn't seem to realise. I didn't mean it unkindly. If she'd tried to humour me, she might have been able to moderate her daughter's dramatic desire! I still couldn't see that I was doing anything *wrong*! The drama didn't last long, and I soon returned to the maternal embrace.

Soon, we were off again to yet another unfamiliar, far away place.

## A farm near Oxford

I don't remember much of this destination, the Staites' farm near Oxford. I have a vague memory of Mrs Staites, the farmer's wife: a short, well-built lady with fair hair, wearing a large white apron. Possibly, there was a Mr Staites, I don't recall. What I do remember well was that Mummy, Daddy and I slept in a white caravan under a tree in the orchard, close to the farmhouse where we ate our meals.

Then, it was back to Blackheath again.

## A chicken farm at Horsepath next

The next family to open their home and welcome this unknown family from London was the Litt family, farmers in the village of Horsepath, near Oxford. The farmhouse was in the centre of Horsepath.

My memories of the Litts' farm are much clearer than the Staites' farm – I was that much older, of course. Mrs Litt was a busy but very welcoming farmer's wife, short and well built; she had her black plaited hair done up as earphones. I don't recall her first name, but her husband was called Tom.

The Litts' kept a poultry farm. The front of the farmhouse overlooked Horsepath's village green and ancient parish church. In the farmyard at the rear of the house, were scores of chicken, ducks and geese strutting around.

Mr and Mrs Litt had three sons: Edgar, 18, Tommy, 16, and William, 8. At mealtimes, we sat round their large square kitchen table, waiting to be served. I was in awe of the boys as they came in for meals. To little me, they were all big boys.

While we were in Horsepath, my father was working at *SS Cars* in Cowley, doing something for the War effort. I don't know what. I was too little to understand.

When the War was over, I recall Daddy pointing out *SS* cars being driven along the road.

After Horsepath, again, it was back to Blackheath and the 'joys' of wartime London.

## I learn to ride Silver - Red House Farm, Chesterton

Our next sortie was the Red House Farm, Chesterton, near Leamington Spa. This was the home of yet another farmer and his wife, Geoff and Vivien Malsbury. They were wheat farmers and also kept a herd of cows and four horses. They ran the farm with their two daughters, June and Jill. Jill taught me to ride a horse, in fact, a grey pony called Silver. In return, my father helped Jill with her arithmetic homework. Or was it the other way round?

Love of horses seems to be a Sutherland family *trait*. My rides on Silver were the start of my affection for horses and horse riding. I continued to enjoy it when older: I went riding for an hour on a Saturday morning, and later joined the Pony Club. Very recently, I rode a horse into Petra, the ancient rose-coloured city. Wonderful! The city of Petra *and* the horse ride through it!

The man with a leading rein soon realised that I was capable of controlling the horse myself, so he let me get on with it!

But I digress.

The Malsburys became good friends of the family, and we returned to visit them at harvest time, after the War. Geoff was one of the first farmers in the country to own a combine harvester, saving much hard labour in the fields. On this, our second visit, one of the cowhands tried to get me to milk a cow. I couldn't bring myself to do it. Even to touch the cow's udders made me sh-sh-sh-sh-udder!

All these farm experiences gave me an appreciation of country life, especially the livestock. But I remain a Londoner at heart.

## Uncertainty casts a dark shadow

The uncertainty and misery of wartime Britain cast a dark shadow over every mind. With the incessant wailing of the siren during the previous night, and hearing enemy planes in the skies above, dropping bombs on us, and later the doodlebugs, one never knew what was next to be hit, possibly destroyed. People made the best of an unnerving situation, but, deep down, they were fearful and tired of the erratic lifestyle, broken sleep and life in the shelter. I couldn't help but hear the tenor of the conversations held between my mother and the neighbours we met round at the shops.

"Weren't the air raids awful last night?" was the sort of rhetorical question frequently asked in a despairing tone of voice. "Mrs So-and-so tells me her mother has been bombed out - her house received a direct hit!" And "How much longer do you think we are going to have to endure this dreadful War?" Conversations revolved around such sentiments and questions, such as these. People were war-weary – the War was a daily torment for everyone.

## Mr Churchill broadcasts encouragement

Mr (he wasn't a 'Sir' until later) Winston Churchill, Prime Minister, broadcast words of encouragement on the wireless to boost the people's flagging morale.

Mummy, Daddy and I huddled round the wireless. We listened intently to what Mr Churchill had to say, with his deep, penetrating growl of a voice, not that I understood. The people of this country were in need of his words of assurance. Mr Churchill's broadcasts raised the spirits of the British, my parents included; he gave them new hope when all was dark, and he assured them that Great Britain was succeeding in fighting off the Nazi evil threatening the country with invasion and occupation. Everyone hung on to Mr Churchill's every word, and they came away from the wireless more able to face another day, which so often seemed bleak. My parents' optimism, of course, made me feel better, too. We learnt later that the war-weary people of the rest of Europe also listened to Mr Churchill and hung onto his words of encouragement.

From the tone of Mummy's voice and the conversation afterwards, I gathered that the War would soon be over and all would be well. I didn't really know what that meant, not having known life without war.

"We're winning the War!" Mummy told me, no doubt to reassure herself, as much as to encourage me.

---

Another source of encouragement during the War was of a very different order...

## 'ITMA' – "It's That Man Again"

"It's that man again" - Tommy Handley and his friends also raised the spirits of the war-weary, taking minds off the misery that consumed everyone. The whole nation tuned in to the Home Service (Radio 4) to listen to ITMA for light relief.

As Tommy Handley's friends came on air, one by one, each character would address him with his or her own catchphrase. Even though there was much I didn't understand, their very inevitability and their familiar voices sufficed to amuse me:

I created a mental picture of the Cockney Mrs Mopp, with her, "Can I do yer now, sir?"; Moanalot, with her misery saying, "It's being so 'appy that keeps me going!"; and Colonel Chinstrap, with his pompous, "I don't mind if I do!" Laughter was a wonderful antidote to misery in the midst of War.

After the War, we learnt that the peoples of Nazi-occupied Europe were also avid listeners; they enjoyed the ITMA jokes as much as the British did, and it helped dispel *their* fear and despondency, too.

## Chapter 7

# NOW THE WAR'S OVER

### *Known as "little" Rosemary*

Air raids or no air raids, in the May of 1945, Grandfather Anderson considered it safe to take us for a short holiday to Sandown on the Isle of Wight, where we'd visited the previous year. We took the ferry across the Solent to Ryde.

On disembarking, we were bundled into a taxi. My grandfather asked the driver to take us to 'Pine Lodge' a small family-run guesthouse where we'd stayed in 1944. As we got out of the taxi, I looked up the drive and saw kindly, smiling, Edna with her long, black, neatly combed hair, waiting at the front door to welcome us. I recognised her from our previous stay.

This visit to the Isle of Wight proved to be memorable, for it was during this visit that we heard the wonderful news:

Peace is officially declared. It was the 8$^{th}$ May 1945.

"We've won the War!" declared a delighted mother. Of course, everyone was delighted that, at last, the War was over:

"Germany has surrendered. What a relief!" The longed-for day, now spoken of as VE Day, Victory in Europe, had arrived. An explosion of joy, tempered with profound relief, rippled across the nation, and across the faces of the people. We could now relax in the knowledge that there'd be no more wailing sirens and no more falling bombs.

The corporate soul of the nation had been through a Dark Night – the nation's life and mine had been turned upside down. The Declaration of Peace heralded the dawn of a new era, and expectations were high.

My expectations were certainly high. My immediate hope was the removal of the nasty metal barricades in the sea, surrounding the coast of Great Britain, the Isle of Wight included.

It had been on our previous visit to the Isle of Wight that I first saw these ugly structures, erected parallel to and a short way out from the shore. When the tide was in, they were invisible, but when the tide was out they were exposed and, to me, looked sinister. Then, of course, the War was still raging.

"Mummy, what are those horrible things for? They look nasty. I'm frightened."

"No need to be frightened," she'd assured me. "They're there to prevent stray bombs being washed up onto the beach and exploding."

The frequently used phrase during the War was, "When the War's over…."

A phrase the grown-ups often used was a wistful reference to life "before the War" - it sounded idyllic.

Now the War was over, the imagination of this littler girl of 5¾ was fired with hope, only to be sadly disappointed. Naïvely, I'd imagined that all our wartime problems and difficulties would be gone in a trice and that the idyllic mode of life that grown-ups had enjoyed "before the War" would return immediately. My naïve high hopes were quickly dashed; it wasn't to be a bit like that.

On this, our second visit to the Isle of Wight, my questioning continued:

"Those horrid metal things in the sea - they're still there. Now the War's over, why haven't they been taken away?

"They must stay, just in case there are still unexploded bombs in the sea. If bombs are washed up onto the beach they still could be dangerous," Mummy explained. [Seventy-two years on, I understand the main function of the barricades was to guard against enemy landings.]

Obviously, things were not going to change as quickly as I'd fondly imagined!

## As Londoners, we were far from home

Here on the Isle of Wight we were caught up in the country's jubilation, but we were far from home. As Londoners, we wanted to get back quickly. Now the War was over, we would return this time without the threat of air raids. However, there was always the possibility that either or both our houses might have been bombed and reduced to ruins whilst we'd been away. What a dreadful thought!

We bade farewell to Edna and Pine Lodge, to resume life in South-East London. We didn't relish the thought that we might have to join the ranks of the bombed out, and the homeless during our time in the Isle of Wight. Anyhow, the sooner we got back, the better. In the event, all was well - both houses were unscathed and still standing.

---

However, not long after the Declaration of Peace, with sighs of relief all round, and just as we thought that bombs were a thing of the past, a bomb exploded in the centre of Blackheath Village. Our lovely Village was devastated, and so was I. The shock and the horror of seeing the bomb-damaged Village was more than I could bear. The only way I could cope with that dreadful scene was to push it down inside me. Fairly recently, the Reminiscence Centre in Blackheath Village displayed a photo which resurrected memories of the devastation.

Devastation has plagued my life. I have hardly known life without devastation. As already stated, "I was born into war and it has been battle ever since!" My world is forever being turned upside down.

---

## The Royal Family and Mr Churchill wave to the crowds below

When Peace was declared, newspapers printed photos of a smiling Royal Family on the balcony of Buckingham Palace, greeting the tremendous crowds of people below. The people waved delightedly, and craned their necks with faces turned upwards - The Royal Family waved back to the crowds below.

Mr Winston Churchill, Prime Minister of Great Britain, though not royalty, was privileged to join the Royal Family on the balcony, from where he gave his now famous 'V for Victory' sign. The peoples' spirits had been kept up by Mr Churchill's wireless broadcasts, encouraging the people that victory was in sight, when, possibly, the situation was far from hopeful. He had led the country to victory. Now he was acclaimed Hero of the Day.

Wartime England was all I knew. My glorious vision of life-without-war was fading fast! I was bewildered by the anti-climax. I am told there was also bewilderment among the grown-ups, for they too were living in uncharted waters.

Peace in Europe may have been declared, but austerity continued and life remained colourless, literally and metaphorically.

Of course, it was a great relief to have no more air raid sirens wailing and bombs exploding, but otherwise not much had changed. Compared with the intense awareness and activity to which we'd become accustomed, there was now nothing to raise the adrenalin. Hope for "normal life", whatever that meant, was dim. Life was tedious, for there is a limit to making one's own amusement. I had to make do with my few toys of pre-War vintage and the few pre-war books already mentioned.

Problems abounded in post-war Britain. Along with the shortage of food, there was the shortage of housing. Dire was the plight of hundreds of people bombed out of house and home. They had lost everything, and alternative accommodation was scarce or unavailable. The shortage was especially acute in London. Many of the bombed-out population became squatters in empty properties whose owners had been killed in the bombing or had moved out of London, staying with family or friends or relations elsewhere. Yet, hope springs eternal.

## Pre-fabs are erected

Speed was of the essence to meet the need. The government partially solved the problem by putting up pre-fabricated houses, colloquially known as pre-fabs. Two rows of pre-fabs were built overlooking the Heath, parallel to St German's Place. Understandably, the residents of St German's Place were not exactly happy to have their fantastic view of the Heath obliterated. The pre-fabs in St German's Place were dismantled soon after the War, but a few remain elsewhere, even today.

With the end of the War, there was a slow return to some sort of social normality. We could now cross the Heath fearlessly, and we could venture further afield, which previously had been unwise.

I have to mention Spam! It was to reach these shores from America in 1941! At the time, it was deemed a luxury, and, as with so much else, tins of Spam were difficult to come by. Its acquisition elicited a cry of triumph. After the daily wartime diet of corned beef for almost every meal, Spam made a *delicious change*. Food rationing remained,

We had to wait till the War was over for bananas to reach Great Britain. One day, as we returned from doing our weekly shop, Mrs Wood, a neighbour, came out of her house in a flurry when we were almost back home, to inform us urgently,

"Bason's has just had a delivery of bananas. Be quick, you might get there before they're sold out."

"Oh dear, we've just been there!" exclaimed my indignant and weary mother. "But, thank you for telling us. We'll see if they've got some left." We hastily retraced our steps in the hope of getting back to Bason's before the bananas had been snapped up. We were there in time to get our ration! As a luxury, bananas were obtainable only with points from a child's ration book. Fortunately, the Bason brothers had kept some "under the counter" for us.

---

## The Conservatoire of Music

Miss Annie M. Morton lived next-door-but-one to us in Langton Way. She taught me to play the piano, and in 1946 when I was six-and-a-half she entered me for my first piano exam, the RSCM Preliminary.

I took the exam at the Conservatoire of Music, next door to the then culturally dead Blackheath Concert Halls, on the Lee Road. I walked into the examination room at the Conservatoire with great aplomb, as "another lady" in the making would. How could it be otherwise? I sat myself down at the piano before the examiner, an 'elderly' gentleman. To me he was elderly. Again, I expect he was only in his forties, if that! I played my pieces and I passed!

However, much to my sorrow, I received no certificate to confirm my pass. Why? Because of the paper shortage of wartime Great Britain. Mean! Life then *was* mean in the original sense of that word. It seemed so unfair not to issue a certificate to me, a little girl. Outwardly, I accepted the situation with stoicism; it was the kind of sacrifice everybody was expected to make, so I understood. But, inwardly, if I'm honest, I was very peeved about it, and there is still a small measure of that inside me, especially when I see the waste of paper today.

[At the time of writing, I believe plans are now afoot to refurbish the Conservatoire of Music.]

In 1940 the Concert Halls, next door to the Conservatoire, were taken over by the Ministry of Works. The Halls were reopened in 1985, having been beautifully refurbished by local enthusiasts.

## Ballet at the Royal Opera House

Slowly, other aspects of life were being restored. In 1946 the Royal Opera House, Covent Garden, re-opened its doors.

Thanks to Daddy's firm, he was given tickets for the four of us to see 'Coppelia', the ballet by Leon Delibes at the Royal Opera House. This was a fantastic experience. As a little girl, I was wide-eyed by the beauty and vastness of the Royal Opera House, and, of course, by the beautiful music of 'Coppelia', danced in such a prestigious venue.

We sat in the front row, and I was enthralled. Alison was not so enthralled - she fell fast asleep. Shame on her! I don't mean that unkindly - to be fair, she was only four, and the stage lights between the stage and our seats gave out an incredible heat, which proved too much for her.

The visit to the Royal Opera House was truly memorable, and the music sowed a seed of my love of classical music, which has since blossomed and flourished.

Even then, I had no liking for "pop" music. The "pop" music of the day was 'boogie-woogie'; nor did I like the singers of the day, known as crooners. Vera Lynn's singing for the troops, "We'll meet again" etc. was in a different category, but it didn't thrill me.

## The Miller Hospital

Alison and I had another – not so enjoyable – sortie, this time to the

Miller Hospital in Greenwich, to have our tonsils out. We shared a room with two other little girls. I went down first to have *my* tonsils out, and then it was Alison's turn. We came back to the ward, both with a rasping sore throat - it helped, having each other for company. I felt sorry for Alison because she was too little to understand the reason for our being in hospital and the cause of the soreness.

We looked forward to Mummy and Daddy coming, though the visiting time was only 20 minutes. It was horrid when they had to go, of course, and Alison cried.

[In those days, visiting time was strict. If visitors arrived late, too bad! No permission was given to stay longer at the end, to make up for a late arrival.]

## Going to the Fair

Apart from the War years, the Fair on Blackheath has been an annual event from medieval times. The end of the War heralded the Fair's return to the Heath, set up close to the imposing main gates of Greenwich Park, the earliest of all the Royal Parks, dating back over 500 years. The fair included dodgems, roundabouts, coconut shies and all the other traditional side stalls, which were assembled and open for business.

I was partial to the dodgems (I still am), bashing into everybody and trying to avoid being bashed into, not, I can assure you, that I exhibit this *trait* in everyday life! Under the parental eye, that was the most adventurous I ever got. I was only permitted one ride! The following year, Daddy relented in a weak moment and gave me the money for a second ride!

Much more recently, my husband, his mother and I paid a visit to Blackheath and the Fair on the Heath, and I took the liberty of inviting my Radley mother-in-law on board. I took the wheel, and we had our measure of bashing and being bashed into. She hung on to the side of the dodgem car for dear life. She didn't dare admit it, but I think she was petrified, poor woman.

Living too far away as I do now, I'm no longer a frequenter of the Fair.

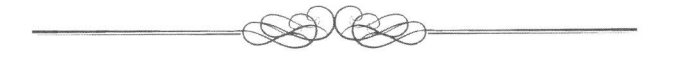

Donkeys have played an historic role on the Heath, and they remain part of the scene, even today. Every weekend, opposite the main Park gates, their owners walked these bedraggled animals up and down, on the equivalent of a donkeys' 'rotten row'. Donkey rides were given to kids, with the donkeys on a leading rein. This short, churned-up, muddy strip of land really did look rotten!

I was never allowed to have a donkey ride because my mother deemed the steeds unhealthy. Maybe they were – I don't know. Anyhow, my innocent request was always turned down flat! The donkeys were part of the scene and were no doubt hired out to many a future Derby winner.

[On the 14th of July 2003, it was announced on the BBC's 'London in the South-East' programme that the donkeys had been stolen, which I was sad to hear. A few weeks later, it was revealed that the donkeys had been found and reinstated, but the newsreader never mentioned where, how and by whom they had been taken and how they were retrieved.]

## The Hong Kong Restaurant

There was a definite loosening of the domestic purse strings when my father decided he could afford to treat us to a meal at the Hong Kong Restaurant, just opened in Shaftesbury Avenue, the first and *only* Chinese restaurant in London! Imagine it, the only one!

I loved that Chinese food, and still do - it was delicious. Not surprisingly, with rationing and wartime shortages, I'd never tasted anything like it before. I think we had to take our ration books with us for the treat, to use some of our points. Such was my enthusiasm, I talked about that meal for years to come, and still do!

Unwittingly, Daddy had fostered my culinary delight in oriental food, just as the Royal Opera House had fuelled my love of classical music.

### "He shall be called Teddy!"

There was a great pageant on the Heath in 1945 to commemorate the meeting on the Heath, of Humphrey, Duke of Gloucester, and Margaret of Anjou in 1445, exactly 500 years earlier. That brings me on to my next 'historical' event: Mummy's acquisition of a little black and white kitten, for which a name had to be chosen.

"What shall we call the kitten?" Mummy asked – rhetorically, I think, for I'm almost sure she'd made up her own mind already. Little did she know, she was in for a tussle!

"*Teddy*!" I replied emphatically, "I want to call it *Teddy*." I admit I had no idea why, I just felt it was right!

Mummy had, indeed, already made up her mind about the kitten's name:

"I think we should call the kitten Henry," she told me, "because the pageant on the Heath today is to celebrate the 500$^{th}$ anniversary of Duke Humphrey's meeting with Margaret of Anjou on Blackheath in 1445. Margaret came to England to marry King Henry VI and to be crowned as his Queen. She was only seventeen!"

I was only six, yet old enough to stick to my strongly held opinion in the matter of the kitten's name!

Obviously, the celebration of the 500$^{th}$ anniversary of Henry VI and the meeting of Duke Humphrey with Margaret of Anjou on the Heath took on added significance, as the date of the anniversary coincided exactly with our WW2 victory celebrations. I have to admit that, at the youthful age of six, I hadn't really understood what it was all about: Duke Humphrey? Margaret of something or other getting married to Henry the something or other? It was all beyond me at the time. Yet I'm afraid I continued to insist, "We must call the kitten Teddy!"

In the end, Mummy gave in and Teddy it was! With hindsight, I now realise that Mummy's choice of Henry would have been far more appropriate, in fact, 200 per cent more appropriate! *Mea culpa!*

"Sorry, Mummy! At least you didn't want to call it Humphrey!"

[I have since come to the conclusion that I have a 'thing' about names.]

## Unlucky Mr Luck

Just after the War, Mr Luck, a professional photographer, came on two occasions to take photos of Alison and me. Finances *must* have improved! But when the photos arrived after one of his visits, Mummy looked at the photo he had taken of the two of us sitting together on the sofa, and she suddenly exploded with indignation:

"Oh! Mr Luck has left his camera case on the chair behind you! Fancy not removing that before taking the photograph!" She was furious about this oversight!

Poor Mr Luck! He hadn't lived up to his name. I still have the photo with the offending camera case on view. It makes me chuckle whenever I look at it.

*Alison and I sweetly sitting on the sofa, with me clutching the primitive rag book. Unlucky Mr Luck's camera case is left on the chair behind!*

With the end of the War, I attended weekly dancing classes at Marjorie Barton's School of Dancing in Independents Road, almost next door to Blackheath Station. I can't say that dancing was my forte! Piano playing was more my scene, not that I was a budding Myra Hess by any stretch of the imagination.

## "Little Rosemary"

Captain Bowen and his wife Rose lived in the semi-detached house adjoining ours.

A long time after the War, and long after we'd moved away, I called on Mrs Bowen. We sat in her front room and reminisced over a cup of tea. I was very touched and amused to learn that when we lived next door, the Bowens had tenderly spoken of me, as "little Rosemary". That was news to me. I hadn't realised they'd thought so kindly of me. I'm sure Mummy would have told me about this affectionate description, had she been aware of it.

---

We were one of the few families to have a car during and after the War. This was an asset, but it meant we went without other things considered essential, such as a fridge; that was how it was for many years to come. The wireless was relatively new on the scene; and television, although it had been invented, hadn't yet reached people's homes. It was a long time before my parents had a television.

As with almost everything else, petrol was on ration; car drivers were issued with petrol coupons. Those who managed to run a car had to calculate how to put their small petrol ration to best use. [On 5$^{th}$ April 1948, motorists were permitted fuel for 90 miles per month.]

'POOL' petrol was the only petrol available during the War and for some time afterwards. The various pre-war petrol companies, Shell, Esso, BP and National Benzole, pooled their petrol, hence the name. Each pump at a post-War petrol station still had a china bowl on top giving its pre-war brand name, but none of these pumps dispensed petrol. The sole functioning pump also had a china bowl on top, appropriately marked 'POOL', as if it were a brand name, and only 'POOL' petrol was for sale.

Our ancient Morris Ten, made an unholy rattling noise as it went along; we were amused to learn that the "less charitably-minded" of my school friends dared to call it the "rattle trap"!

---

Our frequent walks across the Heath gave me the supreme opportunity to keep up my "wanting to be another lady" campaign. I strode out in front of my mother, sometimes my grandmother, as I did in my first demonstration in the Royal Arcade, Norwich, when I first made my declaration

Mummy still complained about my "wayward" behaviour: "Rosemary, please stop your antics and walk with me!" She remained adamant that it had to stop. I too was adamant. I felt like a little person in my own right. I didn't *say* so, but that's how I felt! Mummy didn't understand. I hoped she'd become resigned to the so-called "antics" of her dear, determined daughter, but she never did!

## Chapter 8

# BOXING DAY AT DENMARK HILL

### *"She's my Japanesey girl"*

I have an abiding memory of celebrating the Boxing Day of Christmas 1945 at the home of the Sutherland Grandparents at Denmark Hill.

On Christmas morning, I woke up to find that Father Christmas had made his nocturnal visit and had filled the stocking at the end of my bed. Christmas Day was a quiet family affair spent at home. We went to church in the morning, and after lunch took a walk in Greenwich Park.

Boxing Day was quite different. Mummy, Daddy, baby Alison and I spent the day at the Sutherland Grandparents' house in Deepdene Road, Denmark Hill, in South-East London, with aunts and uncles and cousin John, our sole cousin at the time. Grandmother Sutherland, known as Nan, decorated the hall and downstairs rooms with a great array of brightly coloured Japanese lanterns… red, blue, yellow, green – all pre-war acquisitions, of course.

The War may have ended but not the rationing. That continued long after the end of the War, adversely affecting everyone's Christmas fare. Grandfather Sutherland was Chief Cashier at Hay's Wharf, the last wharf of many before London Bridge, which lined the bank of the River Thames. Ships with cargoes of Christmas fare for the people of London docked in the Pool of London. We did wonder if possibly our meagre Christmas rations had been supplemented! Grandmother Sutherland cooked a lovely Christmas lunch – turkey and all the trimmings. As we ate our Christmas pudding, Grandfather Sutherland "found" a large gold pocket watch in his bowl; a mini-'miracle' he performed every Boxing Day!

An inviting-looking 4lbs Black Magic chocolate box flaunting a beautiful big red tassel on the lid, lay around that Christmas, a leftover from the era "before the War". Of course, when I came across the box, all the chocolates had long gone. This large Black Magic box was the sort of thing I'd assumed would reappear "when the War was over", but didn't! I waited, in vain. I was never to see again, a large box like that, with such a beautiful red tassel.

Nan could play the piano. After lunch we stood round the piano in the front room and sang carols and some of the old songs. I enjoyed the singing. Nan's favourite song was, *'She's My Japanesey Girl'- she* returned to it again and again. She seemed to have a *penchant* for things Japanese, viz the Japanese lanterns. I know not from where the song comes, I still remember the tune and most of the lyrics. They went something like this:

> *"She's my japanesey girl,*
> *She's my bread and cheesy girl,*
> *All the way from Oky-Toky-o,*
> *That's the place, the place I'd like to go.*
> *All the way from Oky-Toky-o,*
> *She is my lily and my rose*
> *She's my jap, jap, jappy*
> *And she makes me happy*
> *Where e'er she goes!"*

I can still sing the tune but, unfortunately, cannot transfer that onto the page! I believe there was a second verse. [I'd be interested to know the origin of the above, and who the writer of the lyrics is and the words of the second verse; also, the composer of the music.]

After Nan had finished playing, it was my turn at the keyboard, but my music making was of a different order! Nan seated me on the piano stool and fitted up the pianola for me. I chose my pianola roll – a roll of paper spattered with hundreds of little holes punched in appropriate places. She then had to convert the piano for the pianola to be 'played' ready for the 'pianist' to demonstrate her prowess!

Nan inserted the chosen roll into a specially designated place in the centre of the upright part of the piano, and then she lowered the special pianola pedals. It was with great delight that I found myself able to 'play' classical pieces on the pianola. I peddled away for all I was worth. Such was the exertion, especially for this little player with legs shorter than the average, that I had to hold on tight to the keyboard! The music boomed through the rafters and I was thrilled to be responsible for bringing forth pieces such as Souza's march "Stars and Stripes" and Johann Strauss's waltz "The Blue Danube". The experience was fantastic!

I hadn't been playing long, before Mummy came in to tell me, "You've had long enough playing the piano. I think you should come and join us in the back room."

"Oh, I'm enjoying myself," I declared. Couldn't Mummy see that? Evidently not! It was as if enjoyment was on ration like everything else, or they thought it should be. I dutifully obeyed, but not without a cry of protest! I didn't see why I couldn't continue 'playing'. I was really delighting in my music-making. I'd have thought my innocent self-entertainment would have met with approval. In those austere post-War days, there wasn't exactly a surfeit of things around to enjoy. Indeed, there was very little. We had a piano at home, in Langton Way, but not the pianola facility!

Anyhow, I was obliged to join the grown-ups in the back room. But life with them was boring - their talk didn't interest me. So I slipped out into the hall to have a pretend telephone conversation on my grandparents' old-fashioned telephone by the front door. The mouthpiece was on the top of a vertical stick about twelve inches tall; the hand-piece was separate and just for listening – hung on a clip on the side of the vertical stick. I held the hand-piece to my ear and conversed with an imaginary friend. Mummy came out and told me off and said I must stop:

"You shouldn't be doing that - you're blocking the line." Someone might be trying to phone Nan.

"Who'd be phoning Nan on *Boxing Day*? No doubt, it was the principle of the thing, as Mummy saw it. I'd heard Nan speak of Mrs Gager. I suppose she just might have wanted to have a quick word with Nan. Again, I dutifully obeyed, though with ill-grace.

We danced the Boxing Day evening away - it was a wonderful evening, and it cheered me up greatly. The vivacious Auntie Rene Winslow, my father's elder sister, was the heart and soul of the proceedings - she had a *penchant* for dancing "In-and-out-the-Windows" and we all followed her; she also excelled at the Gay Gordons, the Veleta, and the St Bernard Waltz. Great fun was had, "Doing the Lambeth Walk, eh!" and then the Hokey Cokey.

"You put your right foot in, you put your right foot out, in, out, in, out, and shake it all about…" etc. etc. We danced until we dropped, or more precisely, until the grown-ups dropped! Boxing Day ended with a heartfelt rendering of *Auld Lang Syne*.

*"Don't be cross with me!"*

Sadly, this wonderful Boxing Day party heralded the end of this epoch of my life: it was the beginning of the end of my happiness living in South-East London. Of course, I was more than relieved that the War had ended, but that Boxing Day of exhilarating pianola playing, singing and dancing at Denmark Hill was never again.

More's the pity, the end of the War seemed to signal a move out of London. The Sutherland grandparents found a bungalow with a large garden in Leaves Green, Keston, near Bromley in Kent. That was to come in useful at a later dates.

# A World Turned Upside Down

## Chapter 9

# GENUINE VICTORIANA

### *The gas mantle had to be lit*

Now the War was over we could leave the house without the fear of air raids, and now we could venture further afield than we had previously dared. The weekly visit to the grandparents and Great-grandparents in Hatcham was usual. It was a very different sort of visit, from the annual Boxing Day party at Denmark Hill.

To get to Hatcham, either we walked up to the Royal Standard, near to the Old Dover Road, where we jumped on a No. 53 bus that took us all the way to New Cross Gate without having to change buses. Otherwise, we caught the No. 108 bus to Lewisham Clock Tower via Blackheath Village, of course, I enjoyed that. The snag, about doing the journey this way, so far as I was concerned, was that we had to catch a tram from Lewisham to New Cross Gate, and I wasn't keen on trams, unless the sun was shining and we went upstairs.

Strange to say, the tram was known as a tramcar. To keep passengers downstairs moving along the centre aisle, the conductor would call out, "Pass down the car, please! Pass down the car!"

As a little girl, I thought: "A *car*? It's nothing like a car!"

The old-style of tram was for me a very mixed blessing. Apart from anything else, we had to walk into the middle of the road to get onto the tram, which had its dangers, not that the volume of traffic then was anything like it is today. The only upside was the upstairs experience, but we only ventured up, weather permitting, with Mummy's agreement - she was never *that* keen! I liked to climb up the outside staircase onto the top deck and sit in the first two rows of seats at the front, that were open to the elements. This was an exhilarating experience, especially when the sun shone warm and bright and the wind blew gently through my hair, not to be recommended if it was raining.

The tram's disadvantages were legion. It was an ungainly boneshaker that swayed horribly; it made a dreadful noise - 'clankety clank, clankety clank' - that could be heard even at my grandparents' house, some way up Erlanger Road; and the tram windows were 'glazed' with orange Perspex, not glass. I tried not to look at the windows - the colour made me feel sick. So, what with the sickening sway, the sickening noise and the sickening orange windows, I was glad to get off!

On alighting, we again had to wend our way back to the kerb, from the middle of the road, when the road was free of traffic of course.

Inflexibility was another disadvantage of the tram. When the overhead power pick-up of a tram came off the electric wire above (which it often did), the pick-up would spring up above the overhead conductor wire. With loss of power supply, the tram was, literally, powerless. Restricted by tramlines, as all trams were, it was not just that *that* tram became immobilised, all the trams behind were also brought to a halt and forced to queue. Yes, trams had to queue too. The result? Gridlock! The impasse continued until a man with a very long stick arrived to re-connect the power pick-up to the overhead power wire: a very tricky manoeuvre. Passers-by would stop to watch on tenterhooks, wishing the man success when, after frequent unsuccessful tries, it appeared to be verging on the impossible.

## Last Tram Week – July 1952

The departure of the trams from the roads of London in the July of 1952 was called 'Last Tram Week – July 1952'. Despite all I have said about my dislike of trams, my father, Alison and I returned to Lewisham to have a nostalgic last ride back to New Cross on a tram. It was just a bit of fun! I still have my 'Last Tram Week' ticket!

I may be wrong, but I believe only a few mourned the trams' passing.

## "Mummy, my legs ache!"

Nowadays, I speak ruefully about my inability to walk far because of aching legs. Friends immediately assume it's due to *anno domini*. Possibly the ageing process hasn't helped, but I have suffered from aching legs, to a greater or lesser extent, ever since I was a little girl.

We had walked only a short way from the house up Stratheden Road to the Royal Standard, when I complained,

"Mummy, my legs ache!"

She preferred not to believe me:

"They can't possibly ache, we've only just left home!" I was told in a disparaging tone of voice.

Yes, I *knew* we had only just left home, but I was telling the truth; my legs *did* ache! I may have been little, but my legs frequently ached when walking only short distances, and especially up hills.

When we got off the bus or tram at New Cross Gate we had to walk up the hill that is Erlanger Road. I didn't look forward to that climb, it was always a struggle, and on reaching No. 100 I was invariably complaining, "Mummy, my legs really *do* ache!"

Much later, as a Girl Guide, when a six-mile hike was expected of me, I could hardly walk one mile, let alone six!

Much, much later, in the nineties, when on holiday in Rome my husband and I were misdirected twice back to our hotel, and my aching legs collapsed - I'd walked too far and I was unable to walk any further. I made for a chair in cafe that, providentially, was close at hand. We were returning home the next day, and my husband had to push me in a wheel chair.

The second time my legs collapsed was when we were in Croydon - a neighbour took me to the osteopath in his car

The third time was at 2.30 am on Boxing Day morning about the year 2,000, when I could hardly get to the loo. I managed it somehow but had to crawl back on my hands and knees to get back to my bed. There must be a connection between my early experience of aching legs and these three collapses.

---

My legs may have ached during the War, but my mind was ever active and prone to asking my mother many pertinent questions.

"What are those funny black knobs?" I asked, as we traipsed up Erlanger Road, noticing the line of black knobs on the low white stone wall marking the edge of the front garden of every house we passed:

"Before the War every house had railings. They were all taken away and the metal was used for the War effort. Those little black knobs are where the railings used to be. Now the War's over I expect the railings will soon be back." She sounded hopeful.

This act of vandalism of the railings was visited upon many an elegant, and not so elegant, London street; but their replacement was to take a long time coming. The tragedy was not just their removal but that the exercise turned out to be a complete waste of time, money and energy: the metal was found to be unsuitable for the manufacture of armaments etc. for the War effort.

## Hatcham is declared a Conservation Area

Quite recently, Hatcham was formally declared a Conservation Area, deemed an unspoiled area of Victorian residences in original tree-lined roads. I'd love to be able to tell my mother about that. She was sad to witness New Cross, in general, and Hatcham, in particular, go downhill after the War. She remembered it as it was before the War when it was "respectable", in the best sense of the word.

---

## Weekly visits to No. 100

On reflection, I think it was a privilege to have been born in one of these genuine Victorian houses, still furnished with genuine Victorian furniture, furnishings, bric-a-brac, and, of course, a wot-not in the corner. For a long time, things Victorian went out of fashion, considered dull and heavy. Recently, victoriana has made a comeback.

On our arrival, Grandmother Anderson was at the front door to greet us, as if she hadn't seen us for months – it was only the day before *chez nous*! When Grandfather Anderson was at home he enjoyed holding my hand and walking me up the beautifully scrubbed, pristine pure white stone flight of steps to the front door, counting them as we went. I have been silently counting steps ever since!

Before we got to the front door the neighbours on both sides would greet us.

On one side, at No. 102, was Mrs Bridges, also known as Ada, with a friendly "Good morning" for us, as she scrubbed *her* front doorsteps, a task that all house-proud women of the day felt obliged to do, week after week, to keep the house looking spruce.

On the other side, Florrie came out of her front door at No. 98, cheerily greeting us, as did her ageing mother Mrs Knight, sporting a large white mobcap, giving us a wave through the net curtains from the ground floor window.

*Telegraph Hill Park, opposite 100 Erlanger Road*

I remember well my Stevens Great-grandparents, Gran and Gramp, who were active around the house. Gran was responsible for lunch, cooking it on a primitive-looking gas stove in the basement. When the meal was ready, she called Gramp, who downed tools and joined us for lunch in the basement.

After lunch, I would wander round to the back of the house and find Gramp in his workshop, making me a beautiful wooden dolls' house, that was to give me much pleasure. Such an item was unobtainable because of the War, and even if one could be found, was expensive. Anyhow, the purchase of anything so trivial as a dolls' house, was out of the question. Gramp made several wooden items, still to be found somewhere in one of the Great-granddaughters' residences.

---

Supper was Grandmother Anderson's responsibility, served in the dining room on the ground floor. The room was furnished with heavy curtains and a heavy oak dresser, table and chairs. Everything was heavy and drab, the brown paintwork contributing to the drabness. A permanent heavy dark green cloth covered the table, legs included, in true Victorian fashion! Every armchair was supplied with a piece of cloth called an anti-macassar, placed where a gentleman might put his head; to stop the oil that some men smeared on their hair in those days, despoiling the back of the chair itself.

Now, here is a mystery concerning the grandparents' furnishings: two large, gory pictures of war. One was hung in the hallway, the other just inside the door into the dining room. They frightened me. The picture in the hallway was entitled The Battle of *Mukden*, showing an horrendous scene of the last major land battle of the Russo-Japanese War, fought in 1905 near Mukden, depicting soldiers of the Japanese Empire trampling the soldiers of Imperial Russia. The Japanese won the battle. I would run past it as fast as I could, hands tightly pressed over my eyes. The picture was really scary.

The other picture was also war-like, though not quite so gory and scary, depicting Prussian soldiers fighting. Thanks to this picture, I learnt at the early age of six that the point on a German soldier's helmet identified him as a Prussian – crucial information told me by my mother, which remains with me to this day!

I was mystified that my kindly, peace-loving grandparents and Great-grandparents, should have chosen two such ghastly pictures to hang on their walls. Having lived through two World Wars and other lesser wars, I'd have thought they'd have had enough of war, without having it hung on the walls of their house; especially when neither picture showed a battle in which Great Britain had been involved, to give it a certain *raison d'être*. Imagine such pictures on the walls of a house today!

## Plus ça change!

Later on, I told Grandmother Anderson how I liked the old Music Hall songs of Marie Lloyd and others:

"I wish I'd seen Marie Lloyd on the stage," I told her. "I do enjoy her songs, such as 'My Old Man says follow the Van', 'Oh Mr Porter' and others."

Nana furrowed her brow and shook her head disapprovingly:

"Tut, tut. In my day," she told me, "respectable people didn't go to see Marie Lloyd. She was a person of low morals and considered very *risqué*!"

I had never thought of Marie Lloyd like that. *Plus ça change*!

---

Grandmother Anderson and Grandmother Sutherland were good friends when they were young girls, and both had lived in Queen Elizabeth Street, Horselydown, just down the road from The Tower Bridge.

"We went together to see the Opening of The Tower Bridge by the then Prince of Wales. That was in 1894. And we were, of course, among the first to cross The Bridge after its Opening."

N.B. Grandmother Anderson always spoke of *The* Tower Bridge, using the definite article. When it was constructed, *The* Tower Bridge was how it was always known: in an article written on the subject or in all the printed publicity material advertising a talk on the subject, the definite article was always included because *The* Bridge was erected near '*The* Tower' (of London).

## Lighting the gas mantle

In those days, many older parts of London, Hatcham included, still had only gas as the means of lighting and cooking. Today, we are so accustomed to just touching the switch as we enter a room and we have immediate light! Then, there was no switch to flick. Members of the household had to think ahead:

"Which rooms shall we definitely be using this evening?' - the question had to be considered, and the gas mantle was lit, ideally, before darkness fell.

Every evening, the dining room table was set, with plates, cutlery, glasses etc. and the family was seated, waiting for supper to be served.

On one particular evening, dusk started to fall extra early and "Oh dear, the gas mantle over the table hasn't been lit," declared my grandfather.

My grandmother, realising the urgency of the situation, got up and stood precariously on a chair. She stretched over to the centre of the large dining room table; match in hand, in an endeavour to reach the gas mantle.

Lighting the mantle was a delicate art at the best of times, and on this occasion speed was of the essence. The room was getting darker and darker: the mantle *had* to be lit - and quickly! We were all getting a little concerned, for not only was dusk fast descending, it meant that Nana's ability to see what she was doing was lessening, moment by every precious moment. Her frustration was apparent when the match went out! She struck a second match, applied it to the mantle, thinking, surely, it would light this time, when, suddenly, the mantle broke! With darkness nearly enveloping us, it was no doubt a case of more haste, less speed.

Knowing the fragility of a gas mantle, my grandmother always kept one or two spares, in case of breakage. By this time, my grandfather had produced a torch to give her short-term light while she replaced the mantle. Once she had lit it, she had to adjust the light by gently pulling the two small chains hanging down on either side of the mantle, until it gave out the light required. What a palaver!

At last, supper was served and we were able to relax to enjoy the meal.

## Chapter 10

# BLACKHEATH HIGH SCHOOL

## *Realising my gift of creative writing*

Blackheath High School was the school intended for me, had the War not intervened. The school was evacuated to Tunbridge Wells. To fill the gap until the school returned, I went to the R.C. Ascension Convent, accommodated in one of the row of little Victorian houses between Westcombe Hill and the Charlton Road. I wasn't happy there. The nuns weren't very kind, at least to this 4½ year old who, for the first time, was away from home and without Mummy.

I was taken away from there and sent to another private school, St Margaret's Preparatory School in Diamond Terrace, just off Hyde Vale, run by a Miss Ribuffi.

I liked Miss Ribuffi, and I was happy at her school.

I was given, 'Excellent' for almost every subject, 'Christian knowledge' included, that is, except Arithmetic.

I stayed at Miss Ribuffi's school until one auspicious day a long-awaited letter dropped onto the mat. Mummy opened it and reacted delightedly,

"Oh wonderful! Blackheath High School has just returned from being evacuated. And they've got a place for you!"

"Oh good," I replied with matching delight, not that I really understood at the time, the reason for Mummy's obvious joy at reading the letter. I was told that the offer of a place at the High School was an opportunity not to be missed.

It was 1946 when Blackheath High School returned to its home in Wemyss (pronounced Weems) Road, Blackheath. I made yet another new start: the third school to get used to. Better late than never – this was where I was meant to be, had it not been for the War.

*Growing in wisdom*

## Settled, at last!?

Here I was, settled, at last, at Blackheath High School - I loved it. I could tell it was a lovely school. I started in the form, strangely called Transition - in transition from Kindergarten to Form 1.

Miss Kemp was my form mistress in Form 1. Thanks to Miss Kemp, I realised my gift of creative writing - stories about wicked witches, congenial gnomes and beautiful mermaids. I was given As and ACs (A Commended) marks. I was asked to stand up in class and read out my stories.

After the tension and turmoil of the War, after the many upheavals of evacuations, here, there and everywhere, and already two changes of school, I treasured this sense of security and stability.

In spite of post war austerity, every girl in the form saved a little money. Miss Skeffington was responsible for coming round every week to collect our money and to issue National Savings stamps, 1/6d or 2/6d (12½ pence), which we stuck in the book that each of us had been given. She was very old-fashioned and demure-looking, her greying hair skewed back into a neat bun and her two top front teeth always protruding over her bottom lip.

No longer was my world being turned upside down. Now, I was on top of the world. The War was over and I had found my *niche*. I felt quite sure that this was where I was meant to be. I was happy and my sense of fulfilment could hardly be bettered. At last, my life seemed to be settling down.

## Murmurings abroad

The operative word is 'seemed', for it was not long before disaster was to strike again!

I was aware of murmurings abroad, and the murmurings eventually became an openly discussed topic of conversation: a *move* was being considered. My father feared that the Labour-controlled London County Council was out to destroy Blackheath. Possibly, he had reason: they had just built an horrendous Council Estate close to the prestigious Blackheath Park, and the next scheme did not auger well: a six-lane motorway was seriously mooted to be driven right through Blackheath Village. A committee representing concerned residents was speedily formed and the proposal was vigorously opposed. The LCC dropped the idea.

My father considered it best that we depart before it was too late. In fact, the LCC didn't come up with further unfriendly developments; but my father's mind was made up, and that was that! A move was now almost certain, subject to our finding a suitable house somewhere out of London.

We usually took a Sunday walk after lunch, through Greenwich Park, but just for a change, we sometimes walked down Crooms Hill. There were, and still are, many gracious large houses in Crooms Hill. My mother nursed a secret hope, which she candidly shared with me at the time of our possible departure from Blackheath:

"I don't want to leave Blackheath," she told me wistfully, "I'd like to live in Crooms Hill!"

The idea quite appealed to *me,* too! I didn't want to leave Blackheath either. A beautiful house in Crooms Hill was a lovely idea. In her heart of hearts, Mummy knew that her dream of a house in Crooms Hill was a mere pipe dream and she dismissed the idea. Far too expensive!

*One of the last school reports from Blackheath High*

## Chapter 11

# ON THE MOVE AGAIN!

### *1841 on a Sunnydale House chimney*

The decision to move had been made. In 1946 our search began for a suitable residence large enough to house all eight of us: our family of four, my two Anderson Grandparents and my two Stevens Great-grandparents. Seeing I had no enthusiasm for the idea, I suppose I was fortunate to be included as a member of the search team looking for a suitable house.

We looked at some lovely spacious residences, from Sundridge Park, near Bromley in Kent, to Bessels Green, near Sevenoaks in Kent. Of all the properties we inspected, Sunnydale House in Farnborough Park, on the border of Bromley and Orpington, had the most to commend it.

Sunnydale House was a large, gracious, white-creosoted residence, wisteria covering the front elevation. It was the old original house of Farnborough Park, set in one-and-a-half acres of ground. Farnborough Park had been built at the rear of Sunnydale House, mostly between the two World Wars. The vendors of Sunnydale House, a Mr and Mrs Gatti and their daughter Angela, were moving to Canada.

The accommodation could hardly have been better: three very large living rooms, one of which was of mini-ballroom dimensions; four very large bedrooms and two smaller rooms; the latter: bedroom and sitting room, presumably, for the maid. The house had a kitchen, with a breakfast room adjoining, the latter, easily convertible into a second kitchen for the grandparents; there were already two bathrooms, already four WCs (two up and two down!). Apart from the need to make the breakfast room into a second kitchen, no adaptation was necessary. The outhouses comprised a garage, a spacious workshop area, a coalhole and a stable for a horse, and, in the far corner of the garden, was a pigsty, which must have set my father thinking!

The house had the date 1841 inscribed on a chimney. It was difficult to actually get to see it: visible only from the loft space, and even then it was a question of a ladder onto the roof where there had to be a straining of the neck. This meant that the date was very infrequently seen, which was a pity - *I had the chance to see it only once.*

Farnborough Park was, and still is, a private estate. The original road to Sunnydale House was a long, unmade-up lane, hard on the feet, which took one onto the Crofton Road, leading down into Orpington. Sunnydale, the road, ran along the rear of the house, and had taken its name from the house, Sunnydale. At the far end of Sunnydale (the road) there was dense woodland. The surrounding area was still very countrified. Down 'the lane', as it came to be known, horses grazed in the fields to the left and to the right.

*Sunnydale House – our mini-mansion*

The property we were considering buying was "Inspected and confidently recommended by Knight, Frank & Rutley, Estate Agents, at the price of £7,500, Freehold, subject to contract." initialled "P.M.A". In those days £7,500 was a *tremendous* sum of money! How on earth could we ever hope to buy the place? My father was determined. He had purchased our Blackheath house,

No. 61 Langton Way, for £1,500 in 1936. Some of his peers at the time thought him crazy to invest so much money in a freehold property. They called it Bill's castle!

Having decided that we were to purchase Sunnydale House, our Blackheath house was sold to a Dr Sanderson from Deal in Kent, for a mere £1,750! My father and grandfather took out a mortgage on Sunnydale House, and the purchase was sealed, signed and delivered.

Spring had sprung early in 1947. Winter returned later, with exceptionally deep snowfalls. The day of our removal to our mini-mansion, in April 1947, was very cold and snow was falling, snow on snow, to quote the Christmas carol. It lay two or three feet high with no sign of a thaw, and so it remained for weeks thereafter.

All our possessions were transported from Blackheath to Farnborough Park by Chiesman's of Lewisham, that respectable old-fashioned department store that once stood on the large, spread out corner opposite Lewisham Clock Tower. Fortunately, the removal men were undaunted by the extreme weather conditions. Off went the van with the home packed in it, we followed on with a little more than the old cock linnet!

My Great-grandmother, Gran, came with us when we moved to Sunnydale in 1947, still quite hale and hearty. Unfortunately, my Great-grandfather, Gramp, was not with us - he had died in the summer of 1946. Gran didn't die until 1954, *just* nine months before her hundredth birthday.

As we drove through Farnborough Park in the deep snow, it looked like fairyland, especially as many of the front gardens and verges were unfenced. These were private roads and the snowplough hadn't yet been this way.

While all our goods and chattels were being unloaded, Alison and I had great fun playing snowballs in the garden and jumping off the ancient tree stump of vast circumference opposite the front door. The tree trunk was quite a feature of the front garden. Mrs Gatti told us that they used it as a table to serve tea in the summer. I think we only tried it out once.

A large conservatory flanked the front and one side of the house, in which grew a grapevine and tomato plants. As we made our way through the conservatory, with Mrs Gatti highlighting points of interest, we passed a shallow tray filled with a mass of little green leaves.

"What's this called?" we enquired.

"Mind your own business!" Mrs Gatti told us, unemotionally and with a straight face.

Her reply took us aback at first. How rude! But our disconcerted reaction turned to laughter when she let on that she was serious. That really *was* the name of the green stuff!

We had great fun on many subsequent occasions when friends came to the house and asked the very same question. Now the joke was on us, when we responded, "Mind your own business!" straight-faced and unemotionally, It was then our turn to observe the bemused look on the questioner's face, not knowing how to take our apparent discourtesy!

*Sutherland / Anderson / Winslow families in the Sunnydale House garden.*

Sunnydale House had a beautiful garden: there was a large expanse of lawn with well-kept flowerbeds and mature fruit trees and nut trees – mulberry and cherry, hazelnut and walnut; and a hazelnut grove lay at the end of the garden. An ornamental cherry tree overhanging the ornamental pond, was just right for climbing. In the spring the artistically designed pond was great for frogspawn and frogs, newts and goldfish; and a very tame heron would sometimes pay the pond a visit. Happy though we were to observe the heron perched at the edge of the pond, its presence and purpose were not so happy: it was waiting to pounce on unsuspecting goldfish, which had to be replenished, all too frequently.

On the other side of the garden a stream flowed between the garden and the adjoining field; a rickety little bridge crossed the stream. The owner of the field was a big kindly man, Mr Butler, a Master Baker, before his retirement.

Mr Butler had a sense of humour; He'd left an old tin kettle in the stream and beside it, a notice stating, 'Beware of the water otter'!

He kept a pony called Tommy in the field. Later, he gave me permission to ride Tommy, which was much appreciated.

## The 1947 freeze-up brings a bumper harvest

The vicious cold spell that struck so late in the spring of 1947 sorely disrupted the rhythm of nature. Birds were deceived by the warmth of an early spring and, as a result, had come out of hibernation before time, only to find that winter had returned in a vengeance. The birds, laid their eggs and hatched their chicks, but so bitterly cold did the freeze-up become, all the family, parents and offspring alike, were decimated. Animals were likewise deceived. They too had come out of hibernation, assuming winter had past, especially the squirrels, and they also died in the freeze-up.

All very sad, but there are two sides to every coin: their demise meant that we had a bumper harvest of fruit and nuts! Our first summer at Sunnydale was gloriously hot and the fruit and nuts ripened beautifully. We picked cherries and mulberries by the bowlful, and walnuts and hazelnuts by the basketful. But, never again was it to be thus.

The decimation of birds and squirrels was a short-term phenomenon. Their revival was very apparent in subsequent years. We made every endeavour to scare off the birds and the squirrels, with silver paper and other devices, but to no avail. The birds pecked away and ate all the ripening fruit; and the squirrels ate all the nuts before we had the chance to pick either.

## Chocolate comes off ration

Four years were to elapse after the end of the War, almost to the day, when the Government announced, that "Chocolate and sweets will come off ration, 24<sup>th</sup> April 1949": a date never to be forgotten! How I looked forward to that date - it couldn't come quickly enough. The wait was an endurance test, beyond measure!

At last, the 24<sup>th</sup> April dawned but, Oh dear, it was a Sunday and shopping on a Sunday was frowned upon, indeed, forbidden! After all that waiting, it didn't seem fair. Constraint until the morrow seemed to be the only alternative - in theory!

In practise, such was my frustration, I made a surreptitious visit after church on my bike to the little sweet shop round the corner in Locksbottom, run by old Mr Sansom, and his two rather quaint, sons, Claude and Harold. I got there just before the shop closed at 12 noon. *Eureka!* I'd made my first-ever chocolate purchase without needing sweet coupons: Cadbury's small milk chocolate tuppenny bars (two old pence).

Unfortunately, only a few months later supplies of chocolate became insufficient to meet demand and the post-War Labour Government had to eat humble pie (or was it humble chocolate?) and chocolate and sweets went back on ration. What a let-down!

The 24<sup>th</sup> April remains a significant date in my life. It's not just history, it's indelibly imprinted on my mind. Even now, I keep the date as a personal private 'feast day', not, I assure you, to gorge chocolate all day, as the description might infer. It's kept more with wry amusement rather than an actual feast!

## My father, the smallholder

My father's time in the RAF, when he lived in the countryside of Warwickshire and Oxfordshire, had given him a love for country life, which had fostered in him a desire to be a farmer. That was out of the question, the nearest thing was to become a smallholder, as a sideline to his work in a firm of City stockbrokers. No doubt, the ready-made pigsty in the corner of the garden of our house purchase was a factor and an inducement, in his decision to purchase Sunnydale House.

It was not long after we'd moved in, that fulfilment of his desire was complete: pigs, chicken and geese were the residents of a mini-farmyard to complement our mini-mansion. Keeping pigs was all very well; but when the pigs got out and my father was at work and unavailable to deal with the escapade of swine, it was another matter. Now and again, it happened and, inevitably, it fell to my poor mother to chase the "wretched things", as she used to call them, back into the sty!

## Fred comes to my mother's rescue

Fred was an unusual character, whom we believed was illiterate. He was possibly of gypsy origin, and he always wore the same dirty old black beret. He spoke with a strange husky, almost cockney accent, which made him hard to understand. I can still put on my "Fred voice" - I'm only sorry that it\s not transferable onto the page.

Fred lived in an ancient hovel of a cottage, not that far along the Crofton Road. Fred became my father's right hand man on the pig-keeping scene, he willingly worked, for nothing, for Fred *loved* pigs; he seemed to have a way with them. Such was his devotion to the animals, Fred would often turn up to deal with something for the pigs' welfare - possibly cooking up the pigswill in the workshop boiler room or cleaning out the sty.

Generally, my mother wasn't keen on Fred - in her eyes, he lacked respect. He didn't always let her know when he was around, but when he *did* knock at the back door – (at least it wasn't the front door!) - he announced his arrival, with:

"Allo, I've come up to feed the pigs for Bill!"

My mother complained bitterly within the family about his cheek! "Whenever Fred speaks to me of Daddy, he will refer to him, as "Bill", not Mr Sutherland".

I'm certain *she* didn't think she had found fulfilment when, single-handed, she had to cope with an exodus! She couldn't deny that Fred had his uses, and she expressed her gratitude when he was around and available to come to her aid, dealing with half-a-dozen pigs running rampant round the garden. In fact, if Fred was on the premises, he was only too happy to help get the "wretched things" back into the sty. Fred could always be relied on to restore equilibrium to the 'farmyard'!

## Pigs are reared to supplement our meagre food rations

My father's intention was to breed pigs – yes, we also had piglets at one point - to supplement our still meagre post-War food rations. He had hoped to produce home-cured bacon for breakfast and home grown pork for the Sunday roast.

Home-cured bacon was not very successful - it was too tough and too salty - better to sell the carcases to the Ministry of Food and use the money to buy the professionally cured shop bacon. That scheme, too, had its problems: It was only worthwhile selling the pig if its weight was propitious on the day of sale - not too heavy, not too light - inevitably, that involved inspired guess-work, which had inbuilt inaccuracy!

Another feature of the smallholding was the gaggle of geese – six in all. Five of the geese were wholesome-looking birds; the sixth was an unfortunate creature - unhealthy-looking, with a scraggy, yellowy-grey, nigh featherless neck. To everyone's amusement, Grandfather Sutherland named it Typhoid. Poor thing, the name stuck, and it was *always* referred to, as Typhoid.

One by one, we enjoyed roast goose for Sunday lunch: the first five were very tasty, but what about the sixth - Typhoid? We didn't really fancy him (or was it a her?) for Sunday lunch. With wartime austerity still in force and food generally in short supply, there was no point in getting emotional about the unimportant! Alison and I had been brought up not to be fussy. Until we'd tried Typhoid, we wouldn't know whether he was edible or not. So, despite all reservations, Mummy served up roast Typhoid for Sunday lunch. A little warily, we all commenced to eat him/her, and he proved to be just as tasty as his brothers and sisters, and none of us suffered any adverse symptoms!

## Surprise, surprise!

Both house and garden were full of surprises, large and small.

Soon after we'd moved into Sunnydale House we came across a disconcerting item hanging behind the back door: a genuine, nail-studded wooden cosh! A rather ominous find that set us speculating:

Why was it there? Had the vendors ever had reason to use it? Perhaps they had left it behind because they knew it would come in useful to us! Presumably, it was put there for good reason…..which was? The answer never came. The nearest we got to a possible answer was in a family dispute, when the cosh was alluded to and its use threatened! In jest, I might add.

I'm glad to say, the cosh was never used, for this or any other purpose; it was finally decided to leave the cosh where it was found – hanging behind the back door, in the hope that the answer to our query might one day be revealed.

## 'Sardines' - our mini-mansion was made for the game!

The house had scope for tremendous fun, especially at parties, for playing 'sardines'. There were many obscure hidey-holes, for example, under the backstairs; participants would find themselves squeezed together like sardines, all in great discomfort, trying to fight the temptation to burst into giggles or to prevent an audible gasp for breath. Our mini-mansion was made for the game!

As, no doubt, you have gathered, Sunnydale House was a very superior residence compared with our 1936 semi-detached in Blackheath, but residing there wasn't necessarily a recipe for true happiness. With all the advantages that the house afforded, and the garden permitted, both far more interesting and spacious than what we'd left behind, many would say, "How fortunate you are. It sounds ideal!" Some did say, as much. It was empty talk!

We were settling in well to life in Farnborough Park. I continued at Blackheath High School, proudly displaying the yellow and black cockade on the side of my black velour hat. In the event, our move to Sunnydale proved to be the preamble to yet another upheaval that again was to turn my whole world upside down, with disastrous, nigh irreparable consequences.

A World Turned Upside Down

## Chapter 12

# DISASTER STRIKES AGAIN

## *From a little somebody, to a big nobody*

Not only was 1947 the year of the move and the year of the April snow, for me, it was also my first year of "commuting" between Farnborough Park and Blackheath.

My father took me in the car in the mornings to Lee Green, near Lewisham, where I caught the No. 75 bus – a short journey along to Blackheath. After school there were three buses I could catch in Blackheath Village: Nos. 54, 89 or 108, all of which took me to Lewisham Clocktower. I changed buses there and got the No. 47 Farnborough bus to Farnborough Park. At first, my mother or grandmother met me at the Clocktower and accompanied me on the No. 47 to home.

But it wasn't long before I was doing the whole journey by myself; it was the early morning start that spoiled the day for me. Even then, I wasn't a lark.

My mother was so worried about my doing the return journey alone:

"Now, make sure you get on a *No. 47 going to* Farnborough, not a 47 going only to Bromley Garage. And you mustn't talk to strangers!" she told me strictly. I may have been only eight, but there was no reason for her to worry. The journey was well within my competence. I sat on the three-seat near the entrance to the bus, where the conductor stood, and three other passengers were sitting opposite and two, on the seat where I sat – strangers, yes, but never in the least dubious: they were ordinary kindly people, generally going home after shopping. They didn't always speak, but when they did it would have been discourteous not to reply. I never had any trouble. Indeed, I've been having trouble-free conversations on buses and trains with all sorts and conditions of women and men, ever since!

I felt "big" when, full of confidence, I said to the bus conductor, "Fourpenny-half, please!" In those days the four (old) pence! fare indicated that I was on a long journey. It seemed remarkable in the eyes of some of the grown-up passengers around me, who, at times, showed surprise:

"You're very young to be going such a long way all by yourself," said the lady opposite.

I beamed broadly and nodded, "Yes, almost to Farnborough," I replied with great self-assurance. I was quite capable of travelling by myself, and I enjoyed it. Perhaps, I was demonstrating, unwittingly, my hope, my desire, my ability "to be another lady"!

## I have an inkling

I was *so* happy, at Blackheath High. I really believed I'd found my *niche*. After the tensions and turmoil of the War when my world was forever being turned upside down with threatening air raids; evacuations here, there and everywhere; and already two changes of school, it was good to be settled - at last. Now, I felt on top of the world. Fear and uncertainty were past history, or so I thought. I seemed settled. Oh dear, that word "seemed" comes up again.

I had an inkling - an inkling that change was in the air, once again. I'd heard some veiled talk between mummy and daddy, indicating the possibility of change. It sounded as if the other BHS "was being considered", and then it was seriously suggested, "as a good idea". I concede, I was finding the early morning start a bit much, but that would mean saying "Goodbye, to *Blackheath* High School!" I could hardly bear the thought.

My inkling proved correct. In the spring term of 1949 transfer to Bromley High took place: it spelt disaster and almost destroyed me! It felt like *the end*! It almost was. With a heavy heart, I was uprooted for the *nth* time, only to be *dumped* at Bromley High – school number four. Inevitably, it *had to be* "Goodbye Blackheath High", and there was no possible reversal. I little knew the desperate unhappiness in which this move would immerse me. I was *brokenhearted*!

This was one move too many and it spelt misery for me; my zest for life vanished, seemingly never to return. At Blackheath High I was a little somebody; at Bromley High I was a big nobody.

I tried to recapture my happy memories: that beautiful school hall in which Miss Janet Macauley took prayers every morning with great sincerity; playing 'Hide and Seek' in the many hideouts on two sides of the playground;

and riding my little blue bike to and from school; and many another lovely memory of the happiness I once enjoyed. I'd had a real sense of fulfilment at Blackheath High, writing stories about snowmen, gnomes and witches. 'A' and 'AC' (A Commended), and was asked to stand up in class to read out my compositions.

Happy memories! That's all I had.

Again, my whole world was turned upside down. I was leaden with unhappiness and was inconsolable! With hindsight, I do wonder if my return to Blackheath High was, even then, *really* out of the question. Blackheath High had "soul" and I yearned to be back.

Bromley High seemed soulless. There, I was not even given the opportunity to use my gift of creative writing. I needed encouragement to do what I knew I was able to do – write my fantastical stories.

## The State Opening of Parliament

There was one event in late 1949 that helped to sustain my hope: before I left Blackheath High School, my name had been put down to go to London to see the Procession for the State Opening of Parliament. So, I had this reunion with my Blackheath High friends to look forward to.

The day dawned cold, grey and drizzly, not very conducive to waiting on a London street. I was overjoyed by being back with my former classmates. I think they were pleased to see me, but I was aware that our reunion didn't mean as much to them as it meant to me. They had no real idea of the extent and depth of my unhappiness.

But, here we were, first and foremost, gathered again to watch the Royal procession for the Opening of Parliament. We waited in the drizzle for what seemed a very long time, getting wetter and wetter, colder and colder.

But, at last, the Royal coach carrying King George VI and his Queen Elizabeth came into view. We cheered their Majesties as they made their way to the Palace of Westminster, where the King was to perform the Opening of Parliament. Not long afterwards, we raised a further cheer for the two Princesses, Elizabeth and Margaret Rose, also bound for the Palace of Westminster. In spite of the rain and the cold, it was worth the wait, just to see the King and Queen and the two Princesses; and, of course, It had been a memorable day for me, in more ways than one.

    The reunion with my Blackheath High classmates didn't really help. The day was memorable while it lasted; its benefit was transitory. I was now back to facing the stark reality of my situation. So deep ran my unhappiness, it issued into blackouts, a life garbled by loss of consciousness.
    I had been such a happy little girl, and, according to my mother's diary, a happy baby too. All I could do was hope that happiness might return some fine day. I was trying, but in vain, to get back to the happiness I'd known at Blackheath. Hope sprung eternal with the end of the War, but now even hope was almost dashed.

## Chapter 13

# BEAUTIFUL THOUGHTS TO HORRIBLE THOUGHTS

*One change too many!*

### From blackouts to blackouts

This change of school was one change too many; it wrought devastation to my life, and my inner world fell to bits. In spite of many obvious attractions and advantages of Sunnydale House, beautiful thoughts were replaced by "horrible" thoughts, over which I had no control. My ability to describe my inner turmoil wrought by the blackouts has defied me since the day the blackouts started. But I will give it another try.

Horrible thoughts, as I called them, frequently assailed me. The initial thought wasn't horrible *per se,* it could be a thought about *absolutely anything*: but that first thought triggered off a connecting thought, which triggered off another thought, and so on and so on – subtle and fast-moving, unexpected and unpredictable and I had absolutely no control over the process - that is what was horrible. Along with these unsolicited thoughts and memories, horrid sensations and emotions rose up from deep within me. All this got jumbled up and became so terrible and frightening, that I needed to hold the hand of the nearest person, as quickly as possible. When the moment came that the brain could take no more. I lost consciousness - the sub-conscious took over.

Outwardly, nothing was untoward, apart from the fact that I had a vacant look in my face and eyes, so I was told. All the untowardness was within, silent and unseen. I would walk around doing things "normally" but was completely unaware of what I was about. I wasn't there, so to speak. Onlookers often thought I'd come round, when I hadn't.

The attacks were also a cause of humiliation. A seizure during a lesson at school usually meant landing up in the sick room - quite inappropriately, because when I came round I found myself alone and unsupported. When

I realised later that my bladder had relaxed my humiliation was complete. Fortunately, this didn't always happen, at school or wherever, but obviously, when it did happen, it was a dreadful embarrassment.

Well might Shakespeare say, "For you there's rosemary and rue" (*A Winter's Tale*). My life has exemplified that - blackouts were to blight the rest of my life.

It was another ten years before I noticed on a doctor's sickness certificate that my attacks were described as epilepsy! I'd never been told that that was what my illness was.

## I pass the Eleven Plus

Initially, despite all, I managed to hold my own at Bromley High School. I passed the Eleven Plus exam, which meant I could stay on at Bromley High School, but it didn't qualify me for a *free* place there. Why? Because I'd *never* been to a Council School! What a crazy ruling: that one had to have spent at least two years at a Council School to get a free place. However, I was entitled to a free place at Bromley Grammar School, a very good school, which possibly, with hindsight, might have suited me better. The powers that be, as they were then, considered rightly that I'd had enough of school-changes.

Grandfather Anderson, who paid for my education and my sisters', agreed to continue paying for me, so enabling me to remain at Bromley High, a very mixed blessing.

Grandfather Anderson was a generous soul in more ways than one. He gave we three Sutherland sisters our pocket money, half-a-crown (12½ new pence), each week - half-a-crown was a lot of money in those days. Most friends only got a shilling or even a mere 6d. Our grandfather magnanimously described our weekly half-crowns as "wages", not that much work had been done to deserve that description!

As already stated, we were taught not to fritter our money away; rather, were we encouraged to save it for something really worthwhile. Three weeks' "wages" paid for me to have an hour's horse ride on a Saturday morning. I enjoyed horse riding.

It wasn't unknown for me to have a blackout while out on a horse, but I never fell off; nor did a fearful event while on horseback result in a blackout happening.

One particular *cause célèbre* comes to mind: two school friends and I were leisurely trotting our horses down Holwood Park Avenue, an upmarket private road near Locksbottom, when, for some unknown reason, all three horses suddenly bolted. They galloped furiously down Holwood Park Avenue, heading straight for the A21, the main Hastings Road. None of us was able to rein in our respective steeds - all three were unstoppable. We just had to sit tight, literally, and hope upon hope that when we came to the busy A21 the horses would stop of their own volition. Fortunately, they did. I kept my head, and I coped. It was a bit scary, but there was no question of it being the cause of a blackout.

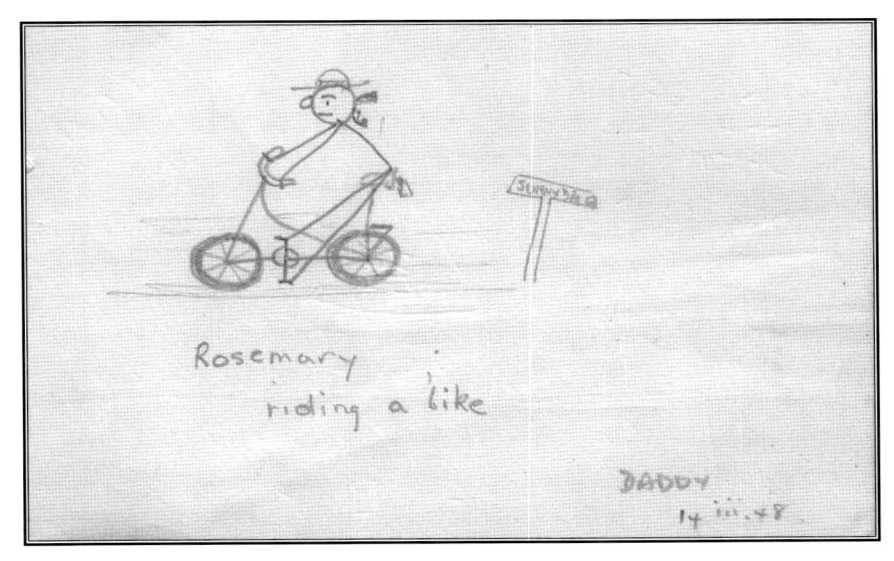

*Rosemary riding her bike – signed Daddy, dated 14.3.48*

As with riding on horseback, I loved riding my bike. I cycled all over the place and, if, as on a horse, I had a blackout, I never fell off.

Come one particular occasion, I had a blackout as I was cycling home through Farnborough Park. The next thing I knew, I was 'coming round' sitting on the sofa in the front room of Sunnydale House. As I emerged from the blackout, a vestige of its horribleness still lurked within me, telling me why it was that I'd suddenly found myself in the house, sitting on the sofa:

"Oh, I must have had a blackout!" I exclaimed.

I went out to the shed to investigate the whereabouts of my bike. No one marvelled more than I, that I had put the bike away in the shed in exactly the right spot! I recalled not a thing.

## Attendants to Mary, Queen of Scots

Alison and I were involved in a memorable occasion. We were invited, at the behest of the Caledonian Society to which our parents belonged, to be attendants on horseback to Mary Queen of Scots in the Pageant at the *finale* of the 1952 Highland Games at The White City.

## The Elizabethan Fayre

Miss Elizabeth East, headmistress of both senior and junior schools of Bromley High School, decided that she should retire.

*Alison and I are Attendants to Mary Queen of Scots, 1952 Highland Games, at The White City stadium*

Miss Harrison, head of the junior school, had the idea of putting on an Elizabethan Fayre in honour of Miss East, who had agreed to be Queen Elizabeth, for the day.

The Fayre was held at Speldhurst, as the house was known, in which the junior school resided, in Elmfield Road, Bromley. The invitation to the departing headmistress to take on the royal part, just for the day, seemed an appropriate farewell gesture.

The day of the Fayre dawned and the weather was fine. Her Majestie Queen Elizabeth, attired in regal splendour, made her grand entrance on the raised part of Speldhurst garden. On her Majestie's arrival, Sir Walter Raleigh was standing close by - fortunately, because it meant that he was available to lay down his cloak for the Queen's Majestie, which he did, most gallantly; that meant that her Majestie did not have to walk through a puddle of dirty water. For that noble action, if for nothing else, I think Sir Walter will be remembered through history.

We, her subjects, were all suitably attired as Elizabethan citizens. We formed various small groups around Speldhurst's garden, representing different aspects of life in Elizabethan England.

My sister, Alison was in the Preparatory form. She and other pupils in Preparatory were maypole dancers. They encircled the maypole set up in the playground, singing and dancing round it, entwining their multi-coloured ribbons round the pole, as they danced.

Six of us in Upper II were Elizabethan seafarers: Jane Basset was the gallant Sir Walter Rayleigh; Mary Vickers, Sir Francis Drake; Barbara Read, Christopher Columbus; Barbara Scott-Wilson, Ferdinand Magellan, and I, Rosemary Sutherland, was Sir Martin Frobisher. When a goodly number of the Elizabethan *hoi poloi*, that is, parents and mistresses! were assembled before our group, we intrepid seafarers stood up in turn to relate the discoveries of distant lands, made on behalf of her Majestie the Queen Elizabeth of Merrie England.

One of our number, Christopher Columbus, had actually made a brave journey right round the world and, thanks to his courageous vision and steadfastness he discovered that the earth wasn't flat, after all; and his presence with us proves that one doesn't fall off the edge! We have a lot for which to thank him, for settling this raging controversy.

The following is the account I gave of my seafaring accomplishments:

"I am Sir Martin Frobisher, born in 1535.

After several years of adventurous trading on the coast of Africa I was made Captain of The *Primrose* on Drake's voyage to the West Indies in 1585.

"I commanded several expeditions in the long search for the North-West Passage, and was on the first expedition that set sail from Blackwall in 1576. Although the North-West Passage was not to be established until over 300 years later, I got further than anybody else at the time and, indeed, for a long time to come. I might add that I had a bay named after me in recognition of my pioneering exploration.

"Later, in 1588, I was with Drake when the Spanish Armada arrived near our shores, threatening to invade England. I was captain of *The Triumph* and we sent the Spanish scuttling. The rogues!

"For this last service I was knighted by the Lord Admiral on the deck of *Ark Royal*. That was my triumphal end."

*"I am Sir Martin Frobisher!"*
*(Early discoverer of the North-West Passage.)*

(Well, not exactly my end. It didn't seem appropriate to tell the audience the date of my death!)

The court photographer came round to take a photograph of our group and the privilege was mine to hold the pointer on the map showing where the

North-West Passage lay.

My mother had made my lovely Tudor costume, including a black hat enhanced by a beautiful black ostrich feather. On seeing the photograph, I was dismayed to observe that I was standing on the wrong side of the map for the feather to be visible. I was cross with myself for this oversight! Really, the ostrich feather 'made' the *chapeau*, no disrespect to my mother's handiwork.

I think her Majestie the Queen enjoyed The Fayre, marking the occasion of her retirement.

It was a welcome interlude for me – temporarily lifting my dismal disposition.

## From Lower to Upper School

A year after our Elizabethan Fayre, our form moved up to Lower III, which took us into the senior school, situated further along Elmfield Road, close to Bromley South Station. Our form started to learn French for the first time. I was fortunate because my father had previously taught me basic French using a book called, *La Vie de Madame Souris*.

It was two years later in the Lower Fourth that I started not to be coping with schoolwork. It was as if I were being bombarded with a plethora of facts, coming fast and furious on so many different subjects. I was unable to assimilate all that was being thrown at me – not helped by my blackout-ridden life impairing my concentration. It wasn't long before I really *wasn't* coping. The only way of dealing with this state of affairs was to give up!

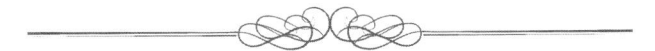

---

Sheila joined us in the Upper School. She was one of the scholarship girls. We became best friends. Relatively recently, Sheila dropped in to see me at home and a discussion started on my unhappy sojourn at Bromley High.

"Perhaps Bromley High School wasn't the school for you," Sheila suggested sympathetically.

"Well, yes and no!" was my paradoxical reply. "I am very grateful to have had a classical education. It was my inability to assimilate so many facts and figures, as they were relentlessly poured into my brain, along with the belief that passing exams was the only thing that mattered. That was pressurising, and I can't take pressure. I quite understand that there has to be exams, but exams didn't necessarily serve to fulfil the potential of everyone. For whatever reason, some were slow learners, others were late developers, whilst others had a disability that held us back. I could identify with all these aspects rolled into one! But despite the inability to pass exams, some of us managed to thrive and find an element of 'success' later on."

Certainly, no allowance was made for my disability. That's how it was in those days, I suppose. I learnt later that there were others in the form that felt similarly, that the school's attitude was destructive. A word of affirmation for us lesser achievers would have been welcome.

**Nobody cared that I had a gift for conversing in French**

French and Classical Music were my two redeeming features of life at Bromley High. I passed French 'O' Level, not that that is anything to write home about, but I have built on it and seem to have a gift for speaking French and, later on, other languages. I may not be able to translate Molière but I can converse with his countrymen. Nobody cared about that. Speaking the French language was given such low priority at school. Little time was spent on finding out a girl's ability to speak the language. Why, I wonder, was it given such low priority?

Four of us took the RSCM Grade V Music Theory exam. I'm glad to say, we all passed that. Quite independently of Bromley High School, and thanks to the Third Programme, as the Radio 3 station was then known, I acquired a good knowledge of classical music. But neither my ability to speak French nor my pass in Grade V Music Theory elicited one word of affirmation. These mini-successes, as I call them, indicated, at least to me, if not to anyone else, that I wasn't the complete good for nothing that the circumstances encouraged me to believe. I left Bromley High School feeling an abject failure.

I was interested to hear Alison, my younger sister, saying only recently and with great emotion, "I left Bromley High feeling a complete failure."

"So did I," I told her.

I hadn't realised how deeply she too felt about her time at Bromley High. Alison is very different from me. After studying Home Economics at the Westminster School of Cookery she proved herself by running a successful restaurant for many years and writing cookery books.

Alison and I are the unfortunates!"

Another aspect of life at the High School that Alison and I had in common was our frequent unceremonious removal from the classroom. When Alison was two she caught Pink Disease. Her lungs and bronchial pipes were badly damaged and they got bunged up with phlegm, and she coughed unstoppably, so had to leave the class.

Similarly, I too was taken out of the class when I had a blackout.

Presumably, our mother had spoken wistfully to Miss East, the headmistress, about her two daughters and their respective health problems.

My mother told me much later how Miss East had commiserated with her, "Oh, Mrs Sutherland, you are unfortunate!"

I wonder if it had occurred to Miss East that, first and foremost, it was Alison and I who were the unfortunates!

## Catherine Mary joins the Sutherland clan

Before I continue, I must add that eight years after our move to Sunnydale another sister, Catherine Mary, was born on the 8$^{th}$ May 1950 in Farnborough Hospital. I was twelve. Children were not permitted in to the Maternity Unit, so Alison and I went to the hospital and Mummy stood on the balcony of her room and waved to us from there. That was the nearest we got to seeing Mummy in hospital!

I have no great significant memories of Catherine, except to say, that her song was 'Sparrow in the Treetops' and that she was a dear little soul. I enjoyed playing with her. She couldn't get her tongue round her name at first, so insisted on calling herself '"Tatty" Sutherland.

## Up the Bürgenstock

My first memory of Catherine, of any significance, was in 1955 on a family holiday in Switzerland. We stayed in a chalet halfway up the Bürgenstock Mountain. Daddy drove us up and down the mountain in the car, to and from the chalet, fearlessly negotiating many a hairpin bend.

Mummy didn't like the hairpin bends, so my parents decided to take the lift as an alternative to going up and down the Bürgenstock via the hairpin bends, by car. We had our sandwich lunch on the bank of Lake Lucerne and, of course, took the lift up the mountain when we returned for supper in the chalet.

*"Look, Mummy! Look at the cows down there."*
*– Bürgenstock Mountain above Lake Lucerne*

The lift had its disadvantages, too. No hairpin bends, of course, but it started a long way up the mountain and the cabin was reached by a considerable length of walkway, high up between the mountain face and the lift cabin that took us down to the foot of the mountain. On either side of the slatted walkway there was a very flimsy inadequate handrail and a sheer drop that didn't bear looking down; and there was a disconcerting gap between each of the wooden slats that went across the walkway from left to right.

One particular memory I have is that of Catherine walking along this slatted walkway, holding Mummy's hand, blithely trying to attract Mummy's attention, encouraging her to look down at something at the foot of the mountain that she wanted Mummy to see far, far below:

"Look, Mummy! Can you see the cows down there?" Understandably, our poor Mother, with no head for heights, at the best of times, was neither willing nor able to look at what her youngest wanted her to see. Mummy was doing her utmost to look anywhere other than "down there"!

"No, darling, I'm afraid I can't look now!" said she, firmly.

Mummy may have found this a greater agony than the hairpin bends. She never said.

"Tatty" Sutherland was only five; she couldn't understand why Mummy was unwilling to share her delight at seeing cows grazing in the field, far below, at the foot of the mountain.

*'Tatty' Sutherland enjoying an ice cream on the beach*

I had great sympathy for Mummy and her very real sense of insecurity, exposed as we were to the great drop on both sides of the walkway and with the gaps between the slats. The walk from the side of the mountain to the lift was quite unnerving; I found it difficult enough to concentrate my gaze on the destination a few yards further along. I wanted to get into that lift as quickly as possible.

That was one of my amusing memories of Catherine Mary when she was small.

Chapter 14

# ON PILGRIMAGE TO ETHIOPIA

## *Providential Encounters*

Generally speaking, I was not a very sporty type, but when I had the energy I enjoyed netball, especially goal-shooting. At lunchtime break I spent much of the time practising goal shooting with a certain Marion Syms and two others from her form. I held my own with them, and was suitably gratified, matching myself with this company, seeing they were three forms above me!

### I meet up with a person with a familiar name

In 2008, we went on a pilgrimage to Ethiopia under the auspices of the Anglican and Eastern Churches Association, AECA. I got talking with a fellow pilgrim, and it transpired that our lives had taken similar paths: we are both committed Anglican Christians and we both belonged to the same two Church Associations: the (AECA); and the Association for Promoting Retreats (APR). And ir turned out that we both support the Anglican Church in Ghana – more of that anon.

There have been many wonderful pilgrimages under the auspices of the AECA, and I cannot do justice to them here. We have visited various countries where the Orthodox Church is the main Christian presence, especially when life under Communism was so often desperate. The most significant pilgrimage, I believe was the one to Russia in 1988, to share in their Millennium celebrations, for 1,000 years of Christianity in Russia. Our visits have been to let them know that Christians in the West remembered them and to assure them of our concern and prayers for their suffering people.

I digress from my meeting up with the above mentioned lady. Neither of us recognised the other so, at first, neither of us was aware that we were renewing an acquaintance of yesteryear. She told me that her name was Marion Syms, and I said to her, "Your name is very familiar, but I can't think how I know you."

Later, we were in the company of a fellow pilgrim, who commented favourably about some small thing Marion had said or done. I don't recall what it was, but in reply she declared,

"That's what Bromley High School does for you!"

"Oh, Bromley High School!" I exclaimed with surprise. "I went to Bromley High School!" My mind went into overdrive as I walked round the hotel trying to recap how it was that I knew Marion's name so well. Suddenly, it hit me - of course, it was our lunchtime netball goal shooting sessions!

Our meeting in Ethiopia was, of course, long after we had left school, and I sought Marion out in the hotel to tell her that I had recalled our netball goal shooting sessions in the playground of Bromley High School! Yes, she remembered it well and we started to reminisce, laughingly, about our endeavours shooting goals in our lunch break.

As we reminisced, we realised that we had both been that same year, at the AGM of the other Church Association, to which we both belonged, The Association for Promoting Retreats, at Launde Abbey in Rutland.

Marion Syms and I had another mutual concern: we were both involved in Ghana. Although Ghana is a very large West African country with many diverse Anglican Church projects, supported by churches in the England, as Marion and I talked it transpired that we both supported the very same venture – the University College project to train post graduate Ghanaians in Environmental Sciences and Engineering, Food and Health Sciences, and Social Sciences, and that we had a mutual Ghanaian friend in Professor Marian Addy, the young woman who founded the college, whom Marion Syms and I had come to know, quite independently of each other. I have supported the college, financially, through my dear, now late, Ghanaian friend, Josephine Armah, who was the bosom friend of Marian Addy, the College founder.

Marion Syms also supports the College, financially, and knows Marian Addy, because the College is the project identified by Portsmouth Cathedral, which Marion Syms attends.

Ghana was yet another strange coincidence that came out of the renewal of my friendship with Marion Syms when we met in Ethiopia.

## Another providential encounter

That brings me to how I met the above-mentioned Josephine.Armah,

Marian Addy's close friend. In the 1980s I was attending St Andrew's Church, South Croydon, when, one Sunday, I sat next to a lady from Ghana, Josephine Armah. I got talking to her and encouraged her to stay for coffee served at the back of the church. I invited her up to our house. We became good friends.

Josephine told me later,

"I went to church that Sunday morning because a Ghanaian Pentecostal friend of mine had encouraged me to go with her into Croydon, for me to find an Anglican church. I didn't know Croydon at all and hadn't the slightest idea where to go to find an Anglican church," Josephine told me. "My friend went to her Pentecostal church. I was left wondering which way to turn, when I heard a church bell ringing and I made her way towards it. The bell happened to be that of St Andrew's Church, and, you came and sat next to me that morning."

Josephine was a very cultured lady, a clever and highly educated scientist. She was Head of Department at the Atomic Energy Commission in Accra. Much later. I learnt that she had led the way for women to be given higher education in Ghana.

The reason for Josephine's visit to England was because she had cancer. She was being treated at a leading London hospital where she was prescribed the necessary drugs, unobtainable in Ghana.

"I didn't want to be a burden on the State or the NHS," Josephine continued, "so I borrowed some money from a Ghanaian friend in London, to pay for my consultations with the specialist and the expensive drugs I'd need."

When we first met, she had omitted to tell me that she was doing a cleaning job to pay for her accommodation in England. She was a sick woman and deserved better. I was very cross with her for not telling me earlier about the cleaning job. We were only too happy to help her with the rent, so she could give up having to work.

"My concern now is how I shall be able to repay the friend from whom I've borrowed the money."

"Don't you worry about that, we'll deal with that," I assured her.

We respected her greatly for not wishing to be a burden on the State.

"Look at it like this," I said, "In England, I see the local doctor or the hospital consultant, all without charge at the point of consulting them; and I have the privilege of not having to pay for my medication for my epilepsy and other medical needs. Now, it's my privilege to pay for your medical needs!"

Dear Josephine, her relief was tangible to learn of the offer; a tremendous burden had been lifted from her shoulders; and she was overwhelmed with gratitude!

As a result of our providential meeting at St Andrew's, her faith in Jesus Christ was deepened, for providential, it was. Also, her commitment to Christ's Church was increased, on her return to Ghana, as a mark of her gratitude. Josephine lived in the village of Kwabenya, near Accra, and she determined to be at Mass every Sunday. It was mooted that a new Anglican church should be built for the first time in Kwabenya - Josephine was a leading light!

We corresponded regularly, and one May she wrote to tell me that Bishop Joseph Dadson of Tamale had given permission for Mass to be said once a month in her house. She felt very privileged and was jubilant at the bishop's suggestion. She wrote and told me all about it.

---

Not long after this, my husband, Robert, went out to Ghana to refurbish and extend the water supply of Accra, the capital of Ghana. He found a modern house near his work, which happened to be fairly close to Kwabenya, where Josephine lived. He had met Josephine, of course, during her time in England, and he was glad to have her and the church nearby, with a ready-made Anglican Christian congregation, which he could join on a Sunday morning.

Because Kwabenya village lacked its own church at that time, the nearest chapel for the villagers to attend Mass was the chapel on the Legon campus of Accra University. Robert joined Josephine and her many friends at Legon and once a month in Josephine's house. He was a regular member and supporter of their worshipping community. Again, all very providential.

The reason for my relating all the above details has nothing, ostensibly, to do with what follows, yet the purpose will soon become apparent.

## Yet, a further providential encounter

Back in England, a small group of us from our Days of Renewal was en route for Walsingham. We were staying the night at St Saviour's Priory, Haggerston, near Hackney, in order to be on the east side of London, ready to go off to Walsingham in Norfolk, next morning.

It was the evening of the 21st September, St Matthew's Day; we wondered where we would go to celebrate St Matthew, one of our Lord's apostles.

"Let's go to St Matthew's, Westminster," suggested Father John, our leader.

"Yes, that's a good idea!" we all agreed.

So, after a light supper, that evening, off we went to St Matthew's Church, in Great Peter Street, Westminster, for the Sung Mass. On our arrival, we found that an African bishop was chief celebrant and preacher. That, in itself, was not that remarkable, but…..

After Mass, all were invited to join the congregation in the church hall for refreshments. I happened to meet up with the bishop and was fortunate to have a conversation with him.

"Where are you from, may I ask?" Just a polite opening gambit.

"I'm from Ghana," he told me.

"Oh, really, my husband is working in Ghana, at the moment." I wanted to mention that "I had a good Ghanaian friend….." but I dismissed that thought. Considering the size of the country and the thousands of Anglican Christians in his diocese/country, it's a bit inane to ask someone, such as he, "Do you know my friend…?"

Anyhow, the bishop and I talked for quite a while. He showed great interest in my husband's crucial work, increasing the supply of water to Accra. I didn't wish to 'hog' the Bishop for too long, after all, I wasn't a member of St Matthew's Church, but as I moved on to let someone else speak to the bishop, I added, in passing,

"I must tell my friend, Josephine Armah, that I've met you!"

The bishop looked at me aghast, "Josephine Armah?" he enquired in amazement, looking at me with a sense of disbelief, "I've said Mass in her house!"

Our amazement was mutual.

"Oh, you must be the bishop who's given permission for Mass to be said in her house!" I replied, also with a sense of disbelief, "Josephine wrote to me six months ago and told me about it!"

This was none other than Bishop Joseph Dadson, about whom Josephine had written to me! What a coincidence.

When I got back home I wrote a quick note to Josephine and told her about my providential meeting up with Bishop Dadson at St Matthew's, Westminster.

The very next Sunday after the bishop got back to Ghana he went to say Mass in Josephine's house and said to her, "I met a friend of yours in London!"

"Yes, I know," Josephine replied. "I've received a letter from her, telling me all about how you met, - and here's her husband!" she added, introducing Robert, standing nearby.

I could, of course, have asked the bishop at the start of our conversation at St Matthew's if he knew "my friend Josephine". But the inanity of such a question prevented me. The possibility of his knowing her was remote, to say the least.

The Hand of God seems to have been at work in these providential links.

Josephine died of the cancer some ten years ago; and more recently, her close friend in Kwabenya, Marian Addy, the mutual Ghanaian friend of Marion Syms and me, has also died of cancer.

## Chapter 15

# AN AFFIRMING VISIT TO FRANCE

### *In France I find myself*

I was 16 when I first went to France, on an exchange visit with Martine Huet du Rotois, my *correspondante française*. This was the first time I'd been away from home alone, and my first opportunity to put my French properly into practice. I loved my visit to France.

I have happy memories of my stay with *La Famille Huet du Rotois* in their small but tastefully furnished flat in Versailles. It was with some difficulty that they fitted me into their cramped accommodation. I slept in the room where we also ate our meals, including breakfast! That meant, of course, I had to be up and dressed before *le petit dejeuner* was served! One morning I overslept and breakfast was delayed, but that didn't seem to concern the family unduly.

Life was very relaxed *chez la famille du Rotois*. Their *apartement* was not far from the famous *Palais de Versailles* with the *Grand Trianon*, and the *Petit Trianon*, the latter built for Marie Antoinette.

It was in that milieu on this, my first venture to France, that I had the sense of finding myself, in spite of the fateful move to Bromley High School. I came alive in France - speaking French!

A trivial aspect though it may be, I delighted in the frequency of cups of coffee served after every meal and at other times during the day. Coffee, not tea, reigned supreme! In most households in England, at the time, ours included, tea reigned supreme. Coffee was considered a luxury, kept for breakfast and after lunch. My French hostesses were surprised to find that their visitor from England was very unEnglish as an inveterate non-tea drinker.

We paid several visits to Paris by train, and I was shown all the well-known sights: *L'Arc de Triomphe, Le Champs Elysée, Le Sacré Coeur, Le Tour Eiffel*, etc. Of course, I visited the wonderful *Palais de Versailles*, down the road. I liked especially *Le Petit Trianon*. Other English people came to stay with friends of

Martine, and they too wanted to visit *Le Palais de Versailles*. I ended up going there three or four times during my stay.

*Martine and me in Paris*

This visit to France really boosted my morale. *Monsieur, Madame* and Martine were a tremendous help increasing my French vocabulary and improving my pronunciation. Their slow, precise enunciation of words remains with me even today. By the end of my stay I was conversing quite fluently. It was good to realise my ability to speak and understand French. I've advanced since then, of course, and now converse with greater fluency.

I had one or two blackouts while there, an embarrassment of course. *Monsieur* et *Madame* coped well and were't too put out.

## My love of words

I have benefitted greatly from having had a classical education. I didn't excel academically at writing essays on the works of Shakespeare, but the language of Shakespeare has influenced my poetry and the articles I have written since.

I am fascinated to know the derivation of English words. Knowledge of Latin is essential if one wants to find out the derivation of words. Of course, the derivation could also be Greek, German or Norman French.

I'm vey glad I did Latin at school, albeit only for two years. I recall quite a lot. I can still decline the nouns and conjugate the verbs.

## Stymied by the lack of choice - my *forte* left undiscerned

Obviously, my *forte* for learning languages and of writing stories was not discerned at Bromley High, for later on, as you will see below. I was not permitted to start learning German.

When we dropped certain subjects and started others, our year's choice was stultifying and inflexible. We could study: Latin and Greek, Latin and German, Latin and Economics, Latin and Physics and Chemistry OR Domestic Science. All the girls in our year were subject to this crazy lack of choice – I couldn't see the logic of it then, and still can't. I wanted to do German but that wasn't permitted me because I wasn't good enough at Latin! Latin had to be dropped because the school considered, quite rightly, that I wouldn't get Latin 'O' level.

Domestic Science it had to be. There was no other option. Presumably, it was assumed I'd be doing Domestic Science for 'O' Level. I could have told them right from the start, I would *not*. Pushed into doing Domestic Science was Hobson's choice for several of us. Here I was, not only *dumped* at Bromley High School, I was now *lumped* with the Domestic Scientists! A double wammy!

I was frustrated to the core (*Core,* Latin, heart). When one's heart isn't in whatever one is doing, the frustration can be unbearable, added to which, in my case, was the frustration of having to listen to some of the inane conversation that took place. Topics discussed by certain girls concerned such things as the latest fashion in shoes, the colour of a new lipstick, and the ups and downs with the latest boyfriend! I shan't forget the day that Veronica, at the age of 16, proudly declared, "I've got 21 boyfriends"; and then there was the dramatic moment when Belinda, her voice filled with emotion, made the great announcement,

"I've fallen in love with film star, James Mason!" She almost swooned as she related this earth-shattering news.

I couldn't have cared less. Not every girl doing Domestic Science was party to this kind of talk but it seemed to predominate. It was an endurance test!

I felt a misfit all round: I belonged neither to the academics nor to the domestic scientists!

I don't know that I've really forgiven Bromley High School for this *faux pas:* forcing me into pastry making. I've never been keen on eating pastry – I find it indigestible. You could say this was rubbing it in!

What a waste of time, what a travesty! Having had my creative potential, my gift of writing, unlocked, I had to endure much that came nowhere near to nurturing me, all the more so, in view of my blackouts. Neither was my ability to speak French affirmed, nor my love of classical music encouraged.

I'd known how I had been at Blackheath High, in the pre-blackout era – alert, fulfilled and, I think, fairly intelligent. With the advent of blackouts, my ability to focus, to concentrate and so to learn, was nigh impossible. I was desolate. A doctor informed me not that long ago that my record shows I had an IQ of 139, which, so she said, is fairly good.

I met a retired schoolmistress when I was serving on the bookstall in Southwark Cathedral. I shared with her something of the above. It so happened she had taught at both Blackheath High and Bromley High Schools and I was very gratified to learn that her experience of the two establishments confirmed me in mine. It wasn't just the experience of an unhappy, disabled little girl.

## Chapter 16

# ST GILES' CHURCH, FARNBOROUGH, KENT

*I took to the Sung Eucharist like a fish to water*

Our move to Farnborough Park was a disaster so far as I was concerned, but there was *some* compensation of whose significance I didn't realise. I was ten when neighbours took me on Sunday mornings in their old Vauxhall car to the 12th century church of St Giles the Abbot in Farnborough Village.

The car was parked and we approached the church through the lytch gate into the churchyard, past a vast yew tree spreading its ancient branches over the many ancient tombs and graves.

The Sung Eucharist we attended was sung to the well-known Merbecke setting, an act of worship that inspired me. Nothing about it had been explained, but that didn't matter greatly. I was told, "It's Trinity Sunday" or whatever Sunday it was. I was shown the place in the Prayer Book for the Collect, Epistle and Gospel, and was left to get on with it, which I did! I took to the Sung Eucharist like a fish to water. So far as I was concerned, it was a great improvement on Sunday School. Halfway through the service, a Mrs Palmer, a kindly elderly lady, took out a gaggle of children for Sunday School, and relief was mine when I knew she wasn't expecting me to join them. I was *so* grateful to be permitted to stay in church and continue worshipping the Lord in the beauty of holiness!

I loved that Sung Eucharist; my heart was truly in it. I was overwhelmed by the Holy Spirit as we knelt to sing the *Sanctus*, Holy, holy, holy, and. Later on, the priest, speaking the words of Jesus Christ, said:

"This is my Body... This is my Blood..."

The words spoke for themselves.

Of course, my understanding was mostly of the heart, but it was real and didn't diminish my spiritual involvement. There was a sting in the tail when the moment came when the grown-ups got up from their seats to receive Communion, and I was left behind – not permitted! I dearly wanted to join the grown-ups at the altar rail to receive the Body and Blood of Christ, but, once again, my need was overlooked. I have wondered since if I was the only Christian believer in that church denied the Blessed Sacrament. Unwittingly, I made what I've heard described since as a spiritual communion. I was doing so, without realising it! We sang the post-Communion hymn, kneeling. My favourite was Bishop Heber's devotional hymn, 'Holy, holy, holy, Lord God Almighty'.

I ventured to tell my mother how I wished I could receive Communion but she gave me short shrift, "You're far too young - you can't possibly understand!"

I was dumbfounded. Oh dear, Mummy had no understanding either of me, or the desire to receive Communion.

I have since thought about the opinion that children were considered too young to understand. The inference is that the adults, because they are adult, *do* understand, which, of course, is all too often not the case. Logically, if every adult understood, at whatever level, my mother and many another would be at the Eucharist every Sunday to receive the Lord in Holy Communion!

One Sunday morning, we had just left the church and were walking through the churchyard, when I happened to overhear a woman giving a friend her opinion of the Sung Eucharist:

"Isn't it *High*!" she declared in a disparaging tone of voice.

I was really shocked! I pondered this woman's remark. How was it that a grown-up should be so lacking in appreciation of the Service that so inspired me? It hadn't occurred to me that some could be so unappreciative of this wonderful act of worship.

"But," I thought to myself, "if the service at St Giles' is considered High, it's alright by me!" I had learnt about High Church and Low Church at school but hadn't quite understood what it meant in practice.

My sense of shock was deepened when I learnt later on that neither parent seemed to appreciate the Sung Eucharist.

How was it that I, their daughter, should so love the Sung Eucharist, whilst they evidently didn't? Was it, I wonder, the innate Scots' Non-conformist genes on both sides of the family - Sutherland and Anderson - that prevailed? I don't know.

Fr Field never knew what the Lord was doing in the soul of a certain "little" Rosemary in the pew. With hindsight, I believe Fr Field was a holy man; something of his holiness came through to me by the prayerful way he celebrated the Sung Eucharist.

Faith and prayer seemed to mean more to my father than to my mother. He had been confirmed while in the RAF, that is, without the veneer of 'respectability'.

## A new Rector at St Giles' Church

There was talk of a new Rector coming to St Giles', a fact that meant little to me at first. However, on his first Sunday, the neighbours took me to church as usual, but things were different, in more ways than one.

The service started. We sang the *Benedictus*, the song of Zachariah on duty in the temple, when an angel appeared to him, to tell him that his wife Elisabeth was expecting a son, the future John the Baptist. I enjoyed the *Benedictus*, the tune and the words. The lines,

"Blessed be the Lord God of Israel, for he hath visited and redeemed his people" are beautiful, but this wasn't the act of worship I'd known and come to love.

The new rector sat in the stall on the right of the chancel steps. On that first Sunday and for several Sundays afterwards I spent all the Service waiting for new rector to use the altar, but he never did. He remained stolidly in his stall. I was disappointed - things were inexplicably different. Something was missing, and I didn't understand. My friend's mother, realising I was perplexed, whispered, "It's Mattins!" Of course, at the time, the significance of this meant nothing, but I soon came to understand – Mattins had displaced the Sung Eucharist.

I couldn't understand my father when he told me that he considered the new rector "great"; my mother tacitly agreed.

With the disappearance of the Sung Eucharist the prayerful atmosphere also disappeared. The praying people, denied eucharistic worship, slipped away one by one, never to return. Here was I, also denied the Sung Eucharist - the Lord's Service on the Lord's Day. What a travesty! Again, something precious was taken from me. I felt cheated. Previously, silence had fed the prayerful atmosphere; now interminable chatter had replaced it; the church became a glorified social club.

## Confirmation comes too late

My Confirmation by the then Bishop of Rochester, Christopher Chavasse, meant a lot to me as he gave me the laying-on-of-hands at the altar rail. I joyfully told my mother: "The Holy Spirit came to me at my Confirmation," and again she gave me short shrift. By then, I suppose I shouldn't have been surprised, but I was. Whenever I spoke about things of the Spirit she seemed to have no conception of what I meant!

Spiritually speaking, I felt I'd "missed the boat". The 8 o'clock Said Eucharist was the service I had to attend, but that meant being up with the lark, keeping the eucharistic fast to receive Communion after quite a long cycle ride. As already stated, I am an owl, not a lark. I have always found it hard to focus on what I'm about in the early morning, especially without first having a little something to eat.

My parents insisted that I get up in time, and showed displeasure if I didn't. They never came with me. If they went to church, it was to Mattins!

"The Lord gave and the Lord has taken away" (Job 1.21) is a verse that has often come to mind since, concerning this and other situations. Time after time, this thread of receiving a gift, only to have it taken away, has been woven into the tapestry of my life.

So, on top of losing Blackheath where happiness was mine, then losing Blackheath High School where I'd found my niche, I had now lost the Sung Eucharist. What with unhappiness at home and at school, and with blackouts worsening, any vestige of faith was gradually eroded.

I felt abandoned by God.

## Chapter 17

# WE SEEK MEDICAL HELP

## *"Rosemary will grow out of the blackouts"*

Blackouts continued, frequent and frightening, horrible and humiliating. I was only too aware how unpalatable my dear Mama found her blackouting daughter. Her "perfect" Poppaloo did not live up to her high expectations. Poor Mummy, she found it hard to accept me 'warts and all'. I think she'd assumed from day one that the blackouts were but a passing blip!

I was an embarrassment and a disappointment. In her eyes, I brought shame on the family! After all, "normal middle class people didn't produce the abnormal, did they?" I realise that that was the attitude her generation took towards people with an aberration! It wasn't very long, since the 'abnormal' had been taken out of the public gaze, sometimes locked up in one of the large mental hospitals built for the purpose. I was instructed not to talk to anyone about the blackouts. In those days, it was considered best if such matters were left unspoken.

But, with the blackouts increasing in frequency, my mother could no longer ignore them. She took me to our fair-haired and fair-skinned doctor, recently arrived from New Zealand, Dr David Rowlands.

"Rosemary is having blackouts and they are getting more frequent," my mother said. "They start with what she calls 'horrible thoughts'. She doesn't fall, but walks around not knowing what she's about."

There followed a short discussion on the subject, which ended with Dr Rowlands advising,

"I think you should take Rosemary to see a doctor at Farnborough Hospital for specialist help."

When we got home Mummy duly phoned the Hospital and made an appointment to see a Dr Leys, one morning before school. So started my traipse to doctors and hospitals.

I don't think we had to wait long before getting an appointment. The day arrived and we were just finishing breakfast when Mummy spoke icily to me: "Come on, we shall have to be off soon."

As we prepared to depart, I could tell, she was feeling uncomfortable at the prospect of having to face yet another doctor about her problem daughter and her embarrassing malady.

On our arrival, a tall grey-haired gentleman welcomed us with, "Good morning, Mrs Sutherland. Good morning, Rosemary. I am Dr Leys, do come in," and he then graciously ushered us into his consulting room.

"We are here because Rosemary is having blackouts. We need your help." Mummy told him. Dr Leys turned to me:

"Rosemary, would you tell me what happens when you have a blackout?"

With my mother's instruction not to speak on the subject, I was still unprepared for giving a description of what happens when a blackout happens, and trying to convey the terror experienced. But, unpractised as I was, this was the reason for our being there, and to the best of my ability I tried to put into words how it was when assailed by 'horrible thoughts'...

"I'm trying to get back to the happiness I knew when we lived in Blackheath and when I was at Blackheath High School. I see or think of something - anything - and other thoughts get added on and they all pile up. I also have nasty sensations coming up from the pit of my stomach. It's impossible to explain how horrible it is. I can't stop it happening and I'm so frightened. I don't fall down. I carry on doing things without being aware of anything I'm doing."

Dr Leys thanked me and then turned to my mother.

"Mrs Sutherland, would you please tell me how Rosemary's blackouts appear to you?"

Mummy, also, still unpractised at speaking on the subject, did her best and managed it:

"When Rosemary has a blackout she's very frightened and needs to hold someone's hand. Her eyes glaze over and she looks distant. Sometimes she's 'out' for a few minutes, sometimes longer. Often, we think she's come round, when she hasn't. Sometimes, she comes round partially, and then she goes back into loss of consciousness. She doesn't fall. Sometimes she makes remarks that are inconsequential."

Dr Leys looked pensive and thanked my mother, as he avidly scribbled notes about his new patient.

"Tell me, Mrs Sutherland, did Rosemary have a difficult birth? Did she knock her head against the side of the pram? Was she struck on the head by shrapnel or similar during the War?"

"No," was my mother's reply to each of these possibilities, shaking her head with a frown. "No! But she did have convulsions when she was a baby."

"Well, that is a *possible* cause," Dr Leys opined. Many babies have convulsions with no long-term ill effect. I think Rosemary's blackouts are the sort she'll grow out of."

Soon after this consultation, Dr Leys arranged for me to have had an Electro-Encephalogram (EEG) at Farnborough Hospital. No MRI scans in those days! At our next visit he informed us: "The EEG shows that Rosemary has a scar on the right side of the brain. I think we have to assume that this is the cause of her attacks."

Dr Leys' first prescription for me was phenobarbitone. It did absolutely *nothing* for me. Back we went to tell him as much. My next prescription was for phenytoin. That controlled the attacks for a while, but later ceased to do so. Our monthly consultations continued and the quizzing each time about the nature of the blackouts became repetitious.

At least, Mummy was now more relaxed when relating what she knew. Well, almost!

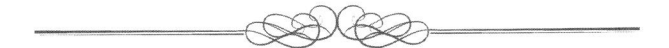

---

There was more to it than met the eye! Years later, I was around 60, when, out of the blue, my mother decided to come clean with a startling explanation for the cause of the blackouts:

"I was going up the stairs holding you when you were a baby," she explained. "I tripped and fell on top of you. I think that's how you got the scar on the brain!"

Such was my surprise on suddenly hearing this unexpected revelation, kept from me for more than 50 years, I was lost for words and ill-prepared to respond. I realised it must have cost her something to tell me. I'd like to have had a few further details. But I'm *so* glad she did tell me because, first and foremost, I wanted to know the truth of the matter.

Her confession also gave me a possible reason for a strange occurrence that had happened some 30 years previously.

I woke up one morning lying on my side in bed, when suddenly there was a strange heavy pressure on my head, for which there was no obvious explanation. It wasn't nice. No one else was in the room. There seemed to be a remote, indistinct voice, too indistinct to hear what was being said. Perhaps, what my mother had just told me was linked to this strange moment. I shall never know for sure. I'm just left wondering.

---

After two EEGs at Farnborough Hospital, Dr Leys made a recommendation:

"Mrs Sutherland, I'd like you to take Rosemary to the Belmont Hospital, Sutton, for a more advanced EEG."

The journey from Farnborough in Kent to Sutton in Surrey was not an easy one, travelling cross-country through suburbia. My father took us by car that morning and we made our way back by bus and train.

An EEG is not in the least painful; it measures the brain's electrical activity and shows up any abnormalities. The set-up was as before. I lay on my back on the EEG bed, with electrodes placed on strategic parts of the skull, stuck on with a special sort of glue to ensure good contact. All I had to do was lie there and obey the instructions given me by the woman in charge:

"Keep perfectly still, Rosemary. Close your eyes," followed by,

"Now open your eyes, Rosemary" – a sequence repeated several times.

"Breathe in deeply, Rosemary; now breathe out; continue breathing in and out until I say, 'Stop.'"

She then hung a flashing lamp in front of my face and gave instructions to close my eyes, then open my eyes etc. etc. All the information garnered was being transmitted to busy needles connected to the electrodes, frantically going up and down, up and down, on a long stretch of white paper. It informed those able to interpret it, either that all was well or in a certain part of the brain, not so well.

Next time at Farnborough Hospital, Dr Leys reported on the EEG. Apparently, it conveyed nothing significantly new:

"I have received the result of the Sutton EEG. It confirms that the scar on the brain is the cause of Rosemary's blackouts. Don't worry, Mrs Sutherland, Rosemary's blackouts are the sort she'll grow out of," he confidently reassured her. "Here's another prescription for phenytoin." But neither Dr Leys' words of assurance, nor the phenytoin put an end to my misery.

### Another truth will out

Over 40 years later, the year 2002, to be precise, "Another truth was out!" I was discussing the history of the blackouts with my GP when she asked me, "How old were you when your blackouts started?"

"I was ten when they started," I confidently replied.

She clicked through my records on the computer and to my surprise, queried this.

"Are you sure? According to the record, the earliest mention of them was when you were twelve!"

"No, I *know* the blackouts started when I was ten!" I exclaimed indignantly. "I know they did!"

"The first record we have here was when you were twelve," she assured me, as she strained her eyes intently at the screen, as if to make sure of her facts.

"Twelve?" I queried again, incredulously, "I *know* I was ten when they started!" I insisted, "I remember it well."

"I'm afraid we are not permitted to change the record," she replied kindly.

"No, quite!" I nodded understandingly.

Later, the reason for the discrepancy dawned on me: the first two years was the duration of my mother's non-acceptance of my affliction. She'd done her best to dismiss my "indiscreet" losses of consciousness, and had hoped they would soon disappear. I realised that it was quite possibly when I was twelve that she realised she must consult Dr Rowlands.

## Dr Leys has a further recommendation:

"Mrs Sutherland, I think you should take Rosemary to see Dr Pond, the well-known child psychiatrist at The Maudsley Hospital, Denmark Hill." Obviously, Dr Leys thought he could do no more for me.

Appointment made, off we went to The Maudsley, opposite King's College Hospital. Dr Pond seemed sympathetic to my unhappy lot. The same old questions were asked of me and I replied with the same old answers. The same old questions were asked of my mother and she gave the same old answers. Obviously, Dr Pond had to know the history of his new patient before he could presume to help, but the question and answer sessions were getting a bit tedious. After several interviews, Dr Pond was to reiterate Dr Leys' advice:

"I think Rosemary's attacks are the sort she will grow out of."

I had great confidence in Dr Pond. Whatever the rights or wrongs of this prediction, ever since my first visit to The Maudsley Hospital, I had a deep down sense that this was where my problem would be solved.

## A brain surgeon is consulted

At a later consultation with Dr Pond a brain surgeon, Mr Murray Falconer, was present. After Dr Pond had given Mr Falconer a summary of my blackouts, Mr Falconer told us confidently,

"I think I should tell you that we could consider an operation. That is a *possible* answer to Rosemary's problem. The scar is on part of the brain that is operable, but I also believe that Rosemary will grow out of the attacks."

This remark should have been cause for hope, but by then it was starting to wear a bit thin.

Far from growing out of them, the horrible thoughts and the nasty sensations rising from the pit of the stomach got worse, and the length of time I was 'out' was getting longer. When feeling particularly yucky I pleaded with Mummy, "*Please*, let me have the op."

She wouldn't hear of it. "No, no, all the doctors say you'll grow out of the blackouts!" I was feeling horrid inside, and Mummy didn't seem to understand. Somehow, I felt she didn't want to.

## Chapter 18

# A DARK NIGHT

### *Abandoned by God -: the worst time of my life*

I had always wanted to be a policewoman, and such was my love of horse riding I'd hoped to be the first mounted policewoman.

Some years later, 'The Children's Newspaper' reported that the Liverpool police force had employed the first policewoman in the country to be mounted. I admit to a slight tinge of envy, but, mounted or not mounted, it had been a dream that could never be fulfilled by me. I just had to accept the fact that I wasn't fit enough. If the truth were known, I felt fit for nothing.

So, what was I to do? A secretarial course seemed a possible idea - at Dartford College of Technology. Free education for the first time!

*Friends at Dartford College of Technology*

The yearlong secretarial course came to an end, but not the blackouts.

Again, I pleaded with my mother, "*Please* let me have the operation, the blackouts are *so* awful – they make me feel horrible. I *can't* go on like this." She continued to adamantly refuse.

"You'll grow out of them, all the doctors say so!" This had become a *cliché*.

"Yes," I thought to myself, "I know the doctors say so. The fact is, I *haven't* grown out of them, and they're getting worse!"

At least, praise, God, I wasn't having the far more dramatic seizures of *Grand Mal* though that might have conveyed better to my mother, the greatness of my need. She just would not accept, believe, understand, how tortured I was within, by this indescribable terror and the nastiness of the blackout sensations rising up from deep within me. Life was now getting more serious, with life in the job-market looming large.

## I came to love the City of London

I didn't know the City until I went up there to start work. It's a fascinating place. History oozes out of every street corner and down every alleyway. One wonders how some of the alleyways got their name: Godliman Street, Pope's Head Alley, Angel Court, etc.

My father's office was in the City and initially he showed me round.

However, with the added responsibility of work, life became even more impossible - indeed life was dreadful - and my parents, especially my mother, just could not accept that I was too ill for words, let alone work. Exhaustion overwhelmed me. I was so slow, and I knew it. I was doing my best but I couldn't function properly and horribleness reigned within.

I managed interviews with confidence: I seemed to give a good impression and I answered questions intelligently. The job was offered to me and, if it sounded suitable, I accepted. I wasn't being fatalistic, but even as I started I knew it wouldn't last. and the inevitable happened. I was asked to go! Time after time, my world was turned upside down.

I came to love the City, yet I've lost count of the times I've walked through those historic streets with a heavy heart, desperate about my lot. What was to become of me? Life was becoming more and more intolerable. I was too ill for work and my mother couldn't accept the fact.

I dreaded my arrival home. I was prepared for the worst. I told my mother

I'd lost my job and she received me with damning words, which poured forth like cold water onto a needy, unhappy heart.

"What's the *matter* with you? Pull yourself together! You *must* go out to work and earn money!" Such were the words that fell from her lips, as if I were a ski-ver. Of compassion, there was none. At other times, her dismissive silence expressed her thoughts. My mother expected the impossible of me. She couldn't cope – nor could I! I knew I let her down. She didn't see that she could have been part of the cure.

My father wasn't quite so damning, yet he was the one who, at times, would glibly say, "There's no such thing as can't." From my unhappy experience it's patently obvious that there is such a thing! Yet he was the parent who *could* show a softer side and would give me limited support.

After a particularly devastating rejection the previous day, Daddy would come into the bedroom next morning to pull back the curtains, as was his wont, and he would greet me lovingly with: "*Sans peur*, Rose. Time to get up. Don't forget, Rose, *Sans peur!*" - the Sutherland motto. It was only fleeting, but it helped.

When Daddy spoke like this, he was speaking from the heart and his words were consoling. Yet he was the one who spasmodically would explode into a fury over some trivial thing I'd done. This emotional battering had nothing directly to do with the blackouts, but it didn't exactly help to build up my general sense of well being. His outbursts continued into his old age.

But my father was the sociable parent, who would talk to anybody: contradictions that as a little girl I found difficult to reconcile. I never knew where I stood.

## A catch-22 situation

My inner being had fallen to bits. I asked myself the very question posed by my mother: "What *was* the matter with me?" I wished I knew! I was doing my best. I couldn't do more. What with the horrid sensations of the blackouts, rejections on the employment scene, and the general lack of understanding at home considering me lazy or feckless, life was one big struggle; Truly, life was not worth living.

It was a catch-22 situation to which there appeared to be no answer. As I said, I really was not fit for work yet was forced to go out and earn money.

Sickness benefit would have been more appropriate, to spare me the ignominy I endured. What was the answer to my dilemma? No one seemed to know! No one seemed to care!

Very recently, I put this query to my local GP and she told me that the problem was partly the epilepsy and partly hormonal.

This, no doubt, was the reason for my lack of strength and my inability to do anything, for come the menopause in my mid-forties, the same thing happened, bringing on the same energy-sapping experience. Again, my mind fell to bits and my body could do nothing; I couldn't make decisions for myself; I needed others to help me with the most simple of tasks. This time I was so thankful that I didn't *have* to go out to work.

At the menopause, it was widely acknowledged that the cause was hormonal imbalance, a problem about which little was known 40 years previously, and hormone replacement therapy unheard of. This time, the doctor immediately prescribed oestrogen, hormone replacement therapy (HRT), and immediately my energy was restored. Even now, in my mid-seventies, with the menopause long over, HRT is essential to make my life tolerable.

And, now, so long as I take my epanutin, and more recently, Gabapentin, my blackouts are kept away. I just have 'auras', as the doctor describes the blackouty feelings that I have sometimes.

## Surrounded by success

In addition to the troubles at home, there were also the difficulties when having to face the world in upmarket Farnborough Park, surrounded by 'success'. `I started by doing my mother's bidding and saying nothing about my troubled life to anyone, even if challenged. I greeted people with a smile and a cheery "Good morning!" as if everything in my world was wonderful. Yet here I was, immersed in humiliation and heartbreak, unknown to anyone, my fragile world forever being turned upside down – weekly, monthly, annually!

I had friends in Farnborough Park, on a superficial level. But to have someone in their midst to be in need, was a contradiction in terms for them.

As a woman "of sorrows and acquainted with grief" (The Bible, Isaiah 53:3), I realise I was in good company. Unfortunately, that didn't occur to me at the time - by then, all belief in Jesus Christ had flown. I felt like one of the poor, not exactly poor financially, but having been ground into the ground, I mean abject spiritual poverty, emotionally and spiritually. I was destitute and feeling utterly abandoned by God.

One day, when I was at a school friend's house and feeling particularly desperate, contrary to maternal instruction I decided to risk telling the friend's mother something of my unhappiness. I'd always thought of her as a nice woman, and I thought she'd have a word of encouragement. She replied with indignation:

"You've got good parents, you live in a lovely house. What more could you want?"

I remained silent. If only she knew! It felt like a slap on the face, I was left in even deeper despair. I resolved to return to the previous policy of saying nothing on the subject and to keep smiling, despite all.

This little incident taught me that however 'nice' a person might appear to be, it doesn't mean that she has true love and compassion. As with everything else in life, something can only be given if the person has it to give.

A tradition had grown up in Farnborough Park during the War that continued for some while after the end of the War: residents in a car would stop to pick up the car-less as they walked through the Park or waited at the bus stop, often if they weren't even known to the driver. Almost every day someone would stop and give me a lift into Bromley. For this kindness I was grateful, but it could be a mixed blessing.

Jill and William were good friends of the family. Their car drew up beside me with, "Good morning, Rosemary. Would you like a lift?"

"Good morning. Yes, please," I replied brightly, and I got into the car, thanking the driver and his wife. As ever, I was giving the impression outwardly that everything in my world was wonderful. But when I asked to be dropped off at a different Bromley station from the previous time Jean concluded, rightly, that I'd changed my job and she thought the worst of me.

"Oh, you young people, you won't settle!" was her indignant, disparaging remark, inferring I was feckless. Feckless? Never! I yearned for a settled life. I didn't dare relate the truth of the matter. No doubt many others came to a similar incorrect conclusion. Again, if only they knew!

I was alone! I was so depressed by the whole scenario in which I found myself. Leading a double life went against the grain, depressing me further and adding onto my already depressed life. I cried out silently for help, but there was none.

Truly, this was the most dreadful time of my life! Was there really no one around to meet my need?

Of course, through all this angst, the thought ever hovering at the back of my mind was: "There's always the op!"

## The Dark Night of the soul

Much more recently, I told a priest about this dreadful time, and in passing I referred to it as my 'atheistic' era.

"I suggest that it was the Dark Night of the soul!" he said.

Although his suggestion changed nothing, past or present, it was helpful.

"Yes, thank you," I replied. "Of course, it *was* the Dark Night of the soul'. Thank you."

It is an apt description. Having read St John of the Cross I knew about the Dark Night of the soul - again, I am surprised that I hadn't applied it to my own life

[Today, one hears the phrase 'dark night of the soul' used for many a bad experience, often devoid of Christian faith or belief.]

## Chapter 19

# A HEART OF STONE INTO A HEART OF FLESH

### *Getting Too Serious?*

*The Daily Telegraph* dropped on the mat every morning. Straightaway, my father picked it up and handed my mother the Woman's page, of no interest to me! After my father had scanned the news at home and abroad he would pass on those pages to me, that's where my interest lay. He turned to the financial and business section.

Lately, people have made complimentary remarks about my dress sense. I tell them, "I've never read a fashion magazine, nor the Woman's page of the D.T.!"

The Sutherland family was 'true blue'. My father was very proud of the fact that Bermondsey, where he was born, had once returned a Conservative Member to Parliament. Incidentally, the well-known Dr Alfred Salter was the Sutherland's family doctor. My father told me what a wonderful doctor he was, but couldn't understand the doctor's extreme left-wing political affiliation.

I didn't follow unthinkingly the family's 'true blue' tradition. As might have been guessed, I do have a mind of my own! I took an objective look into political allegiance and considered the matter for myself. The issues at that time were more clear-cut than they are today. Basically, the Left wing or Socialists advocated nationalisation of industry; the Right wing or Conservatives were anti-nationalisation of industry.

In those days, the Young Conservatives (YCs) was a thriving national organisation, especially so in the Orpington Constituency, in which Sunnydale House was situated. Orpington YCs had the second largest membership in the South-East. I attended the meetings of our local Crofton South Branch and found them interesting. I already knew several of the members. I said I would like to join and was told that the official age for joining was 14, but such was my interest in politics I was permitted to join at 13½!

I may have lost my love of God but I hadn't lost my love of people. And, despite all, I managed to retain a modicum of self-respect. This love of people and the ability to get involved socially with all sorts and conditions of young women and men kept me going in the worldly milieu in which I lived and moved and had my being. My membership of the Young Conservatives helped keep me sane during this "dark night" of abandonment by God.

My mother complained that I was getting too serious. I was a seriously-minded person because life for me was a serious matter. I enjoyed the serious side of the YCs but our gatherings were by no means *all* serious; many were in a lighter vein. Every Saturday evening there was a YC dance at the Daylight Inn, Petts Wood, arranged by one of the eight branches in the Orpington Constituency, and every branch held its own social events.

Crofton South Branch meetings were held at St Paul's church hall, then they moved to the Candy Café in Locksbottom. I built up the membership of the Branch, from a mere handful of about a dozen members, to over sixty and I was officially made Membership Secretary. I didn't feel much like going out as chief encourager in my miserable zombie-like state but somehow I managed it. I had to push myself to get on my bike to visit possible new contacts or chivvy along those we hadn't seen for a while.

Once out and about, I found engaging with people was a partial answer to my depressed state. I would gently encourage young people between ages 14 and 30 to come along. The reaction I got at the front door usually determined the meeting I thought might interest them: I invited those of a non-serious disposition to a Beetle Drive; those of a more serious bent I encouraged to come to a semi-serious talk, such as, 'Saunas in Finland'. I gave our programme to those who showed interest and encouraged each to come along. We had a varied programme, including quizzes, outings to the New Theatre, Bromley, and talks by local councillors.

---

Despite the beneficial spin-off as YC Membership Secretary, my parents' complaint remained, that I was getting "too serious". They considered my involvement in the YCs as "not good for me". Yet, they still didn't know what to do about the blackout situation

It sounds rather trite to say, as many another son or daughter has said, "My parents didn't understand me." It was certainly true in my case, *viz* their lack of appreciation of the Sung Eucharist at St Giles' Church. From the War onwards, life had been a serious matter; the trivial holds little interest for me. My parents' ideas were almost always inappropriate because of their lack of understanding.

In their endeavour to "remedy the situation", they took steps to get me interested in something else. They sent off for information about the English Speaking Union, in the hope it might fulfil that end. I don't recall much about the brochure received, but it sounded dull. I really didn't understand why they should have considered it as an appropriate diversion.

After all I did have other interests: there was my love of classical music, which I found healing, but my parents didn't share my enjoyment listening to the concert on a Thursday evening, broadcast on the Third Programme, as Radio 3 was then known. If I remember rightly, it was the only concert of the week. My mother tolerated it in silence – she realised it meant a lot to me. My father, on the other hand, would enter the room, make a cryptic remark about the music and turn it off without consulting. Classical music helped lift me out of my depressed state, especially the compositions of Wolfgang Amadeus Mozart.

[Professor Paul Robertson, first violin of the Medici String Quartet, has recently done tests that have proved scientifically that music has the power to heal or, at least, alleviate the pain of a wounded mind.]

My parents were closer in their understanding when they considered my love of singing, and it was suggested that I join the Ravensbourne Operatic Society, that produced Gilbert and Sullivan operas. Singing releases the spirit. I wasn't a *great* G and S lover, but my time with the Society gave me a greater appreciation of Gilbert's witty lyrics and Sullivan's lively music.

I sang in 'The Gondoliers' and 'Trial by Jury'. Much as I enjoyed my time with the Society, I didn't believe that singing G & S was for me, long term. One obvious difficulty was not having my own transport, which made attendance difficult, especially when rehearsals were held in an obscure part of

Bromley, nowhere near a bus route.

I told Francis Steptoe, the conductor, that for this reason it was impractical for me to continue. He spoke most appreciatively of my contribution to performances and tried to persuade me to stay. Although I was heartened by his words of affirmation, I felt my decision was the right one.

## Chapter 20

# WARD 2 AT THE MAUDSLEY

*"Whatever will be, will be…"*

Life had become intolerable: far from "growing out of the blackouts", as the medical profession had unanimously predicted, their frequency continued *ad nauseam* and the length of each attack increased. Words cannot describe how ghastly I felt, caught in a vicious circle. I do wonder if the doctors were aware of my lack of support from home. Even if the medics were aware of it, there is no medicine to meet that need. There was no obvious answer to my dilemma.

However, in early 1957 Dr Pond recommended that I come into The Maudsley Hospital, under observation, so the doctors and nurses might see for themselves what the blackouts were like and try out different medication. I was on Ward 2 for just three weeks. It was a 'mixed' ward, with men and women suffering a variety of illnesses: from mild depression and deep depression to epilepsy of various kinds: *petit mal, grand mal*, etc. My aberration was described as *petit mal* at the time (no mention of the word epilepsy); much later mine was called *temporal lobe epilepsy*.

The Hungarian Revolution had happened five months before, in the October of 1956. Two male *emigré* Hungarian nurses were on the ward, and I was happy to help one of them, Lazlo, with his English, for which he was grateful. My other pastime on the ward was writing doggerel lyrics.

The doctor on the ward was a Greek Cypriot, Dr Serafetinedes, known as Dr Seriah for short (pronounced like the 'iah' of *Uriah*). Aptly, for the pop song of the moment was, "Che *sera-a, sera-a*, whatever will be, will be; the future's not ours to see. *Che sera, sera*, what will be, will be."

The wireless was on much of the day and this song poured forth incessantly over the airwaves. I composed some doggerel to be sung to the same tune, a parody on Doctor Seriah's name and my time on Ward 2. (I wrote it with the Spanish spelling 'Che',)

## *CHE SERIAH, SERIAH*
(Pronounced like the '*iah*' of *Uriah*)

*Verse:*
>When I was ill at Denmark Hill,
>I asked Seriah, What can it be?
>Will I get better, or will I get worse?
>That's up to you, not me.

*Chorus:*
>Che seriah, seriah,
>Whatever will be, will be.
>My future's at stake, you see.
>Che seriah, seriah,
>What will be, will be!

>Now that I'm feeling so much worse,
>I ask, Seriah, What can it be?
>Can I be cured, or am I a clot?
>Seriah, please answer me.

*Chorus:* Che seriah, seriah…

>Thank you, *Seriah*, for all you've done,
>Thank you for saying what it might be.
>Now that AEG* burst open my head,
>*And* almost murdered me!

*Chorus:* Che seriah, seriah…

*See next page

Obviously, I hadn't lost my sense of humour! I never knew if the good doctor heard his patients sing this ode to his doctoring abilities. If he did, I trust he realised it was all meant in fun. No disrespect intended.

I'd had several EEGs (Electro-Encephalograms) over the years and I had a further two while I was an in-patient. Still no MRI scans!

The EEG was completely painless but the AEG* (Aero-Encephalogram) mentioned in the last verse of my doggerel was a different matter. It was *very, very* painful. Garbed in one of those formless hospital gowns I was seated on a stool, bending forward with forehead resting against a pane of glass. The doctor instructed:

"Now, you *mustn't* move!"

The doctor sat behind me, pumping air up the spinal cord from the base of the spine, displacing the spinal fluid and filling the space with air. It was *excruciating*! But I was forbidden to move!

Photos of the brain were taken from various angles to help pinpoint with greater accuracy the position and size of the scar on the brain. Stillness was essential. The pumping of air up the spinal cord resumed, more air and yet more air, and with every pump the pain became more *terrible*. So great was the pressure, it really felt as if my head was about to burst. There was no chance to writhe with pain, which is what I felt like doing. The order to maintain stillness continued.

---

My short sojourn on Ward 2 was a welcome break, but the problems remained. I was put on new medication, mysoline and mesantoin, which seemed to control the blackouts but, as before, I was drugged up to the hilt, and was even more zombie-like, feeling "good for neither God nor man", as the saying goes; though apparently neither has proved to be the case!

Yet again, either I walked around like a zombie and couldn't work, or if I reduced the medication, was plagued with blackouts, and lost the job.

How I desperately needed someone to understand – gender didn't matter, though I'd assumed it would be female. But, as before, I faced the world with a smile as if I hadn't a care. I felt so alone and was left to smile at myself in the mirror! Again, I asked myself, "What *was* to become of me?"

God knows our need, even if it doesn't seem like it; and he meets our need, in his good time. One never knows who or what is round the corner!

## Chapter 21

# THE CZECH CONNECTION

*A remote young man was at the bus stop*

**Czechoslovakia held fascination for me**

Czechoslovakia, as it used to be known, has always held a fascination for me. I don't know exactly why. Maybe it has something to do with the alleged laid-back, 'bohemian' lifestyle, Bohemia being a part of Czechoslovakia.

"She's a bit bohemian, you know!" is the sort of glib remark, made with slightly derogatory overtones, about a particular sort of person considered a little eccentric, leading an unconventional lifestyle.

It also speaks of someone content to be herself and not ashamed of it; a person, hair done up in a bun (usually, but not always, female!) whose attic flat tends to be untidy, *viz* my front room office; someone whose intellectual bent is interwoven with a creative artistic streak, (I can identify with some of that, though not the bun!).

Latterly, our Czech friends have seriously queried this description of the supposed bohemian lifestyle. They assure me that it has no factual connection with today's Bohemia.

Not long after my time under hospital observation, I and several others were at the Farnborough Park Avenue bus stop, waiting for the Nos. 47 red London Transport bus or 402 green Country Bus into Bromley, to catch the train for London. Also waiting at the bus stop was a rather remote young man, dressed for the City with bowler hat and rolled umbrella. The young man was ill at ease and with no obvious inclination to communicate. I was always on the lookout for new YC members. I wondered vaguely if he might be interested. Somehow, I doubted it.

"I expect he's got plenty of other interests and no time to spare," I thought to myself.

One day, a while later, as I waited at the same bus stop, along came the

No. 402 bus. It was often full, but on this occasion everyone waiting got on. I managed to get a seat downstairs and the young man mentioned above found a pitch, standing nearby. I wasn't convinced he was the sort who would appreciate the social *milieu* of YC gatherings, whilst I was almost sure he would say, "No." it was *just* possible he'd say, "Yes!" Anyhow, it was worth a try. Nothing ventured, nothing gained, I plucked up courage and, as with every other chance encounter, started to converse with small talk as the bus trundled into Bromley.

I seem to have, a gift for bringing out the withdrawn personality, though I'm not aware of doing anything special.

"Hallo! How are you, this morning?" I asked cheerily. After an appropriate pause, I restarted the conversation: "I wondered if you might be interested in the Young Conservatives?" I said tentatively. Another pause. "Perhaps you'd like to have a look at this," I added, and handed him our YC branch programme.

Interested? That's putting it mildly! He responded with delirious delight! "Oh, yes!" he exclaimed, and took the programme with the joy of a little child who had known only repression, which turned out to be the case. His name was Derek Vanek. He had lived in the neighbourhood almost all his life and this was the first time anyone had approached him with anything like this. He was overjoyed.

He was soon to tell me that, officially, his surname was Bourne-Vanneck, which obliged him to give an explanation of its history:

"Vanek is the original Czech family name, spelt V-A-N-E-K", he explained.

"Oh, Czech!" I exclaimed appreciatively.

"My grandfather Henry Vanek was a tailor and furrier from Prague. He left Czechoslovakia and came to England before the First World War and set up in business as a tailor in Bournemouth. That's where the 'Bourne' bit comes from. Before the Second World War, my father decided to anglicise the name Vanek, using the old English spelling, V-A-N-N-E-C-K."

The significance of the history of Derek's surname will become apparent later, as my story unfolds.

[It was said that Derek's grandfather knew Mazeryk, the Czech Prime Minister in Czechoslovakia's pre-Communist era.]

Not long after our first cursory conversation on the No. 402 bus, Derek started to share the sufferings of his strange, unnatural childhood. Our meeting seemed too good to be true.

Derek's life story was bizarre. I was soon to learn how the sensitive Derek had suffered at the hands of an insensitive, domineering mother, and a hard-hearted father not averse to writing his son solicitor-type letters, some of which I was to read for myself later on!

The weeks and months passed and he shared with me more and more of his sad story. In his youth, he had been denied friends and a normal social life. His parents had a Victorian attitude to life, verging on the cruel where the upbringing of their two children was concerned – treatment so foreign to the lifestyle of the average 20th-century child. No toys, no fun, no friends permitted home from school, and later, no normal socialising. Even if possessions were acquired, he had nowhere to keep them, certainly not in his bedroom. He had a 'precious' radio waiting to be taken apart and put back together again – his *forte*. He had hidden it under the floorboards for "safe keeping", but it was found and thrown in the dustbin!

So the peculiarities of his family life came pouring out. There was no love lost between him and his parents. He had been disowned. To Derek, our family life seemed idyllic and looking in from the outside I suppose it was! No wonder the delight he showed at a simple invitation to join the Young Conservatives!

He enjoyed the first YC meeting he attended. But, Oh dear, he took the "dreadful liberty" of inviting his purely platonic girlfriend of the moment back to his parents' bungalow to have a cup of coffee – in the opinion of most, a perfectly normal, acceptable thing to do.

"My parents are out this evening, so do come and have a cup of coffee," he said.

On arrival at their beautiful bungalow in Elm Walk, Farnborough Park, Derek cautiously opened the front door, making quite sure before we entered that his parents were not around. He breathed a sigh of relief, "They're definitely out!" he told me in relieved tones.

Obviously ill at ease, he led me surreptitiously into the kitchen where he made two surreptitious cups of coffee, warily offering me a seat at the kitchen table. He had a shrewd suspicion his parents might return early, so he considered it wise that I leave sooner rather than later in case they did turn up early. Obviously, he didn't want his parents to know he'd had someone back for coffee.

The next time I saw Derek I learned that the following morning he was severely taken to task for inviting me back - he was 25! He had unwittingly left a teaspoon lying around,

Here we were, both living in upmarket Farnborough Park, a moneyed area that oozed success in ways that had eluded us. Both of us had been to a public school: Derek to Dulwich College and I to Bromley High School. Both highly academic schools, but neither Derek nor I had been able to achieve the academic level that the schools expected of their pupils. Despite outward prosperity, we both felt like two of the poor. Again, not primarily financial poverty, though neither of us was earning a high salary; but again, I speak of spiritual poverty.

---

In former times of crisis, Derek had left his parents' house and taken refuge with his grandmother in Hampstead or his Godmother in Earl's Court. Each time, after a while, he had convinced himself it was right to go back, in the hope that things would be better this time, but they never were. When I met him he was again finding life at home intolerable. He was very unhappy, not knowing which way to turn.

When I took the liberty of inviting Derek to join the YCs, believe me, romance was furthest from my mind, but, as time went on, it transpired that there was more to our encounter, than my empathy with his Czech connection. At last, both of us had met someone with whom to empathise rather than disparage. Literally and metaphorically, we fell into each other's arms. Derek had saved me and I had saved Derek, just in time for both.

My dear Mama was not convinced about any possibility of my marrying Derek, in some ways, understandably, for, at times, he would act a little strangely and unpredictably, and, like me, found sustained employment difficult, albeit for different reasons. But, she told me much later, how she'd seen the difference Derek had made to me after we had met.

## An interview in Westminster, SW1

I had an interview for a job at a firm of Architects and Surveyors, in Buckingham Gate, a small, friendly firm with three partners.

Mr Graves, a Chartered Surveyor, the partner looking for a secretary, interviewed me. I had learnt from grim experience not to breathe a word about blackouts at an interview. Sharing that bit of information was a sure way of not being even considered. Mr Graves offered me the job; it sounded as if I could cope with it, and I was happy to accept.

The new medication prescribed by the hospital was keeping the seizures away, but I was *so* tired and zombie-like, and unable to function properly. If I were to make a success of this job I'd have to reduce the medication. I had no option. Gradually, I reduced some of the mysoline, and the tiredness receded.

Mr Graves was pleased with me, and I enjoyed working for him. I found the work interesting and informative, and not often was there undue pressure. From the reports I typed on the surveys he made of various properties, I learned many new and interesting facts about purchasing a property: some basic, like ground subsidence and ageing water tanks; others peripheral, such as the missing escutcheon on the cloakroom door or the broken hopper at the top of one of the down pipes; flaws that had to be pointed out, but not so crucial that a prospective purchaser might have to reconsider his or her decision to purchase. Unfortunately, the highlighting of minor blemishes could make the report sound as if the whole house were falling to pieces. It was all most informative.

Thanks to Derek's support and a kindly Mr Graves, I seemed settled at last. Don't get too excited. Once again, "seemed" was the operative word.

A World Turned Upside Down

## Chapter 22

# ALMOST BACK TO SQUARE ONE!

### *And back to Mr Falconer*

Having reduced the medication in order to stave off the tiredness, horror of horrors, I had a blackout – in the office. This was a dreadful blow. It lasted for more than an hour and was the cause of consternation all round! I emerged from the blackout, unscathed but disconcerted. It was as if I was back to square one.

Not long after that, I had yet another blackout, possibly the most dramatic so far, not to mention the most disconcerting. It started one morning as I walked across the concourse of Victoria Station on my way to the office in Buckingham Gate. As usual, the subconscious took over. I emerged from it half way down Victoria Street and found myself hugging a lamp post. I then regressed into the blackout, and when I next emerged I was back at Victoria Station. That had involved having to cross two busy main thoroughfares, Vauxhall Bridge Road and Wilton Road, twice. Of this, I was completely oblivious. I phoned the office from Victoria Station and my colleague answered:

"Hallo, Lyn, Rosemary speaking. I'm at Victoria Station. Have I been sent home because I've had a blackout?"

"No," she replied, surprised by my question, "You haven't been in yet!"

"Really!" I blurted out, "I didn't realise that!" My mind was a complete blank.

What irony, just when I think I'm happily settled, my world is again turned upside down.

I still had Derek's support, but the blackout problem remained.

"I *must* have the operation!" I told my mother adamantly, "I *can't* go on like this."

Having sternly refused to entertain the very idea up to then, my mother at last accepted the seriousness of the situation: the blackouts were worsening and getting longer in duration. She now needed little convincing:

"Yes, if you think it's the right thing to do, you must go ahead and have the operation," she conceded. At last, the gravity of the situation had impinged upon her and she accepted that a drastic situation called for a drastic measure to resolve it. The operation seemed to be the only possible answer.

Feeling not a little desperate, I made an appointment to consult Mr Falconer, the highly esteemed brain surgeon at Guy's Neuro-Surgical Unit, to see what he had to say.

Mr Falconer, a man of small words, sat at his desk pondering my case, his silver-rimmed spectacles perched precariously on the end of his nose.

"Now, Miss Sutherland. Tell me, what has been happening?"

"The blackouts have returned," I told him, in desperation. "It's a real shock. I reduced my medication because I was walking around like a zombie, and conldn't function properly, and now look what's happened - the blackouts have returned, worse than before, and I'm engaged to be married.

It may sound a bit dramatic to say it, but life is dreadful and isn't worth living. *Please* help me!" I pleaded. "You did say once that an operation was a possibility."

"I am sorry to hear your news, Miss Sutherland. Yes, we can certainly consider an operation," he confirmed, nodding his head understandingly... "But get married first. Go away and think about it, and come back and see me in a month's time."

I thanked him, rose from my chair and off I went, my heart feeling a little lighter, and the possible answer to my problem a little nearer. As may be imagined, it didn't take me long to come to a decision!

As instructed, I returned to see Mr Falconer, to tell him my decision.

"Well, Miss Sutherland, what have you decided?"

Without hesitation, I gave my consent, "Yes, please, I definitely want to have the operation."

Mr Falconer confirmed his agreement to operate to remove the scar on the brain. He told me it wouldn't be long before I'd receive a date to come into hospital. "At last," I thought, "a glimmer of hope."

## Chapter 23

# SECOND CONVERSION EXPERIENCE

*"Seek, and you will find"*

Not only had Derek saved me on the natural human level, his witness had contributed to my restoration on the supernatural spiritual level, that is, to faith in Jesus Christ. The spiritual life is not an end in itself. We pursue it that the Holy Spirit of God might enhance our everyday life.

I had dropped away from God for what seemed an interminably long time. In fact, it was only two years, but certain things occurred before my return to faith.

The year was 1958. One evening as we were saying goodbye at the front door, Derek and I started to discuss the subject of our respective Churches. A heated argument ensued. I told Derek I couldn't accept certain Roman Catholic beliefs and teaching. Although I was out of touch with things ecclesiastical, my side of the argument was not conveyed in complete ignorance. My mind referred back to the belief I'd come to for myself when I was fourteen, and, equipped with that, I told Derek in no uncertain terms:

"I believe the Church of England, is the Catholic Church of this country!" Not the Roman Catholic Church!"

I was surprised that this belief had surfaced so naturally in my mind; it was not something I'd thought about for some while. That belief, though significant to me at the time, is not of the essence of faith in Jesus Christ, but in the context of an Anglican/Roman dispute it is very relevant.

Later on, I told him, "I would object strongly to being called a convert! If I were to believe, it would be conversion to Jesus Christ; and were I to return to faith in Jesus Christ, it would be to the Church of England I'd go. I couldn't join the Roman Catholic Church!"

After a heated exchange of words, Derek departed very downhearted, thinking he had lost me. Despite an unhappy childhood and much later suffering, Derek had remained a believer and he still went to church. His faith in

God prompted me to reappraise my own position.

"Perhaps," thought I, "there's something in this believing in God after all."

## Preparation for the return of God to my life

In those days, there was no ecumenical movement, as we know it today. Vatican II had yet to happen. The Roman Church in this country was very antagonistic towards us 'heretics' - Anglicans and other Christians wouldn't accept the R.C. Church with the Pope at its head, claiming Infallibility. And there was still much anti-Roman Catholic emotion around, in the country.

About this time, the witness of two friends came my way.

I was putting on my coat at the end of a birthday party in Orpington, when I happened to overhear Barbara, a good friend of mine, being asked by another girl,

"Are you going to the cocktail party next Sunday morning?"

"No, *I* shan't be going," came Barbara's reply, "I'll be at church."

That took me by surprise. It hadn't occurred to me that Barbara went to church! Instinctively, I thought, "That's where I should be!" Barbara's word of witness sowed a seed in my mind. Deep down, I knew that belief in Jesus Christ had once been mine, and that being in church on a Sunday had once held a normal place in my life! Yet, I kept on asking myself,

"How could anyone believe in God?" At the time, it seemed an insuperable problem.

The second seed of witness was sown when I happened to meet a certain Caroline in Mortimer Street, parallel with Oxford Street. She was in the form above me at Bromley High School, and I knew her also at St Giles' Church, Farnborough.

"Haven't seen you at church for a long time?" she said enquiringly.

"Not interested!" I replied, shaking my head.

"Oh, I'm sorry," Caroline, replied. "You should go to All Souls' Church, Langham Place. There's a good lunch time talk, at one o'clock every Thursday."

"No," I frowned and shook my head firmly, "I don't think so."

I knew *nothing* about All Souls', Langham Place, at the time, but I pondered Caroline's suggestion and decided to give it a try, just to see what it was like.

I settled uneasily into a pew. I didn't feel at all at home in this bare church.

It wasn't the sort of church I'd been used to. The preacher went up into the pulpit and his talk commenced. I have no idea who he was, nor exactly what he said. He quoted St John, he quoted St Paul and he quoted many another! So what?

Sorry, Caroline, the sermon did absolutely *nothing* for me. It was irrelevant. I was bored stiff, and I sat there feeling disenchanted. The preacher could have quoted the Bible till he was blue in the face - it left me cold. I was anti-Bible because its contents *proved* nothing for me. It was just words relating stories of yesteryear.

I could relate the basic tenets of the Christian faith, but without belief in God and His Son, Jesus Christ, quotes from the Bible meant nothing to me. My problem was, my deep unhappiness and abandonment by God! I left that - to me - empty church, feeling antagonistic and depressed. I walked away, muttering,

"There's no point in quoting the Bible if a person doesn't believe in God or the Bible."

To me, what I'd just sat through was empty rhetoric. I felt, not just empty like that church, but even emptier than when I went in!

But, something, or should I say Someone? stirred within me. Caroline's suggestion was not completely in vain. I was prompted to explore further:

"I must look in that other church we pass in the lunch hour," I thought.

I plucked up courage and announced rather embarrassedly to the friends I was with, "I want to have a look in here." With that, I gingerly slipped into All Saints' Church in Margaret Street. As with All Souls', I had absolutely no idea of the significance, of this church in the Church of England. I stood at the back of All Saints' and gave a silent gasp:   "What a wonderful church!"

Spiritually, this church didn't feel at all empty: It felt full of the Presence of God. No service was in progress, just a deafening silence, and there were a few people kneeling in prayer. The atmosphere was tangible." Surely, this is the House of God!" I thought to myself.

All the above was preparation for what the Lord had in store for me. This, my first visit to All Saints', was another determining moment on my way back to Faith in God.

A year or so later, I was seeking God, silently praying, "Lord, if you exist, reveal yourself to me." And He did! Before it happened I'd had two flashes of God's enlightenment.

The first flash was when I was sitting on the lawn at Sunnydale. I was contemplating the blades of grass around me. I discerned God as the One who had created those blades of grass, as a flash of the divine presence came to me and disappeared, as quickly as it had come.

Mr Graves, my boss, had been elected Mayor of Hendon. I attended his installation. His chaplain spoke to the assembled company. I don't recall what he said, but as he was speaking, suddenly the second flash came to me, granting me another moment of God's enlightening presence. Again, it departed, all too quickly. This is the only way I can put into words what happened.

Not long after this, on a March day in 1959, as I was walking along Victoria Street in SW1, to the office in Buckingham Gate, SW1., I was uttering my heartfelt request, "Lord, if you exist…" when I had yet a further flash of divine enlightenment. This time, it was more than a flash: it remained and the Holy Spirit of God fell upon me. I call this my Second Conversion experience.

As a little girl I'd known deep faith in our Father God, a true love for His Son, Jesus Christ, and the Presence of the Holy Spirit with me. Now, having waded through a mire of desolation, I was once more being blessed with God's consoling presence, being equipped for the future. Words cannot express my gratitude.

Much was being restored to me: something of the happiness I'd experienced at Blackheath; something of the faith and prayer I'd known at St Giles' Church. I could hardly contain myself for joy. The desire to pray was insatiable! It was wonderful - I just wanted to fall on my knees. Obviously, this was impossible in street or office!

I yearned for my lunch hour to come - it seemed a long wait. As soon as I was free, I made my way up Victoria Street post haste to Westminster Abbey. I fell into the nearest pew, praising God from the depth of my soul, oblivious of the hundreds of tourists milling around. How I thanked God for my faith in Jesus Christ restored and for the renewed Presence of his Holy Spirit. It was all too wonderful for words! Time permitting, I made my way to the Abbey every lunch hour; later I came across St Faith's Chapel, the most ancient part of the Abbey, with its ancient painted mural above the altar. Here was silence and seclusion away from the madding crowd.

Not long after that, I came upon St Matthew's Church, tucked away in Great Peter Street, near the Abbey, one of those beautiful Anglican churches built for the Anglo-Catholic revival in the Church of England. I made my first sacramental Confession in St Matthew's.

Much later I was to learn that St Teresa of Avila had also had a Second Conversion experience.

Not that long after my heated argument with Derek and then my Second Conversion experience, Derek and I met up again and there was reconciliation. We were about to say farewell, again on the doorstep, when I plucked up courage to tell Derek what had happened to me as I walked down Victoria Street. Our conversation ended, I dared to speak out further,

"I'd like to go to Mass with you next Sunday!"

Derek was astounded. The request came out of the blue. This didn't sound like the girl with whom he'd had the recent argument. He hadn't lost me after all.

Come the Sunday, off we went to St Joseph's Church, Bromley. I wasn't really looking forward to attending, for the first time, a Roman Catholic Mass. But I was suitably surprised by what I witnessed. With his hope of being a priest, Derek was well versed theologically; he gave explanations when he thought it might be needed.

Whilst the Latin was unfamiliar, *much* was familiar: the fact that the set parts never changed, but the Collect, Epistle and Gospel readings changed every week. It didn't take long for it to dawn on me that, in essence, the R.C. Sung Mass was, in essence, the same as the Sung Eucharist I'd known as a little girl. I found the gabble of Latin that the priest had to utter at certain points, unedifying, unnecessary and unintelligible. This was the only real discordant note that struck me.

---

Now, as a restored believer in Jesus Chriat, I took the first opportunity to go back to that church I'd come upon two years previously - All Saints', Margaret Street - I had difficulty finding it - I'd started searching in the wrong corner of Oxford Circus!

When I realised my mistake, I found the right corner, and, in the end, All Saints' Church. It was good to enter All Saints' again, this time as a believer and, now, as one of the pray-ers! Also, I was now aware that All Saints' was known as the Anglo-Catholic cathedral. The act of worship at All Saints' was likewise similar to what I'd known as a little girl.

I had known deep spiritual satisfaction, as a little girl, in the Catholic, or High Church, tradition of the Church of England. Here I was two years later, having been ground into the ground, picking up the threads in that very tradition of the C. of E.

---

I had started reading the Bible again, and also the lives of Christian Saints and mystics, and I became interested in Christian mystical theology, or "the science of Love", as St John of the Cross calls it, which helped to affirm my spiritual experience.

I came to see the importance of taking the spiritual life seriously: our need for forgiveness; the need for our inner wounds to be healed; and, most importantly, that we are not to lose hope whatever life brings.

I came to see that the spiritual life is not and end in itself: we pursue it, that the Holy Spirit of God might enhance our every day life. And Love is His meaning.

Transformation of our inner being is what we Christians are to be about, first and foremost, by prayer that we might be changed into the likeness of Christ; as St Paul puts it: "It is no longer I who live, but Christ who lives in me" (The Bible, Galatians 2:20).

---

Pope John XXIII called the Second Vatican Council in 1962. He was the catalyst that changed the attitude of he R.C. Church towards us non-R.C. Christians. Up to then, we were still deemed heretic. Vatican Two, changed that, and we became known as "separated brethren". A new spirit was abroad, with many ecumenically-friendly declarations and greater openness. This was a real help within our marriage. (See Addendum 6.)

Not long after my second conversion experience, I was walking home through Farnborough Park, when I met up with Brian, who lived near us in Sunnydale. I knew that Brian was a Christian; he belonged to Crusaders, to which I didn't exactly warm on hearing about it.

I wanted to tell him what had happened when God came into my life as I walked along Victoria Street. My lack of ability to describe the things of the Spirit still made it difficult. At that point, I didn't even know the expression "second conversion". Brian told me he was an Evangelical, which, at the time, I hadn't the slightest idea what that signified. Falteringly, I tried to tell Brian about my life-changing experience and my need to find a church:

"Brian, I want to find another church, I can't go back to Farnborough Church," I said… "I want 'something more'!" That was all I could say; I didn't know really how to explain what I meant. Significantly, Brian the Evangelical, understood, despite my un-theological expression, 'something more'.

"Well, there's St George's, Bickley," Brian suggested.

One Sunday morning, Derek and I went to High Mass at St George's, Bickley: it was just what I was looking for. Brian's suggestion exactly fitted my spiritual need. I felt I had come home. This was a wonderful act of worship, "all done decently and in order" as the Book of Common Prayer directs. The sermon was inspiring, given by the vicar, Father Hugh Glaisyer.

High Mass celebrated at St George's was a real eye-opener for Derek. It was with some trepidation that he had accompanied me because it was his first time in a non-Roman Catholic church. Derek could hardly believe his eyes at what he beheld: vestments, candles, incense, bells, etc. He too felt at home, well, almost, for in those pre-Vatican II days, the Roman Church deemed it mortal sin for one of their adherents even to *go into* a non-R.C. church, let alone to attend a non R.C. service. A mortal sin was categorised as sin that was beyond God's forgiveness unless mentioned in sacramental \Confession.

Little did Brian know how significant his suggestion would be, long-term, for my life, in so many ways. Unknown to me, Fr Glaisyer was to be of tremendous pastoral help, later on – not just to me, but to Derek too!

**Queen of the Sciences**

Theology, sometimes known as "the queen of the sciences", was to be my interest, along with my love of people and my desire to help suffering humanity.

I'm quite sure, it didn't occur to my parents that, whatever my subject of interest, it would be of a serious nature and I would be inevitably drawn into it deeper. But, theology? At the time my parents were trying to stop me from "getting too serious", theology would have been furthest from their mind, as it was from mine. The word had never before been in my vocabulary - or theirs!

I didn't know that the Man, Jesus the Christ, who came to live among us, would help me make some sense of my life, particularly the sufferings. I little dreamt that, in the power of the Holy Spirit, Jesus Chris would become my Companion and my Lover, to whom I would give my heart, in the hope that my life might give glory to God. Obviously, I was too young to give a theological description of my early encounter with Jesus Christ as I walked across Blackheath, and my spiritual involvement in the Holy Eucharist at St Giles' Church, Farnborough. All this was the start of my theological understanding. I came to realise later.

---

Others, evidently, didn't see things quite like that. In the mid-Sixties, I had met a young woman in London, who told me,

"Now I have been filled with the Holy Spirit, there is no need for theology!" That sounded very dangerous! This woman always had her Bible on her but she hadn't understood the meaning of the word 'theology': *Theo Logos* Gk. Word of God. The purpose of the Bible is to speak to us of Jesus the Christ, who *is* the Word of God.

My response was to tell her that our theology matters crucially.

"We only have to make a statement such as 'Jesus is the Word made flesh' and we have made a theological statement!" I told her. She was silent.

Theology is not necessarily highly academic unless, of course, one has the intellectual ability and desire to study the subject at degree level. However, knowledge of God is *much more* than what is grasped by the intellect. Intellectual attainment alone is empty rhetoric if not underpinned by prayer.

We don't have to go through academia in order to know more of God's ways. "The true theologian," says the monk Evagrius "is one who prays"; and the one who prays is the true theologian! That opens up the way for us all, from the greatest intellectual to the greatest failure.

# A World Turned Upside Down

## Chapter 24

# PREPARATIONS FOR HOLY MATRIMONY

*He'd saved me and I'd saved him*

### Marriage Arrangements discussed

When Derek had told me quite early on that he was a Roman Catholic, my heart sank. That didn't augur well if/when marriage was considered right.

With Mr Falconer's instruction in mind, that I should get married before being operated on, Derek and I started discussing in earnest possible dates for our wedding and to finalise where the wedding ceremony should be held.

As already stated, in those pre-Vatican II days, unbelievable as it may seem now, it was deemed mortal sin for a Roman Catholic even to enter a non-R.C. church; and, officially, they were not permitted even to pray with non-R.C.s; there was one exception: they could say the Lord's Prayer with us, and that only.

In view of all this, Derek's allegiance to the Roman Church meant that wedding arrangements would be far from straightforward.

For a start, tradition has it that the marriage takes place in the bride's church, but my circumstances made that problematical, nay impossible. I'd like to have been married in St George's, but if our marriage was considered invalid because it had taken place in an Anglican church, there was a possibility that some or all of the Vanek family might absent themselves.

I'd already met most members of the Vanek family before our wedding, but only cursorily. I didn't wish to give any of them, especially Derek's parents, reason not to be present. Derek's father was the R.C. and, so far as Derek was aware, his mother had no religious belief. It seemed wisest and would save a lot of trouble if we were to be married in the Roman establishment and that, was definitely problematical. Hence, I signed their wretched piece of paper, under duress, to satisfy the Pope!

## The first hurdle - the Grand Introduction

Before we got married, obviously, it was only right that Derek introduce his future wife to his mother and father. We received a formal invitation to visit them for the purpose.

It was a cold, dark winter's evening and the first time his parents and I had even set eyes on each other. With some trepidation, we arrived on the front doorstep of their superior modern bungalow in Farnborough Park, sorely wondering what our encounter on the other side of the door held out for us.

Derek's mother opened the door and we were greeted with a frosty, "Good Evening". We were ushered into the sitting room, with a curt, "Like a sherry?"

We both politely accepted, and sat ourselves down. Ma and Pa sat on either side of the fireplace; Derek and I sat on the sofa, facing the fire. At least, *that* was warm!

The entire conversation that evening was held between Ma and Pa, discussing the welfare and the whereabouts of their two (ugly!) bull mastiff dogs; then the subject changed to the neighbours on either side of their bungalow, whom they proceeded to pull to bits; and, finally, the discussion turned on "that dreadful man opposite", the *nouveau riche* Donald Davies. More of Donald later.

Derek and I were left gazing into the fire as silent, embarrassed spectators. To speak of the set up as "most peculiar" is an understatement. No interest was taken in their son nor in their son's future wife.

We just *sat* there! And we continued to just *sit* there. We were getting a bit fed up with this strange procedure and exchanged a fleeting glance, with a slightly furrowed brow and a slight shrug of the shoulders, both of us wondering what on earth should be done about the situation. Derek was embarrassed by their indifference towards us and he plucked up the courage to say something to draw our visit to a close.

"I think we'd better be going!" We both silently arose from the sofa, thanked Ma and Pa for the sherry, and made for the front door. Neither Derek nor I could make any sense of my so-called introduction.

With an unemotional "Goodbye!" we departed, bewildered and mystified.

## Now for the next hurdle

The next hurdle was our interview with Canon Edmund Grady to inform him of our wish to get married. Obviously, I would have preferred it to be married at St George's, my spiritual home where I was a regular attender at Sunday Mass, but I was resigned to having the wedding at St Joseph's.

Canon Grady was grudging about my Anglican allegiance. All went fairly well until, almost at the end of the interview, he presented me with the form that *had* to be signed, promising to bring up any children of our marriage as Roman Catholics.

I objected strongly! However, my signature was essential if the Canon were to marry Derek to the likes of 'heretical' me. I refused to sign and I walked out. Derek followed, not a little concerned. Again, he thought he'd lost me. I think the venerable Canon was a bit taken aback. Why should I have to sign away my children to the Roman Church? It was an imposition.

Derek told me afterwards that he sympathised with the stand I made.

I went to discuss the matter with Father Glaisyer, "I'd much prefer to be married at St George's," I told him. "And I'd like to have a Nuptial Mass. If I *have* to be married at St Joseph's I object strongly to *having* to sign the form I was presented with when we went to see Canon Grady."

Fr Glaisyer nodded understandingly. "You are very welcome to get married at St George's. I'd be very happy to celebrate a Nuptial Mass for you," he assured me.

"I don't want to be married in the R.C. church, but I've decided it's the wisest thing, in all the circumstances. I think it will have to be St Joseph's because I don't want Derek's parents to have *any* excuse for not attending the wedding."

What else could be said? Fr Glaisyer knew my situation and the difficult decision I had to make.

A week later, Derek and I returned to see Canon Grady. I submitted to Rome's requirement that I sign their obnoxious piece of paper! I made sure that Canon Grady knew I was signing under duress. I was angry! Believing that Derek and I were meant for each other, what else could I do? I had no choice. I realised that the priest had no choice either - the Pope insisted on a signature and Canon Grady was only obeying his boss's orders.

In those days, the "mixed" marriage was looked upon as very second class. The unofficial R.C. way of expressing disapproval was to make things difficult for the couple and by denying them the "extras" at the service: hymns, organ, flowers, that in any other church were normal.

At our second meeting I told Canon Grady that my faith had been wonderfully restored, "I'd like to have a Nuptial Mass," I told him.

My request was abruptly turned down - far too much for him to even consider – it was 200 per cent against Rome's rules and regulations, "Oh no, out of the question!" was the reply.

I shrugged my shoulders slightly. I told the Canon that I could have a Nuptial Mass if I got married at St George's! He remained silent. Whether I liked it or not, St Joseph's it had to be.

## Chapter 25

# THE SWINGING SIXTIES? NEVER!

### *A house in the country*

I sometimes hear the decade of the 1960s spoken of as "the Swinging Sixties", which annoys me. It *might* have been swinging for some: rock 'n' roll, jiving, skiffle bands and the late night café culture, etc., most of which I deplore anyhow. For many of us, the Sixties were *far* from swinging.

**No house-hunting hurdle to jump**
However, there was one hurdle we didn't have to jump was the house-hunting hurdle. Just as we were preparing to get married in 1960, the Sutherland grandparents' bungalow in Leaves Green, Keston, providentially, became available for Derek and me to purchase. This was the property my Sutherland grandparents had bought when they moved from Denmark Hill, after the War.

Grandfather Sutherland had died a few years previously and now Grandmother Sutherland, suffering from dementia, was unable to look after herself. She moved out and was looked after by her three children in turn: my father and his two sisters.

My parents assisted Derek and me to make the bungalow ready for us to move into after our wedding.

Leaves Green was surrounded by lovely country: fields at the bottom of our back garden, and, at the front, fields could be seen from our front door, beyond the houses on the other side of the road. Many a visitor waxed lyrical about the bungalow's situation: "What a wonderful place to live!" I was told. When visitors praised the bungalow's countrified situation, I held back my reservations.

Leaves Green was a remote hamlet on the main road leading up to Biggin Hill Airfield renowned for the crucial part it played in World War Two. Our address was Leaves Green, Keston, but the Village of Keston was some way away and inaccessible by public transport. At least, we were on a bus route but the service was infrequent.

Leaves Green may have appeared an idyllic place to live, it was five miles from Bromley - *not* ideal for a city girl whose heart is in London. Don't think me ungrateful. Of course, the bungalow was a Godsend becoming available, as it did, just before Derek and I were married! But…. I'm not a country girl.

## Chapter 26

# DEREK AND I ARE WEDDED AT ST JOSEPH'S

### *The problem of the name*

**Two minuses make a plus!**

Our wedding day, Saturday 21st May 1960, was a cloudy, grey day, but we weren't rained on. We had what used to be known as a "white wedding" - we don't hear that expression these days!

"I've decided to revert to the original Czech family name, Vanek. I'm really not keen on having a double-barrelled surname."

"Yes, I think that's a good idea," I agreed. "I can't say that I like the prospect of having a double-barrelled name." No way had I influenced Derek in his decision.

Marriage seemed obvious and marry we did, as Mr and Mrs Vanek, and our difficulties were faced and lived through.

Our 'mixed' marriage was deemed second class in the eyes of the Roman Church. With so much negativity swirling around in the lives of both Derek and me, the outsider not knowing half of it, it could be said, "What a pair!" I referred back to my basic school algebra and I recall that two minuses make a plus! Fancy, even knowledge of algebra contributing to an understanding of a marriage relationship. I didn't get algebra at O-level, either!

---

The ceremony proceeded and, all things considered, Canon Grady seemed to have shown a little more leniency towards us than might have been expected. He had bent the rules a little, for we were permitted a hymn with organ, the church was graced with flowers, and the organist played a voluntary at the end of the service. I wonder what his 'boss' would have said! Maybe the Canon was glad that Derek had found a wife!

What a pity the woman flower arranger felt constrained to tell us next day, that the flowers had been arranged "for the Sunday Mass!" said, as if she had to justify the presence of flowers at a "mixed" marriage!

Thank goodness Derek's dear old Grandmother Vanek, together with all his aunts, uncles and cousins, came to the wedding. For whatever reason, Derek's parents decided not to attend. We had no idea why.

The Vanek family happily welcomed me into their midst. And I am glad to say, not one of them suggested I join the Roman Church, though I expect they harboured a silent hope that I would! Fortunately, thanks to the revised thinking of Vatican II, attitudes and beliefs were changing as they permeated the ranks. The Vanek family graciously accepted that I was a practising Anglican and that as an Anglican, I practised the Catholic Faith. R.C.s generally, were getting used to the idea that we non-R.C.s were acknowledged as separated brethren.

Only Derek's godmother had the temerity to pose the question, "Had I ever thought about becoming Catholic?"

"Grrrrrr!" I thought silently. "No, I had *not*!" I replied, firmly shaking my head. The question was quite irrelevant!

I told her firmly,

"I don't have to join the Roman Church to be a Catholic! I am an Anglican and I practise the Catholic Faith as an Anglican. I would object strongly to being called "a convert". I'm converted to Jesus Christ! Anyhow, why should *I* change? I have a very spiritual, pastoral priest who is always available when I need help, and I've many lovely friends in the Church of England." My indignation remains!

Apart from any other consideration, I could never deny the validity of my Anglican past; and there are still R.C. beliefs, moral and theological, that I could not accept.

Derek *never* suggested that I join him. He knew what Fr Glaisyer and St George's meant to me. In fact, in the end, Derek joined *me*! He too went to see Father Glaisyer for his pastoral care, and, he too was acquiring friends at St George's.

Life was difficult. In addition to the sufferings of the moment, much energy was expended coping with the problems caused by the sufferings of yesteryear.

At one point, when I had thought that things were improving, they worsened, to the point of verging on the impossible. We both hoped and prayed that our sufferings would some day somehow be redeemed by the Man we call our Redeemer - Jesus, the Christ, but it didn't happen quite as we had hoped. I could never have envisaged how deeply scarred Derek was, nor could I have known the unforeseen problems of my own life, as a result of the brain operation.

In spite of much adversity, Jesus Christ remained our Rock we were faithful worshippers at Mass every Sunday, at our respective churches.

Derek came to pick me up afterwards, and found me chatting to other members of the congregation: This friendship with church members was another eye-opener for Derek. Things were very different at St Joseph's. The vast majority of the congregation spoke only briefly to the priest at the door and departed without a word to another!

## The problem of the name

As already stated, at the time of our wedding we had no idea why Derek's parents didn't come. Some time later, we received a letter, from which we learnt the reason: "the problem was the name"! We frowned. What did they mean? It sounded crazy!

At some point, after Derek's birth in 1933, his father had decided to anglicise the name and Vanek was changed to Bourne-Vanneck": the 'Bourne' part is taken from 'Bournemouth', the town where Derek's grandfather first set up in business on his arrival in England, the second part of the new name, is an old English spelling - 'Vanneck'.

---

Mr and Mrs Eddie and Millicent Bourne-Vanneck became known, rather disrespectfully, as "the B-Vs". It was shorter and easier and also became a cause of cryptic amusement. Such were the tragic scenarios they created for us and for their next-door neighbours, if we hadn't laughed, we'd have cried.

Derek and I had problems enough within our own four walls, without having to cope with the troubles that the B-Vs threw up in our face! The postman delivered many a solicitor-type letter, usually written by Derek's father. We did wonder if his mother had been responsible for the hurtful tone and contents. We pored over every missive that dropped on the doormat from them, and, having read the letter, a decision had to be made whether it warranted a reply or was it best just to ignore it? We came to dread the post.

---

## The next hurdle comes into view

About seven years after we had been married, we invited Derek's parents to come up for coffee – the first time ever! For the explicit purpose to discuss "the problem of the name", that being the reason, evidently, so we learnt later, for their non-attendance at our wedding. This was only the second time we had met: the first was the 'joyous' occasion, already related.

We politely welcomed them in, invited them into the sitting room and served coffee. The atmosphere was tense. The evening started with an exchange of a few strong argumentative words between father and son. I don't recall what was said; it was irate and not very edifying. After they had calmed down, a short but stilted discussion commenced.

Ma-in-law then proceeded to tell us in no uncertain terms why they had found it *impossible* to come to our wedding. The problem was "the name".

I feel quite sure it was she who had decided to make "the name" a bone of contention.

I became the spokeswoman on behalf of Derek and me, not by design. I just found myself in that role. The conversation went something like this…

"We couldn't *possibly* come to your wedding when the name was different!" Ma-in-law informed us, in a haughty tone of voice.

"But Vanek is the *original* Czech family name," I protested politely. I can't see what's wrong with the name Vanek. It's a lovely name. All the other members of the family, Grandma and Derek's aunts and uncles, have Vanek as their surname."

"It's foreign!" Ma-in-law retorted sharply.

"What's wrong with it being foreign?" I asked, again, politely but a little indignantly. "I get on well with foreigners!"

I'm not convinced that Derek's father was wholly behind his wife on this particular point. I sensed Pa-in-law softening with a slight approving nod of the head, observed out of the corner of my eye. Understandably, he had retained an affection for his family's origins and the traditional Czech surname with its original spelling. He remained silent.

I was well aware that, because of the War, many people with a foreign surname anglicised it to prevent their coming under suspicion. My mother's cousin, Ann, and her French husband had done just this.

I suspect that the well-heeled Mrs Millicent Florence Bourne-Vanneck rather fancied herself sporting a double-barrelled surname!

With some irony, Vanek is the surname on Derek's birth certificate, which definitely states that Derek was *born* Vanek!

Somewhat facetiously, I ask, "Apart from the spelling, what's the problem?"

[I didn't put that to Mrs B-V - I thought of it afterwards!]

The B-Vs departed, no more agreeable to Derek's decision to revert to the family name than at the moment they had walked in through the front door. I suspect they had come to our house with little or no desire for reconciliation.

### *Bonhomie* when the two fathers meet

Some while before the B-Vs' visit, my father was picking up Mr B-V in true Farnborough Park tradition, long before my father realised his identity, as he took him to Bromley South Station. Apparently there was much *bonhomie* between the two of them. I don't know how the two fathers came to realise the identity of the other, but my father told me, "I thought Derek's father was a jolly good chap." Not that he continued to give the gentleman a lift, once he'd realised his identity.

Derek's sister has confirmed since, "My father told me how well he'd got on with your father!"

I was able to tell her, "My father thought the same about your father!"

It made me think that Mr B-V was under his wife's thumb and when away from home, he was relaxed and convivial. As already mentioned, I got on well with all Mr B-V's brothers and sisters and other members of the Vanek family. One of Mr B-V's sisters later admitted that their opinion of Mrs B-V was *very* similar to mine/ours!

## Donald, the inveterate joker

Derek's tale of woe as a child growing up was almost too dreadful to be believed. Now we were hearing about Derek's mother's atrocious behaviour from a completely different source, Sarah, the B-Vs' next-door neighbour.

The B-Vs were responsible for many a threatening letter or verbal abuse - at times physical abuse, of the neighbours. On both sides, the B-Vs neighbours were quiet, inoffensive souls who would never do or say anything to deserve such treatment. The persecution became intolerable. Poor Sarah was often in tears, she seemed to take the brunt of it. When desperate, she would make her way over the road to see Donald (we heard Mrs B-V describe him as "that dreadful man opposite") and his wife Rosina, to relate the latest hurtful episode.

The brazen Donald was a very different type, so unlike Jim and Sarah Guy on one side of the B-Vs, and the elderly Mr Ridley and his wife on the other side. (Mr Ridley had the hosepipe put on him.) All were sensitive and easily upset, understandably, by what emanated from their mutual neighbour. Donald was a *nouveau riche,* extrovert and self-made man. He drove an ostentatious Rolls Royce and had gold taps installed in his bathroom!

Little did Mrs B-V know that Sarah was a *very* close friend of my mother; and, from Sarah we would get to know about all the horrendous experiences that were being perpetrated.

Derek had long before told my parents about his unhappy childhood, and teenage life at home, and the dreadful treatment he received, generally, and he told them about the solicitor-type letters that he had received more recently from his father. Thanks to Sarah's experience at the hands of the B-Vs, my parents were more willing and able to understand and fully accept Derek's bizarre story of unhappiness - almost too dreadful to be believed.

Derek had left home to become a teacher; he had hoped to be an R.C. priest, but his unstable background put paid to that. His sister advised me later on that she became a nun to get away from home.

---

This ridiculous scenario was ripe for ribaldry. Mrs B-V did her best to ruffle Donald. Donald, who made light of any offence perpetrated against *him* from the house opposite. He enjoyed playing jokes on the establishment across the way, and he gave as good as he got, always without malice. My parents, the distressed Sarah and Jim, Derek and I, not to mention Donald and Rosina, discussed *ad nauseam* the problem of the B-Vs – the topic consumed us. Donald, the inveterate joker, was a wonderful antidote to the prevailing situation, which saddened and disconcerted us all. There seemed to be no obvious answer.

Every so often, Derek and I would drop in on Donald and Rosina, sadly, to hear the latest bit of 'aggro' and Donald's latest joke. He told them with great gusto. One had to laugh!

I recall one particular joke. He enjoyed letting off champagne corks, which sounded just like a gun going off. On one occasion, fulfilment was complete, when Mrs B-V came storming out of her front door in a fury, believing it to be just that – a gun. Donald put two fingers up. Donald's ability to lighten the misery of the situation was just what was needed. If we hadn't laughed, we'd have cried.

Sarah and Jim had a lovely house in Farnborough Park. However, sad to say, the day came when they decided that they could take no more of the abominable behaviour issuing from next door. Enough was enough. They sold up and moved to the little village of Cudham, to be free – free to walk out into the garden without the fear of verbal abuse!

---

## Why am I waiting?

I had to wait a long time to be admitted to Guy's Neuro-Surgical Unit for the brain operation. At the start of 1961, I was in limbo, feeling too ill to do housework or anything else, just waiting for my marching orders.

I was very relieved that my mother now accepted my plight and my decision to have the op. During this anxious time of waiting she came up to the bungalow to keep me company. We sat in the front room discussing the situation.

"I think you are very brave to even consider having the operation," she told me.

"Oh, no," I replied, "It's the only answer. I just wish Mr Falconer would let me know when I shall be going into hospital. I am having blackouts, day in, day out, and even when I'm not having a blackout, I am plagued, body, mind, and soul, with horrible thoughts and nasty blackouty sensations. It may sound a strange thing to say, but I feel like an old woman. I can't do anything round the house, I'm worn out and weak right through! And there's *nothing* I can do about it. I wonder how much longer I'll have to wait before I hear from Mr Falconer."

I wanted my mother to know that the horrible sensations continued and had, in fact, worsened, first and foremost because it was true. But also, in case she changed her mind and her approval of my decision to have the op.

---

Mr Falconer's letter arrived, at last, giving the 26th March 1961 as the date to go into Guy's Neuro-Surgical Unit. I had no idea how long I'd be in hospital, nor the length of time I'd need for recuperation, so I'd already said my farewells to my friends at Stevens, Scanlan & Co. They were very sympathetic and wished me well.

## Ida is informed of the op.

My mother and I had been doing our annual stint helping at the jumble sale in Farnborough Village Hall to raise money for Dr Barnardo's Homes. My father came to pick us up and was driving us home. I was sitting in the front seat next to him, and my mother was on the back seat with Ida Becket, an old friend of the family, who lived near us in Farnborough Park. I had a shrewd suspicion that Mummy wouldn't have told Ida about the op. so I was considering telling her myself – the first time I'd told anyone outside of the family. Ida supported the charity MIND, so I knew she'd be sympathetic, but to speak about it in front of my mother was another matter. Anyhow, why shouldn't I speak out about it? Farnborough Park was like a village: the gossip web would soon disseminate the news, so Ida might as well hear it straight from the horse's mouth. I turned round to face Ida and my mother, behind me:

"Ida, did you know I'm going into hospital next week, for a brain operation?"

"No," Ida replied incredulously, "I didn't know! What are you going to have done? And which hospital will you be going into?"

Ida was interested and asked pertinent questions. I wasn't able to give an answer to all of them. I didn't know then exactly what they were going to do to remove the scar on the brain!

"I'm going in next Tuesday to Guy's Neuro-Surgical Unit, at the rear of The Maudsley Hospital, Denmark Hill. Blackouts have blighted my life since the age of ten. They are going to remove the scar on the brain. It's getting close now! Doctor after doctor has said I'd grow out of the blackouts. Not only did I *not* grow out of them, they've got worse and life has become intolerable. I'll tell you when I come out what they do to me!"

Ida was most interested to hear my news: "Thank you, Rosemary, for telling me about the op. I hope all goes well. I shall be thinking of you."

A World Turned Upside Down

## Chapter 27

# UNDER THE SURGEON'S DRILL AND KNIFE

*Some past memory might be recalled!*

### Awake on the operating table

On the 26th March 1961, Derek took me in the car to Guy's Neuro-Surgical Unit at the rear of The Maudsley Hospital. I was settling in to life on the pre-op ward when, two days later, Mr Falconer, the eminent surgeon, called me in. I was an in-patient now, of course, and he wanted to tell me something of what I was to expect during the impending operation.

Sitting at his desk, this man of few words had serious matters to share with me. He looked at me intently over his narrow, gold-rimmed reading glasses:

"We have considered your case, Mrs Vanek. We think you are a suitable person for the operation to be performed under a local anaesthetic," he told me in his slow, deliberate voice. I grimaced.

"But, of course, we need your consent. When we put an electrode on the brain we get a more accurate reading from the electro-encephalogram if the patient is conscious," he explained. "Also, we want to stimulate the brain with an electrode and I will ask if you hear anything, smell anything, see anything, or you may have some past memory recalled. Would you be agreeable to this?

"Go away and think about it and I'll see you tomorrow. You can tell me then what you've decided."

Back on the ward, I pondered long and hard the prospect of a brain op. only under a local anaesthetic. It sounded a bit scary. Mr Falconer had spoken about past memories. All my blackouts involved past memories. It would be great if I recalled a memory or two that had lain dormant for years. That would make consent worthwhile, but, of course, an even better reason for giving consent was that a more accurate op. could be performed *because* the patient is under a local anaesthetic instead of a general one.

On my return next day, I confidently told Mr Falconer my decision:

"Yes, I agree to have the operation done under a local anaesthetic." A further grimace. I could only hope that I'd made the right decision.

## The long-awaited day arrives

The day of the operation, 28th March 1961 dawned, with all the dramatics that I described back in chapter one. The itch had been scratched, and the skull had been cracked and removed, and I lay there waiting for the surgeon to begin the procedure.

Mr Falconer's first words were addressed to the team looking on round the operating table:

"See what a small temporal lobe she's got!" he said. I imagine this was part of the learning curve - mine as well as theirs! Evidently, a small temporal lobe is connected with my sort of epilepsy.

I don't quite understand why – but that was what they had expected.

Then he called upon me:

"When I say 'Now', you must tell me if you see anything, hear anything, smell anything, or have any past memory recalled." Ah! The crucial moment had arrived.

At each "Now", I am sorry to relate that my answer was "No" - every time. Not a thing did I see, hear or smell; and never was there the slightest recollection of a past memory occurring! What disappointment. So far as that was concerned, there was no benefit, by my being semi-conscious - apart from accuracy, of course, and, I must add, interest!

During the removal of the scar, an EEG, with electrodes placed actually on the brain, was in progress. With the patient semi-conscious, this indicated with greater accuracy what the surgeon needed to know, indicating when and where the 'scraping' process, if scraping is the correct word, was to begin and, of course, end!

## Back in the post op. ward

I came round in the post op. ward with a very, very tight bandage wound round my head to help the removed piece of skull bone to re-join its place in the skull. The headache was excruciating, *so* tight was the bandage.

It so happened that the operation was done on the Tuesday of Holy Week – a Holy Week I shall not forget: in great pain and confined to bed. Thursday of Holy Week, otherwise known as Maundy Thursday in the Christian Church's calendar, is the day we meditate on the Agony of Jesus in the Garden of Gethsemane, when He prayed to His Father that the cup of suffering should pass Him by. This made my physical agony all the more poignant, a supreme opportunity to enjoin my pain and suffering to our Lord's.

Come the next day, Good Friday, in fact, a little relief was permitted me: the bandage was taken off and replaced with a fresh one; and then on Holy Saturday, it was changed and tied just a little looser; and tremendous was the relief when, the bandage was removed for good, providentially, it happened to be Easter Day! Resurrection Day!

This episode in my life was not the end of my suffering; there was more resurrection life to come!

My unsuspecting family, visiting me on that Easter Day, had the surprise of their lives. Not only had they not expected to see me with the bandage removed, they hadn't expected the Yul Brynner effect – what a shock! My poor mother, especially, was horrified to see her daughter's new 'hairstyle'!

The pressure of the bandage was gone; but the right side of my head was still very tender and sore. For two weeks I could hardly lift my head from the pillow. The muscles of my right eye were badly affected, and the eye could hardly be opened. I had to prise it open with my fingers, but when both eyes were open at the same time I saw double. Double vision remained for some time and disappeared very slowly. Two years later my head remained tender, and sleeping on my right side was uncomfortable. Even 50 years later, the tenderness remained.

As I lay in the hospital bed, I suddenly had a bad turn. It was as if the whole of my head and mouth were full of writhing, wriggling snakes. It was horrible! I was petrified. A lovely Maori nurse of large proportions happened to be nearby and she held me and comforted me till this strange occurrence faded. I'm glad to say, that this was a one-off.

I was very grateful to all my friends at St George's Church and others, who were praying for me.

I emerged from all this with a great desire to pray, and the desire increased. I needed desperately to go apart to be with the Lord, but that was not possible. I was too ill, and, anyhow, there was no hospital chapel at that time - a lack, I believe, that has been rectified since.

One of the doctors in Mr Falconer's team, who was involved in the op., came into the room where I was recuperating to find out how my recovery was progressing.

"I'm not feeling too bad, apart from the headache," I told him. I got to know this doctor – he seemed the most open of the team. At an appropriate moment I took the opportunity to ask him to furnish me with some details:

"I want to know the facts of the operation," I said. "Friends and family will be asking me, also wanting to know details of what was going on above me during the op. and I want to be able to tell them."

I could see the doctor was reluctant to speak on the subject, so I pressed him to tell me more. He overcame his reluctance and when he got into his stride he explained what he could, the best he could:

"In cleaning up the old scar that was causing your blackouts, and which did *not* heal, the surgeon has created another scar that *will* heal."

"Oh really, I see! That's interesting." I told him.

He continued:

"After we had stitched you up, you were given the full anaesthetic – to relax you – that is, after the piece of skull had been replaced, and the flap of skin covering the piece of skull had been sewn back into place."

"Oh thank you for telling me all that." I was profuse in my thanks. "That's a great help!"

With that, the doctor departed.

How ironic: to be given the full anæsthetic after the operation had been performed!

## 'Iolanthe' and immersion in the Spirit

To celebrate my homecoming my parents had bought tickets for the four of us to see *'Iolanthe'* (a comic opera by Gilbert and Sullivan) at the Bromley New Theatre. It was a good performance. I enjoyed it, but I was elsewhere - I was with the Lord. His presence was tangible. He evoked spontaneous praise and thanksgiving – first and foremost for the operation, and also for my return to Sunnydale House until well enough to return to our bungalow.

Before getting into bed, Derek and I knelt to pray, as we had always done. The Holy Spirit continued to fill me, yet as I knelt there, the Spirit was welling up from the depths of my being and gloriously overflowing me. Praise and adoration also flowed from the depth of my being. This glorious, awesome event revealed to me something of eternity. I couldn't get up from where I knelt.

That night I also discerned how death is the gateway to enter into His glory – eternally. Death need not be feared; it will be the final hurdle by which we shall enter into the nearer presence of God. I also learnt that we don't have to wait for our final death; even while we are still earthbound God uses the little deaths we experience on the way. We seekers after God are also seekers after our inner transformation, to be the person we are meant to be, and in readiness for when the soul is liberated from the restrictions of our earthly body.

Prayer and thanksgiving will be offered up by all those who are pure in spirit, that is, single-minded in their desire for God, unhindered by sin and the effect of our unhealed wounds, spiritual, emotional and physical. Prayer will be made that all may be healed, and that the rubbish we carry around within us, is thrown out of our being. Our spiritual nourishment on earth is the Eucharist (Gk. thanksgiving). We are to make eucharist in our heart. One day, we shall be nourished at the eternal Eucharist, the heavenly banquet. Now we see only darkly, then we shall see God face to face (The Bible, 1 Corinthians 13:12). That will be glorious.

"You must come to bed," Derek cajoled, "it's getting late."

Late it was - past midnight! But I was enjoying such blessings as the Spirit of God filled me with His overflowing Love. I didn't wish to do anything to despoil the Holy Spirit's presence. It was awe-inspiring. I hardly knew how to deal with the situation. I was tired and I knew I had to get into bed, but still I couldn't get up. I had to force myself off my knees with a supreme effort of will.

At the first possible opportunity I went to see Fr Glaisyer, an Anglo-Catholic priest of the old school. I wanted to share with him something of this wondrous experience of the Holy Spirit. I knew he was a man of prayer, but I wasn't quite sure how he would react to my experience. Again, I was all too aware of the inadequacy of words: trying to describe the indescribable:

"So, powerful was the Holy Spirit's presence that night. I just wanted to pray and still do." I told him. "It was absolutely wonderful! "Oh, good!" Father

Glaisyer exclaimed."

"Not only does Father G, accept what I'm saying,' I thought to myself, he understands – he's delighted!" That made me glad.

All this may sound spiritually upbeat, as if it presaged the end of my problems. Far from it: deep down I somehow knew that this unexpected outpouring of God's Spirit was preparation - I was being strengthened for the task ahead, whatever that might be.

## Chapter 28

# OVERWHELMED BY THE SPIRIT AND PROBLEMS GALORE

### *"I need the patience of Job"*

It was the wonder of the brain operation and the wonder of the Holy Spirit's operation that occupied me in the early Sixties. Both had changed my life, and for both, I praised the Lord. This little phrase can become a cliché, but when the power of his Spirit overwhelms, the praising of God is a blessèd reality that flows incessantly from the heart.

St Paul tells us that we are to pray without ceasing, be it in our native tongue, or in another tongue – a gift of the Spirit; not that I'd received the gift of 'tongues' at that point - that was to come.

To return to the start of post op. married life, whilst Derek and I had saved each other on the human level, our marriage proved to be a very mixed blessing: I was to be confronted with Derek's strange, irrational outbursts, when I would need the wisdom of Solomon and the patience of Job. These outbursts were triggered by something so trivial. Had it not been for the Holy Spirit upholding me, I might very well have gone under spiritually, mentally and physically.

I owed much to Father Glaisyer, who had 'open door' at the vicarage on a Wednesday evening. One could go and see him about anything – matters great or small; problems profound or trivial – no appointment needed.

For me, Father G's ministry of pastoral care and his availability was a wonderful and necessary bolt-hole: I never knew when it might be needed. On the occasions I had to use it, I always left his study feeling strengthened and encouraged; he gave an understanding ear when desperation or depression had overwhelmed me; he helped me understand Derek's problem:

"Derek is letting out all the anger he feels towards his mother onto you," he explained.

### Snow is falling, snow on snow

In early 1963 I was working for a firm of solicitors in Throgmorton Avenue. It was a good firm to work for. I was secretary in the conveyancing department, and was also on reception. I enjoyed meeting the firm's clients in reception; and I found the work undertaken behind the scenes by the solicitors acting for the parties involved in the sale and purchase of a house.

This was the year when snow was falling, thick and fast over all the South-East of England and, most unusually, in the Square Mile of the City of London. The daily train journey up to London was difficult because of frozen points, which, when freed, quickly froze again, such was the cold. Once off the train at Cannon Street Station, office workers were faced with a hazardous walk to work.

It was *very* cold and the snow was unbelievably deep. Incredibly, the snow never melted, even in central London. Workmen had already done a good job, banking the snow up on each side of the City streets, but there were fresh falls. Indeed, snow was falling, snow on snow, making deep snow even deeper.

I wonder if such were the conditions that Christina Rossetti witnessed one winter, which inspired her to write the christmas carol, in 'The bleak mid-winter!'!

Yes, it was cold, but the power of God's love pervaded my body with a glowing warmth, as I made my way from Cannon Street Station, through Pope's Head Alley, past the Royal Exchange and the Bank of England, then right to the Stock Exchange and left into Throgmorton Avenue. I walked through the snowy deeps all the way to the office, with the Holy Spirit of God wonderfully present.

### The famous 'Honest to God' debate

In the early Sixties, just as I was experiencing this wonderment of the Lord, the Church was deep in debate on what came to be known as the 'Death of God' theology. The debate was raging in the Church as a result of the book entitled *Honest to God*, by Bishop John Robinson, the then Bishop of Woolwich.

Some time later, I happened to meet Deaconess Elsie Baker, when she was at the Church of the Ascension, Blackheath. She had worked with John Robinson, so knew him personally. She gave me some interesting insights into the origin of the book.

"I think John Robinson has been greatly misunderstood," she opined. "He'd started writing his thesis as he lay sick in a hospital bed, with no intention that his writings should be published as a book At the time, he was a university lecturer, and he'd intended to challenge his theological students with what he had written," she told me.

I was new on the theological scene, and had learned much of the Christian faith as a child and as an adult Anglican in the Catholic tradition. I tried reading John Robinson's 'Honest to God' book, published by SCM Press, but I didn't get very far - it was a difficult read. What he was purporting didn't seem to tally with what I'd come to understand of the Christian Faith, either from my own received knowledge of Jesus Christ or from what I had been taught.

I read the letters in the Church press, as I tried to discern better what John Robinson was trying to say. Evidently, the book had helped some people in their faith, while others declared it had destroyed their faith. I had difficulty untangling the conflicting views expressed.

Some correspondents complained that his approach was not the line that a bishop should take, in his teaching role, whilst others pointed out that the title of the book was not the opinion just of an upstart suffragan bishop: Bultmann and other theologians had already put this case in the pre-WW2 era.

Others complained that it put man at the centre of things, not God.

John Robinson was being honest to God by accepting the prevailing Church's malaise, and was trying to address it. From my limited understanding, I couldn't see that the medicine he'd prescribed was the right medicine. His thesis should have been kept to the world of academia.

Generally, the Church did appear spiritually moribund - respectable churchianity prevailed. The bishop was being honest to God about the situation, as he saw it. He'd hoped to enliven the Church by giving a fresh perspective of God. The traditional belief of an "unapproachable God up there in his Heaven" was out! Perhaps, after all, the bishop was saying that the Church should give greater stress to the Christian belief in the Incarnation, that is, to recognise God present in every human being.

Later on, I came in contact with charismatic renewal, and that, was much nearer to providing an answer to the church's malaise:

## The grace of the Holy Spirit

While all these arguments in the 'God is dead' debate were being thrown back and forth, I was experiencing God in such a wonderful way, affirming truly that God was gloriously alive!

I got off the train at Cannon Street Station, one particular morning, not feeling in the least bit exalted; indeed, quite lacking any sense of inspiration. Derek had yet again lost his job and I walked to work through the deep snow suffering yet a further 'little death', when suddenly I was taken up into the presence of God. Not only was I surrounded by banks of snow, more significantly I was now surrounded by the glory of God. As I wended my way along the narrow streets and alleyways of the City and so, to the office, I was filled with awe and wonderment, the Holy Spirit was gloriously present, within me and without, above me and below, to the right of me and to the left. I gazed upon this vision of heaven and beheld the saints and the angels close at hand. I was oblivious of all else. I was aware of the freezing conditions but I didn't feel cold: the fire of the Holy Spirit warmed me.

When I reached the office door in Throgmorton Avenue, I was sorely tempted to go on walking, that I might continue my enjoyment of eternity. A difficult decision, but I believed it was the right decision, to go into work. Of course, I breathed not a thing to anyone about the wonderful vision I had just been granted, a tremendous and privileged moment in my life.

Once again, my world had been turned upside down, this time, in a simply glorious way, to which words can never do justice.

---

I was diffident about telling anyone, except Father Glaisyer, about what the Lord had revealed to me amidst the snowy deeps. I felt presumptuous. I could hardly explain it to myself, let alone, to another. In a way, The Spirit continued to bestow upon me instantaneous prayer and praise; and I had a tremendous desire to go apart and pray. For this, I turned our walk-in larder into my "glory hole", as I called it.

Later on, the opportunity came and I plucked up courage, rightly or wrongly, to tell Derek what had happened to me on that snowy morning as I walked through the City of London.

## Derek is perplexed

Derek was perplexed. He was consumed with sad incomprehension and hopelessness, nay despair. The following is my paraphrase of what Derek had said to me some time previously. His thinking went something like this:

"Dear Lord, help me! Here I am, a member of the (Roman) Catholic Church that we used to believe was the 'One True Church', and here's Rosemary, a "heretic", as we were taught to call the likes of her, having a deep experience of the Holy Spirit.

"I can see how you are helping her to deal with her troubled life and having to cope with me and my troubled life. I don't know how she sticks me when I have one of my unpredictable outbursts. I'm afraid that one day she might find me too difficult to live with.

"Why don't you bless me, Lord, as you have blessed Rosemary? Here I am, sitting around, sick in body, mind and soul, having difficulty keeping a job, ever hoping and praying that you will help me in a similar way. But it doesn't happen. I just exist with no sense of your presence. It doesn't seem fair, it doesn't add up. Please help me! Why don't you do something for *me*?"

I understood how Derek could feel that God didn't love him. His plight *didn't* seem fair, and from Derek's point of view, it *didn't* add up. With his lifelong faithfulness to Jesus Christ, in spite of all, I realised his quandary. But I wasn't God, so was ill-equipped to pass comment when such questions were asked of me! I had not spoken greatly of my own inner experience of love, peace and joy. I could only try to love him and compensate a little for what had been denied him as a child.

## Deep depression and grand mal!

I felt wonderfully, spiritually transformed, but recovery from the operation proved to be a long, drawn out process, and a year later, in 1964, a deep depression encompassed me. There was much confusion and contradiction, with so many different things going on within me and around me.

### Life is lived on a knife

We had our good moments, but they were all too few and far between, illogical and erratic, life was lived on a knife-edge; I never knew what would induce a flare up – when or why or where it might occur. I endeavoured to dot every 'i' and cross every 't' in all I did or said, when dealing with the most trivial and inconsequential of matters. It is impossible to be objective when the thought process of the other is illogical, unpredictable and violent. I knew in my heart of hearts he couldn't help it, governed as he was by stored-up fury and the lack of maternal love of yesteryear. The consequences of that were terrifying.

Derek's behaviour became more and more irrational. I never knew what I was coming home to. He It could be over the top with a loving welcome or he could be cursing and swearing over some triviality. It could be both.

On one occasion when I was returning from work in London, he saw the bus pass by the house, and having a shrewd idea that I would be on it, he came skipping along the pavement, like a little boy glad to see his Mummy. I would be walking along the road having got off the bus and he showed inordinate pleasure at seeing me, with a big warm hug, as if I'd been away for months.

We were having our cup of coffee at the end of the meal. Derek was looking through some papers, when suddenly he came across the previous week's Radio Times, *not* thrown away. His short fuse went, and suddenly, this became an earth-shattering oversight and he blew up in a rage, out of all proportion, telling me it was all my fault, and asking me:

"Why haven't you thrown away the out-of-date Radio Times?"

*Mea culpa!*

To the best of my ability thereafter, I made a point of throwing away the Radio Times as soon as it became out-of-date. A few weeks later, Derek wanted to refer to the previous week's issue. He couldn't find it and, as before, went berserk, because I *had* thrown it away! I couldn't win.

### Derek attempts to set up his own business

Derek had a real gift for mending things. He could mend almost anything mechanical - clocks, radios, TVs, and items of jewellery. He took on commissions from friends, neighbours and family and had many satisfied customers. Mrs A was glad to give him her broken down radio, to mend; Mr B was grateful to find someone who could mend his prize antique clock; Mrs C put her broken necklace into his hands, to be re-strung, etc. etc.

His aim had been to start up his own business, like his father and his grandfather, but it could never be. Had his childhood been stable and loving, I'm sure he could have been successful, but his circumstances were otherwise.

I'd become his surrogate mother! I stuck it out to the bitter end, and it *was* bitter, too!

I managed to endure with a certain equanimity these demented flare-ups of shouting, swearing and accusation. I let him get on with his abusive torrent of words while I got on with the washing-up or whatever I was about. Retaliation was pointless. I held my ground and didn't crumple. With raised voice, he accused me of not loving him and not caring if he lived or died; he'd then accuse God of not loving him etc. etc. With that, he made his exit:

"I'm off. You'll never see me again. I know you don't love me – I hate myself. I know when I'm not wanted. You'd be better off without me. This is the last time you'll see me!" And so on.

With that, he stormed out of the house, got into the car and revved up the engine to let me know what he was about, and he was serious, implying that I should go out and rescue him – a cry for help. This emotionally battered wife felt duty-bound to venture out and use all her power of persuasion to get him to come back into the house. Difficult, but I managed it, by the grace of God.

Threats of suicide were an oft-repeated scenario. On one occasion, he got hold of the kitchen knife and walked out of the kitchen: He came back into the kitchen while I was at the sink; he had stuck the knife into himself. I turned round, to see blood running down his white shirt, a dreadful sight - I just gasped with horror! Derek then took it upon himself to phone for the ambulance, and off we went in the ambulance to Farnborough Hospital, where he stayed for some weeks. It had pierced his liver.

After one or two more of these irrational flare-ups, he was full of remorse for what had happened and was unable to explain the whys and wherefores of the explosions, often adding that he couldn't understand how I could stick him. Many were the times when I was on the brink of not being able to do so.

The thought of departure occurred to me at times, but I managed to stick it out Anyhow, there was nowhere obvious to go.

Poor Derek, his hope that marriage would be the answer to his problems was far from the mark. Life was too much for him. He couldn't cope with the increased responsibilities that life laid upon him. His inner turmoil continued. I had to remind myself that he had saved me on the human level and his witness had helped restore my Christian faith. For both, I was very thankful.

In the June of 1968 I went to see our GP with earache. He was looking through my file and, 'out of the blue' he took the opportunity to inform me of Derek's mental sickness:

"Your husband is somewhat schizoid – somewhat schizophrenic, somewhat paranoid," he told me. These terms were not in common use in those days as they are today. But I understood.

"Your husband's mental condition is inherited!"

[Derek also had a kidney disease, a form of Bright's. He'd told me himself how the consultant had said to him, that goodness was going out of his body and badness was staying in. They knew *what* was happening; the condition couldn't be treated because they didn't know *why* it was happening.] The mental condition and the kidney disease played one against the other.

The doctor I was seeing that morning was candid, when he added, "Your husband might die at any time – it could be six months. You mustn't have a baby – you couldn't cope." He was adamant.

I received this news with a mixed sense of shock and relief. By this time, I'd forgotten about the earache!

So much for the Swinging Sixties!

In fact, Derek died exactly six months later, as the doctor had warned.

---

As is patently obvious, Derek was in need of a caring priest to help and encourage. So was I, but I had Father G! Derek was attending a new church, closer to home. None of the three priests there ever came to visit us, even though I'd told one of them something of our problems. So disillusioned and disgusted was Derek by their lack of pastoral concern for him/us that he came with me to see Fr Glaisyer to get the help he needed, *and* then started coming regularly with me to Mass at St George's! What should we have done without dear old Father G?

## The Rector of Keston calls

Now and again, the Rector of Keston called on a pastoral visit. I greatly appreciated his concern for me.

Derek sat glued to the television in the living room, as was his wont; the rector and I sat in the kitchen and we had helpful chats over a cup of coffee, He was a kindly man, and I felt sorry that I couldn't support him at Keston Church.

I shared with him some of the difficulties of the home and how Fr Glaisyer had helped both Derek and me, the rector certainly understood:

"Fr Glaisyer was a great help to me when I first came to Keston. I too owe him a lot. I quite understand," he graciously told me.

"I'm sorry I can't get to Keston Church," I added. "I can't drive, and there's no bus to take me from Leaves Green to Keston Village. I've been going St George's, Bickley, for some years now.

## Gratitude for having known Father Glaisyer

Saint George's Church was my spiritual home for eleven years. Fr Glaisyer, the parish priest, tirelessly taught the Catholic Faith, year after year. On this, my return to my pilgrimage of faith, it was a privilege to have sat at his feet. I praise God for his ministry, which met my need in so many ways: for the biblical sacramental teaching he gave us in his Study Circle; his fuelling my interest in theology; his encouragement in my early poetry writing; and, last but not least, for his availability at crucial moments when I was desperate. Father Glaisyer was a great priest.

In 1971, Father Glaisyer celebrated the 50th anniversary of his ordination to the priesthood: he had been vicar of St George's Church, Bickley, for 51 years.

## The Queen honours Father Glaisyer for his ministry

For over 800 years it has been the custom of the monarch to present gold, frankincense and myrrh to mark the Epiphany of Our Lord in 1973. The Queen gave royal recognition to Canon Hugh Glaisyer, and presented him with the gift of frankincense, "in honour of his long and notable ministry" in the Church. The formal presentation was made in the Chapel Royal, on 6th January, the Feast of the Epiphany.

Fr G. died in harness in January 1981. He was 90.

*Father Glaisyer's celebration on the occasion of the 50th anniversary of his priesthood*

## Chapter 29

# GRAND MAL SEIZURES STRIKE ME DOWN

### *From seizures to panic attacks*

I'm sorry to say, the epilepsy story did not end with the brain operation. There was more to come, which, it has to be said, was a disappointment.

I mentioned at the start of the previous chapter the deep depression that encompassed me and disabled me. To my horror, the depression issued into a *grand mal* epileptic attack. I'd not known *grand mal* before, it was horrendous, but when I emerged from it the deep depression had gone. That was a bonus.

### *Grand mal* attack no. 1

Six months after I came out of hospital after the operation, my whole world was again turned upside down. I was working for a firm of solicitors in Queen Street, at the northern end of Southwark Bridge, as secretary to a young solicitor. I was getting on fine.

One day, things were not so fine. I couldn't function.

O dear! Deep depression filled my mind and weakness overwhelmed my body. I was unable to do *anything*. I was petrified! I sat at my typewriter, when suddenly and without warning everything was going haywire. I didn't know what it was all about.

So started my first *grand mal* epileptic seizure.

After two and a half hours I found myself lying on the floor, slowly starting to emerge from it. I lay there terrorised, tortured by hellish voices going on inside my head. It went on and on, seemingly never to stop, as I lay there. Then, horror of horrors, as I came round further I realised the bladder had relaxed, and I was vaguely aware of two or three secretaries, kneeling on the floor around me, all wanting to do something to help.

"Where am I? Where am I?"

I kept on asking the same question of them,

The senior partner's secretary was one of the helpers, and she kept on telling me in a kindly, reassuring voice,

"You're in the office." But it didn't sink in.

"Where am I?" I asked, again and again. Truly, I was in a terrifying place: I was in Hell, overwhelmed and consumed by fear!

At last, I emerged completely from this terrible two-and-a-half-hour scenario. I truly believe I had been to Hell and back! To put it mildly, it seemed a real setback. As may be imagined, this *grand mal* attack was a real disappointment. But it had cleared the depression.

This was the first of four *grand mal* attacks after the op, and they occurred at six-monthly intervals with a very similar sequence. Each one was preceded by the same deep, deep depression. I cried copious tears, ostensibly for no reason, on each occasion. When I had fully come round I felt great! Better than before.

## *Grand mal* attack no. 2

Six months after the first attack, my grandparents came to tea at our bungalow in Leaves Green. I'd made egg sandwiches – crusts removed! The table was set with the pink rose tablecloth I'd embroidered, and, as usual, I had put out my beautiful delicate pink and green Wedgewood Hathaway Rose bone china tea service.

We were seated round the tea table and I was pouring out tea from my antique silver teapot, when suddenly the teapot started to lurch at speed, from left to right, left to right, left to right. I couldn't stop it. My second *grand mal* attack had started. I recall grimly hanging on to the teapot handle, tea sloshing everywhere, spoiling my beautiful tablecloth.

I vaguely recall Derek trying to loosen my hand's tight grip of the teapot handle and my resistance.

He told me afterwards the difficulty he'd had in getting me to let go. I realised he must have succeeded because the next thing I knew, I was lying on the bed, again filled with terrible fear, and again, slowly but surely, emerging from a veritable hellish place. This, of course, was the first time that Derek and my grandparents had seen a post op. seizure. They had seen many of the pre-op. attacks but this was quite different.

When I'd fully come round, Derek was bending over me, explaining that he was about to drive the grandparents back home to Sunnydale. That's all I remember of the afternoon.

### *Grand mal* attack no. 3

The third *grand mal* attack occurred when I was on holiday in Spain, at San Feliu, a small village on the Costa Brava. Derek would never go away on holiday so I joined my parents on this, my first visit to Spain. We were with four friends: a husband and wife, and two mature girls who were friends, and, both of whom were nurses. It so happened I was sitting next to one of the nurses, as we were sunning ourselves on the beach, when I had yet another attack! The nurse friend helped me through the dreadful fear-filled state until I'd come through it. This, of course, was the first time my parents had witnessed a post op. sort of seizure. I recall no more, apart from the nurse who was helping me, as I emerged.

### *Grand mal* attack no. 4

Mrs Bull was our kindly next-door neighbour in Leaves Green. Because we were both out at work she helped us deal with our laundry. The Glennifer Laundry van called every Friday to collect our dirty sheets and pillowslips. A week later the clean laundry was returned to Mrs Bull.

One particular Friday evening after supper I was doing the ironing in the kitchen and Derek went next door to collect our laundry. He stayed to have a chat with Mr and Mrs Bull, as he often did, but, ironically, on this occasion he stayed a little longer than usual; ironically, because on his return, he came into the bedroom to find me lying on the floor, emerging from a *grand mal* seizure. I was trying to get undressed ready for bed, but couldn't manage it, as I lay on the floor!

When fully emerged, I got up from the floor and, as before, was gratified, that the deep depression had disappeared. I returned to the ironing board, where the attack had started, and I found, much to my surprise, that the sub-conscious had taken over: I had finished what I was ironing and had unplugged the iron, I'd stood it up vertically on the work surface. It was difficult to work out the sequence of events - there was an iron scorch mark on the kitchen lino. At some point, I must have laid the hot iron across the back of my left hand, leaving small burns along all my knuckles. Bits of skin and flesh had got stuck to the iron! I was completely unaware of doing *any* of the above, nor do I recall leaving the kitchen and going into the bedroom and falling onto the floor as I tried to undress.

Derek returned and was concerned to find me lying on the bedroom floor, all while he'd been next door. Straightaway, he took me in the car to Farnborough Hospital to have the burns dressed. I needed a skin graft for the worst burn – on the knuckle of my little finger. This is the only time that I'd hurt myself as a result of an epileptic attack pre op. or post op.

Before all four *grand mal* attacks I had the same deep depression, crying my eyes out, and my body drained of strength, during which time I was unable to do anything. However, I emerged from each seizure with the depression gone and my physical strength restored.

This fourth seizure proved to be my last; six months later the deep depression returned but no blackout occurred to 'clear the air'. The absence of a blackout was, of course, good news, but it meant that there was nothing to take away the depression - not a very happy situation; in some ways, *almost* worse. I'm not sure that I really mean that!

The surgeon had cleaned up the original scar and in so doing had created a new scar that was in the process of healing.

As already stated, the *grand mal* seizures occurred at six-monthly intervals, but six months after the iron-scorching event, just when an attack might have been expected, I had a panic attack, as if it was *in lieu* of a seizure. The fear that filled me during the panic attack was very similar to the fear I knew when I started to come round from each of the *grand mal* seizures.

## Petrifying panic in Paris

I was on a pilgrimage to Italy in 1966 with a group from St Mary Aldermary Church in the City of London, where I went in my lunch hour. We visited Florence, Rome and Siena, seeing much of ecclesiastical, historical and cultural interest. The parish priest of St Mary Aldermary led the pilgrimage, greatly assisted by his wife, Dorothy, a fluent Italian speaker. She was, of course, an incredible help on the pilgrimage, in more ways than one, as you will learn!

Dorothy was a very special person: she had recently translated Pope John XXIII's diary into English, the Pope who had died only a few years previously, and she was a tremendous help to me, personally. On our homeward journey I had my first ever panic attack in Paris, not that I knew at the time that that was what it was.

Our train was late arriving at *Gare du Nord,* so we wasted such a long time standing on the platform, with nothing to do.

We had been told that we wouldn't need French currency. There was time to have a coffee but without French francs I was not able to leave the group even for that or to buy *un jeton,* the disc required for making a telephone call from a French public telephone.

I'd wanted to contact Martine, my French penfriend, and here I was in Paris, trapped; surrounded by French people yet denied the possibility of speaking a word of French. Oh, the frustration! The panic attack commenced.

At last, after a very long wait, the train to Calais drew into the platform, and we s clambered on board. The train moved off and the panic continued. Fear consumed me. My body was immovable and my fear turned to terror. I fixed my gaze on the door handle of the carriage, and kept it fixed there, all the way to Calais. I couldn't talk because that would have created even greater terror. That's the only way I can describe how it was.

Fortunately, I was sitting next to Dorothy. I clung onto her all the way back to England. Dorothy was a brick: she valiantly stuck by me, without seeking explanation. Obviously, she knew less than I did, as to what was going on within me. The panic continued as we crossed northern France to Calais and it gradually waned as we crossed the Channel. Normal service was resumed as soon as the ferry slid into Dover harbour. What relief!

The fear I experienced while the panic attack lasted was so similar to the fear I'd known after a *grand mal* attack. It seemed to replace a full-blown seizure. Dreadful though it was, it proved to be "goodbye to *grand mal*". Praise God for that.

Praise God, also, for Dorothy. Truly, I don't know what I'd have done without her. We may have been on a pilgrimage, but there were one or two in our party who were not very charitably disposed towards me.

It was only when I went to the doctor when I got home and tried to describe to him what had happened, that I learnt that it was known as a panic attack.

## Chapter 30

# HOLY SPIRIT RENEWAL (1)

### *From small beginnings*

Over 40 years ago, in 1969 to be precise, five of us gathered to celebrate a Pentecostal Mass, as we called it. The Intention was for the Catholic tradition of the Church of England, that its adherents might know renewal in the Holy Spirit. Our hope and prayer was that we might act as a catalyst for a spiritually renewed Church, and in a *milieu* where the participants would feel comfortable.

---

Let me start at the beginning, which was 1964.

I was in an employment agency, close to St Paul's Cathedral, reading the Church Times. I had a vague feeling that the young woman sitting next to me was wanting to speak to me. She had observed the subject matter of the paper I was reading and at last plucked up courage:

"I see what you are reading – you're a Christian believer, are you?"

"Yes, I certainly am." I replied. We got into deep conversation.

"Have you heard of the Baptism in the Holy Spirit?" she enquired.

"No," I replied, "what's that?"

She then told me how she had received the Baptism in the Holy Spirit that had changed her life.

"You have to pray for the Spirit to fill you," she added.

"But that's very similar to what happened to me – about four years ago," I exclaimed. "The Holy Spirit filled me to overflowing and surged up from within me. And he kept on filling me. But I hadn't prayed for Him to come. It happened quite unexpectedly."

She seemed taken aback that I hadn't actually prayed for the Holy Spirit to come.

Anyhow, she advised, "You should go to St Martin-within-Ludgate, on the right hand side down Ludgate Hill from St Paul's cathedral. You'll find others there who have received the Baptism in the Holy Spirit. They hold a prayer meeting, one o'clock every Tuesday lunchtime."

At the time of this chance encounter, all spiritual consolation had been withdrawn and I was experiencing great desolation. I'd been put off prayer meetings, but I decided I would give the prayer group at St Martin-within-Ludgate a try and see how it was.

I went along, when my lunch hour permitted, and I met up with Christians for whom it was a natural thing to share with others the joyful experience of being filled with the Holy Spirit. I appreciated their openness of heart and mind but remained a little wary. Up till then, I didn't have the terminology to describe the indescribable, that is, the wondrous mystery of the Holy Spirit of God filling me body, mind and soul with His overflowing love.

I had learnt to be circumspect about relating my sufferings and believed that one had to be likewise circumspect about relating one's blessings. I still haven't quite squared the circle. In some respects, the two aspects overlap.

My involvement with this group was instructive and affirming. I was led into pastures new and my horizons were wonderfully broadened while remaining in the traditional pastures of the Church of England, first and foremost, because I was already being spiritually nourished at St George's, Bickley.

The 1960s came to be known as the era of the Holy Spirit, who was moving in countries all over the world. It came to be known as the charismatic movement or charismatic renewal. *(Charismata,* Gk is the plural for gifts).

It has often been my experience that the Lord has seen fit to bestow on me a spiritual gift when I least expect it. One such was speaking in another tongue. When I was first filled with the Holy Spirit I didn't speak in tongues. I had to wait another 15 years before that happened.

I was on a traditional pilgrimage to the Shrine of Our Lady of Walsingham, at a Low Mass celebrated in the Holy House. I had just received Holy Communion when, suddenly, yet silently, I started speaking in another tongue! I hadn't been thinking about it nor praying for it, at the time; it happened, quite unexpectedly.

I told Fr Glaisyer, the most traditional of priests, about what had happened and he exclaimed quite ecstatically, "That's wonderful!" Obviously, he wouldn't have countenanced speaking in tongues out loud at Sunday High Mass, nor would I, but he understood and accepted what had happened to me at Walsingham.

Things were beginning to change. It seemed as if the era of 'respectable' Christianity was starting to lose its hold, but it was only the start. Of course, there is nothing wrong with being respectable *per se*, I don't wish to infer that Christians *shouldn't* be respectable, but it occurs to me that 'respectability' is the Enlightenment's counterfeit of holiness.

Numbered among the respectable are those that imagine "they've made it", socially and materially, perhaps, but spiritually? Sometimes, one is left wondering! Even the innately good can be counterfeit, for goodness is not of the essence of Christianity, whatever the worthy hymn writer might have stated! Growth in the life of the Spirit is so that our desire for holiness is fulfilled and, ultimately, achieve union with God.

It will be "by their fruit you shall know them" – the fruit of the Spirit (the Bible Galatians 5:22-23).

## Fountain Trust

Michael Harper founded Fountain Trust in 1964 to promote Baptism in the Spirit and to encourage the use of the gifts of the Spirit in England.

I went to Fountain Trust with my new found friends from St Martin-within-Ludgate. The meetings were held at Spurgeon's Metropolitan Tabernacle at the Elephant and Castle. We learned a lot from well-known speakers such as David du Plessis and Jean Darnall of the 'old' Pentecostal tradition; also, from the late and much revered David Watson, one time Vicar of St Michael-le-Belfry in York; and Dennis Bennett, the Anglican priest of *Nine O'clock in the Morning* book fame, and many another.

We heard about the Lord's power to heal the sick, to release those in bondage, to deliver those oppressed by evil spirits. The work of the Spirit is the inner trans-formation of Christian believers.

It was an exciting time to be living, hearing about renewal in the Holy Spirit of God and learning of the growth of churches in many parts of the world.

I had already learned about the healing ministry from Father Glaisyer.

What we were witnessing now was something more open and many faceted, a healing ministry in which lay people were encouraged to share in the laying-on-of-hands with prayer for a person's need, in their own home church situation.

Fr Glaisyer believed in the Lord's power to heal - he had the gift. I knew several people in the congregation whom the Lord had healed through his ministry. With hindsight I wished I had asked him to anoint me with holy oil before I went into hospital for the brain operation. More's the pity, one had to ask to be anointed in those days and at that point I hadn't been back in church life long enough to have been aware that that was what I should have done.

One particular healing at St George's at that time remains with me. It was so unusual and hadn't been requested, as such.

It was Christmas Eve and Father Glaisyer was celebrating Midnight Mass at St George's. That night a young couple was present with their baby; they were unknown to Fr G and anyone else in the congregation. The baby was ill, almost to the point of death, so we learnt later. The doctor had made his diagnosis and the verdict on the dying infant's condition was conveyed to the parents as the doctor handed back the baby to the parents, because there was no hope of its survival. For some reason the parents were moved to come along to Midnight Mass and they brought the baby with them. They couldn't say exactly why they had come.

I had noticed them in the congregation and had thought to myself, "Fancy bringing a small baby to Midnight Mass!" I was all for babies being present at the Sunday morning Mass, one never knows how they might be influenced by the presence of the Lord at the service. But Midnight Mass seemed a bit inappropriate!

Fr G. and the altar party processed to the back of the church for the Blessing of the Crib. He happened to see the couple with their baby in the congregation, and, completely unaware of their circumstances, had stopped the procession in order to give them a Blessing. Next day, he heard from the couple that their baby had been healed! They then, of course, knew why they had felt impelled to take their baby to Midnight Mass at St George's.

So did I! "Tut, tut, Rosemary. 'Judge not!'"

## Chapter 31

# HOLY SPIRIT RENEWAL (2)

### *"He will baptise you with the Holy Spirit and with fire" (Matthew 3:11)*

Fountain Trust meetings had started in 1964 at Spurgeon's Metropolitan Tabernacle, Elephant and Castle. Having already received the Baptism in the Holy Spirit, I could empathise with what speakers were saying: I learnt much and felt greatly affirmed.

The word of knowledge is one of the gifts of the Spirit mentioned by St Paul (1 Corinthians 12:8). Jean Darnall, a Pentecostal minister from the USA, had a powerful teaching and healing ministry through words of knowledge and the laying-on-of-hands. Jean was the speaker at one particular Fountain Trust meeting at which I was present. As usual, the church was full, and, as usual, Jean gave an inspiring talk. During the evening's proceedings, the Lord gave her a word of knowledge:

"There is someone here with an ear condition that needs healing."

I thought of my ear infection, but the thought departed as quickly as it had come. "It can't be me!" I said to myself. Quite a long pause followed, and Jean repeated, "There is *someone* here with a bad ear condition; this person doesn't realise that they are being healed. Would they please stand up!"

Deep down, I had the sure conviction that it was me to whom she was referring. I duly stood up, the likes of which I had never done before! And straightaway a comforting heat filled my ear, and it was healed – on the spot.

Those of us who lived when the charismatic movement was at its height were mightily blessed in so many ways. Many new doors were opened and many new encounters with Christians of different Churches were made. The Spirit was a reconciling power among Christians: the Evangelical tradition converged with the sacramental life of the Catholic tradition, and when both traditions embraced the Pentecostal dimension, the Holy Spirit was the source of reconciliation. Evangelism is not a separate issue, but is part and parcel of our daily Spirit-filled life. We witnessed the early shoots growth in charismatic renewal.

The Holy Spirit is no respecter of persons; the outpouring of the Holy Spirit is available to all Christians. Apparently, there was grave doubt and misunderstanding spread abroad amongst those who lived, and still live, the sacramental life of the Catholic or High Church tradition of the Church of England. There is no *real* contradiction, as I can bear witness. Rather, the Spirit leads us along unknown paths, renewing the spiritual life, enhancing the sacramental life, and, so, transforming our inner self. Again, by their fruit you will know them. Yes, the Spirit can take us from one degree of glory to another, as St Paul puts it. That speaks of growth. Lack of growth breeds stagnation and stagnation halts the inner transformation, for which we pray.

We don't hear much about the work of the Holy Spirit today. Charismatic renewal has left its mark on the Church; yet who dare deny their need of spiritual renewal and spiritual growth? Who can deny their need of inner healing? Who can deny the Churches' need of spiritual renewal and reconciliation? Wherever we are on the spiritual ladder, growth is an on-going need. We can never say that "we've got there on this side of death!"

The Church needs to be a praying Church!

---

Fountain Trust in the mid-Sixties arranged an International Conference based at the Methodist Central Hall, Westminster. This was another tremendous corporate experience of the Spirit, attended by Spirit-filled Christians from all over the world and from many different Churches.

Every day there were many inspiring speakers to choose from. Unfortunately, one couldn't go to them all! I think the most memorable speaker at the conference was Fr Francis MacNutt, O.P., when as a Dominican Friar he gave a daily inspiring series of talks on the gift of healing.

The Holy Spirit and the hot sun blessed our lunch break as we sat on the grass of Dean's Yard and witnessed the unity of Christians surrounding us, a wonderful mixture of all traditions: Baptists joyfully singing and dancing with Roman Catholic nuns! Little moments of reconciliation as Christians of the once antagonistic and hostile traditions were growing together, brought about by the power of the Holy Spirit, unheard of in the not so distant past. Christendom in all its facets was changing.

Of course, theological disagreements remained, but the Spirit came in power and great love that ultimately gifted us all with a unity of faith, albeit our beliefs were not 100 per cent identical.

---

Spurgeon's Baptist Tabernacle, Elephant and Castle, or Methodist Central Hall, Westminster, was suitable for the mainly Evangelical clientele of the time, but it was not a *milieu* to which I could happily bring my Anglo-Catholic friends and acquaintances. I could quite understand that it could invoke a reaction similar to mine on the occasion I ventured into All Souls, Langham Place, in a state of unbelief.

My prayer and my hope was to find somewhere that met this need. But how and where?

---

## Our Pentecostal Mass is established

One day, a certain Bertie Pope came along to St Martin-within-Ludgate and enthusiastically declared to the six of us present:

"There are three priests in the East End who have just received Baptism in the Holy Spirit! We are holding a Pentecostal Mass next Friday at St Margaret's Settlement, Bethnal Green."

My ears pricked up immediately and I voiced my support. This sounded hopeful – it could be what I was looking for.

"Really Bertie! I'll be there," I gave him my firm assurance.

Bertie was an Evangelical who told us what had happened soon after he'd received the Baptism in the Holy Spirit:

"I found the Church of Our Most Holy Redeemer in Exmouth Market, Clerkenwell. It's quite close to my office. That church has such a prayerful atmosphere. I love it. In my lunch hour I enjoy great blessings standing before the statue of the Sacred Heart, praising the Lord in tongues. It's wonderful!"

Thanks to his Pentecostal experience, the Lord had led Bertie into the sacramental way of understanding and living the Christian life, without losing his evangelical zeal.

Bertie was so grateful for this enhancement of his spiritual life. He made it his mission to get over any vicarage doorstep to tell the priest about the power of the Holy Spirit. He managed to talk to one of the priests at the Church of Our Most Holy Redeemer.

"The Holy Spirit will enhance your preaching of the Gospel, and through prayer He will give you the power to heal the sick in the name of Jesus Christ. Let's pray together to receive His blessing."

So started our Pentecostal Mass, thanks to Bertie Pope's faithful witness. Teresa Fleming, Warden of St Margaret's Settlement, invited us to use the chapel for our Mass and time of free prayer. The small basement chapel was just the size needed at that point in our history: small, warm and intimate. The alternative, a large East London church, dark and cold, especially in winter, was not necessarily inviting when there is only a handful of people present.

Five of us were present at that first Mass. Our hope and prayer was that we might be a catalyst to show how the gifts of the Spirit were complementary to the sacraments, both being outward and visible signs conveying inward invisible grace; that celebration of the Eucharist does not preclude *extempore* prayer and spontaneous singing; and, most importantly, that baptism in the Spirit involves no denial of grace already received, be it Baptism in water, Confirmation or Ordination, it is release of the Holy Spirit already received.

The likes of Bertie had embraced the Catholic, sacramental understanding of living the Christian life; whilst we in the Catholic tradition became more evangelical in our outlook, as a result of our Pentecostal experience. Having had our spiritual eyes opened, our little group had to consider how best we could share the Holy Spirit with others in the Catholic tradition.

One of our group suggested that we embark on a communal social ministry to 'justify' our existence. I didn't consider that was our vocation. Apart from anything else, it was impractical, coming as we did, from different parts of Greater London and its *environs*. I believed we were called to be a praying presence: 'being' not 'doing'.

At the time, the charismatic movement was spreading its influence; and there was also much misunderstanding. Critics were often ignorant of charismatic renewal's true *raison d'être*, that is, to pray for the release of the Spirit within each of us; to pray for the transformation of our life by a deeper indwelling of the Holy Spirit; and to inspire personal prayer and communal worship, especially in the context of offering eucharist (Gk. thanksgiving)! Our group's little rivulet of praise and thanksgiving flowed into the great ocean of Spirit-filled worship.

Once a month we met in faith at St Margaret's Settlement, praying the Holy Spirit to show us the way forward. We were most fortunate to have Teresa Fleming among us, who happily offered us hospitality. Teresa was sympathetic to both our Catholic tradition and our charismatic witness. She prepared the chapel for us, and joined in our worship, after which she provided us with coffee and biscuits. Unfortunately, I had to cut short that part of the evening, a great pity, but I had to get the tube that would catch the train that would catch the last bus home from Bromley South station to Leaves Green, Keston, quite a way out of Bromley.

We earnestly hoped and prayed for others in our tradition to know more of the transforming power of God's Spirit. But things didn't happen as we had imagined!

---

Some years on, one of our number who had joined us much later, having heard how the Lord had transformed the lives of so many people since our start, had assumed erroneously that our early gatherings "must have been exciting". That was far from the case! Spiritually-speaking, our early celebrations were mostly uphill. We were often dispirited by general lack of support: we didn't grow as we had hoped: one person joined and two left, so to speak. We wanted to share the love, peace and joy of the Holy Spirit that we had enjoyed so abundantly, but for a long time, there was no obvious fulfilment to encourage us on our way. At times, our venture appeared not a little foolish.

## From small beginnings

Eventually, from our small beginnings at St Margaret's Settlement came our London Days of Renewal. Someone came up with an all-embracing motto

P-E-A-C-E, describing ourselves as Pentecostal Evangelical Anglo-Catholic Ecumaniacs!

Our Days of Renewal started small, but gradually our numbers increased and we flourished, spiritually and numerically. At one point, over 200 people were attending our Days, filling a well-known Anglo-Catholic church in London, St. Alban's, in Holborn. We lay-men and women were encouraged to join with a priest to share in the prayer and the laying-on-of-hands of all who came up to be prayed for. the time we set apart, on each day, specifically for the ministry of healing. Lay involvement in this ministry was a privilege that became the norm. We prayed in English or we prayed in tongues, silently or out loud, – a worship language when English didn't suffice. This proved to be a blessing for many.

Anglicans from Peterborough, Leamington Spa, Bristol and other towns and villages in England, joined us at our London Days of Renewal.;and we continued to be greatly blessed by the Holy Spirit. As time went on, these loyal supporters from afar started Days of Renewal in their own town or village. It transpired that our witness to the Catholic or High Church tradition of the Church of England was not our sole *raison d'être*. As indicated above, we were also a catalyst for introducing those of other traditions to the sacramental way of life.

## Twelve years later, a providential encounter

I was eating a light supper in the Pret à Manger overlooking Trafalgar Square. It was full, except for a vacant seat opposite me. A gentleman came along to the table and politely asked, "May I sit here? Is it free?"

"Yes, of course," I replied, "Do sit down." The gentleman thanked me and took his seat. He sipped his mug of coffee and I continued to eat my salad.

I glanced up furtively and observed that the gentleman had a leaflet on London bus routes (presumably a visitor), and also had a brochure on The Prayer Book Society (presumably an Anglican!). I debated within myself whether or not to speak. I hesitated, but "Why not?" I thought, so I plucked up courage:

"Are you a visitor to London?" I asked.

"Well, I was born in Greenwich, so I'm a Londoner, but now I live in Norwich, so I'm really a visitor," he replied.

"I see you have a brochure on the Prayer Book Society!"

At that point, the conversation revolved, generally, round things ecclesiastical. In the midst of our conversation my acquaintance interjected:

"I think I should reveal my hand, I'm a priest of the Church of England."

"Oh really!" I exclaimed, with some interest. I began wondering if I dare enquire after his name. It might sound a bit cheeky, but again, "Why not?" So, here goes: "May I ask your name?" I enquired.

"Patrick Phelan", was his reply.

Immediately, I thought to myself, "I *know that* name!" and my mind started fumbling hard, trying to recall why the name was so familiar. I don't think he was aware of my silent fumbling. Suddenly, it dawned on me, and I exclaimed:

"Of course!" our London Days of Renewal! We shared the laying-on-of-hands, praying for people. I'm Rosemary… Radley!" I exclaimed.

What a surprise, meeting up so inauspiciously and unexpectedly! The year was 2013. After twelve years, we could hardly believe such a providential encounter. The strange thing was that neither of us had recognised the other.

Our meeting up in the *Pret à Manger* was so providential, we both felt there must be some further purpose in it. I wrote to him to find out if he were still involved in the ministry of healing the memories. He wrote back assuring me that he was, and inviting me to come and see him, if I wished to.

I arranged to visit Norwich, the place of my earliest memory, to talk with him as a spiritual friend for the healing of memories that still haunt and hurt me. This was a very beneficial visit, the first of several to come.

---

## The Shrine of Our Lady of Walsingham

Alongside our then well-established London Days of Renewal, in 1974 a few "fools for Christ" made a five-day mid-week pilgrimage to that charismatic place, Walsingham. At the start, there were just a dozen of us, but these foolish few were soon to become a flood of pilgrims at a flourishing annual event.

On the fourth pilgrimage we were full to capacity. Supporters joined us from all over the country: Manchester, Glastonbury, Derby, etc., even from Wales and Scotland. Some came already Spirit-filled, others booked, wanting to "dip their big toe in", metaphorically-speaking of course, to find out what it was all about. There was a tremendous communal outpouring of the Holy Spirit, in a way not known before. We had a wonderful Spirit-filled five days. The presence of God was tangible. We were all greatly inspired and blessed during our informal daily Masses and our informal Services of Benediction.

The spiritual climax of that pilgrimage to the Shrine of Our Lady of Walsingham came at the celebration of our final outdoor Mass at the old Halifax Altar. We were privileged to have the Bishop of Lynn as our celebrant and preacher. He entered joyfully into our charismatic worship of God in the power of the Holy Spirit. We were all, as a body, spiritually uplifted by the presence of the Holy Spirit of God. The singing in the Spirit was ethereal, literally out of this world, when everyone was praising God in the tongue given to each, in a beautiful Spirit-given tune. Words can never do justice to its beauty – it has to be heard to be believed. Truly, the Spirit had set us on fire!

Those of us who had laboured long and hard since the early days of our Pentecostal Mass at Bethnal Green could hardly believe what we beheld: something of our original vision was unfolding before us. It was a tremendous, miraculous moment. Again, words cannot do justice to our immersion in the glory of God at that Mass. We 'old-originals' were overjoyed. A new chapter was ushered in. It was around this time that some found themselves 'slain' or 'resting in the Spirit'. Whilst this was not the main focus of our gatherings, it was a time when people fell backwards and then lay on the floor for a while, resting in the Spirit, for the Spirit to further His work in that person.

It happened to me on one occasion, when the Spirit was doing a deeper work within me. However, on the whole, my function seemed to be that of a catcher of bodies as they fell back!

The waiting list continued to grow; numbers of those wishing to join us were now too great for the accommodation at Walsingham. After much prayer and deliberation, it was decided that we should move to the High Leigh Conference Centre in Hoddesdon, Hertfordshire. It was with great sadness that we left Walsingham, the very place that was an unspoken witness to our Catholic tradition. But larger accommodation was necessary if we were to welcome the many people still wanting to come for the first time but whom we had to refuse, for lack of space.

The move to High Leigh was an act of faith: it was a *much* larger place to fill, but fill it we did. Not long after the move to High Leigh, the waiting list re-appeared. Many have been the testimonies of spiritual renewal, healing, deliverance from evil, deepening of faith, etc., for which we give praise and thanks to Almighty God.

---

## My very first pilgrimage to Walsingham

My very first pilgrimage to the Shrine of Our Lady of Walsingham was in 1962, just after the parish church was burnt down. Because of the fire, all the villagers had to gather in the Shrine Church for their Sunday Sung Mass.. Father Colin Stephenson was Administrator of the Shrine at that time. He had taken over from Father Hope Patten. He had restored the Shrine while he was Anglican Vicar of St Mary's Church, Walsingham.

Pilgrim numbers going to Walsingham then were comparatively few, compared to the hundreds of today.

Supper was served in what is still called the pilgrim hall. Before the official pilgrimage proceedings commenced, we had to wait for those travelling by train to join us.

In those days, Walsingham had a station and a few pilgrims would come by train. Had the railway authorities known then how the number of pilgrims to the Shrine was to increase, as it has, they would surely have revised their thinking on the closure of the rail link.

On this, my first pilgrimage, in 1962, I was gratified to find that the large crucifix hanging closeby the Shrine Church, was known as the Hatcham Crucifix, in memory of Father Tooth, who in 1868 became Vicar of St James's Church, Hatcham, the next-door parish to St Catherine's, Hatcham, where I was born and baptised. He was to make a valiant stand for the Catholic Revival in the Church of England, and was persecuted for introducing High Mass to St James's. He was on the receiving end of dreadful persecution by a mob of extreme Protestants objecting to his Anglo-Catholic beliefs and worship, and at whose hands he suffered other vile behaviour.

Walsingham is a very prayerful place. I have been going to the Shrine almost every year since 1962.

## Chapter 32

# A MOST FULFILLING POST

### *Secretary to the senior chaplain*

After my *grand mal* attacks ended, my health was improving and I got a lovely job at the Anglican Chaplaincy to the University of London, as secretary to Prebendary Gordon Phillips, the senior chaplain.

This job really suited me. It comprised my interest in the Church, the world and academia all residing in the one job. I was involved with people of faith, students who had problems of faith and life, contact with the world, and a ministry to lecturers in the academic world.

I was in touch daily with one or other of the assistant chaplains, each of whom had responsibility for a particular College attached to the University. Fr Ron Swan was responsible for trainee doctors at King's College in the Strand; Fr Michael Marshall was chaplain to University College, London, and priest-in-charge of the beautiful Church of Christ the King, Bloomsbury; and Fr Peter Mason to a college in the East End, and Fr Ron Swan, with a ministry to trainee doctors, at King's College in the Strand, to mention a few.

Gordon Phillips was also Rector of St George's, Bloomsbury. The Rectory of St George's, at No. 6 Gower Street, Bloomsbury, doubled-up as headquarters of the Anglican Chaplaincy to the University of London. The office was a very relaxed and friendly house. It was such varied work. One never knew what the day would bring; or who might be the next visitor of the day might be.

I worked not just for Father Phillips but also with and for Sister Edna Mary CSA, of the Deaconess Community of St Andrew, all of whose members were both nun and deaconess. Sister Edna Mary was a lovely person, and great fun to work with and for. I think everybody loved and respected her, with her infectious laugh.

As usual, I never mentioned blackouts or brain operation at my interview. I did 'spill the beans' to Sister Edna Mary later, and went on to tell her about my brain operation. She was cross with me for not having said anything about this before. I don't know why. Maybe she thought she had been inconsiderate or put too much on me, but so far as I was concerned, she had always been more than considerate in whatever she had asked me to do.

Sister Edna Mary had just written a book on *"The Religious Life"*. She had it accepted for publication as a Penguin Original, a rare occurrence, and it proved to be a very informative and readable book. I must read it again some time.

Sister Edna Mary had cancer. I visited her in St Mary's Hospital, Paddington, where she died in 1968. She was 43, living just long enough to see her book published. I think the prospect of its publication helped to keep her alive. I missed her greatly.

Father Phillips went back to his beloved Wales to be Dean of Llandaff. A group of us went down just for the evening, for his Induction, in a mini-bus, driven by Peter Mason, mentioned above.

I received a very appreciative letter from Gordon Phillips, thanking me for the good work I had done at the Chaplaincy, which was most affirming.

With Father Phillips' departure from the University Chaplaincy, Ron Swan and I held the fort, for a while, at No. 6 Gower Street, expecting a senior chaplain to be appointed at any time. This wasn't to be, for whatever reason, and, much to my sorrow, my lovely job at the University Chaplaincy, came to an end, and the Chaplaincy, as a real entity, seemed to disintegrate.

The Bishop of London had asked me, previously, at a plenary session of the council meeting of chaplains, if I would agree to stay on until another senior chaplain was appointed.

"I certainly would," I told him, with an assuring nod of the head.

The bishop thanked me, but it was never followed up. Once again, something good was given to me, only for it to be taken away!

---

During my time at the Anglican Chaplaincy, Pope Paul VI issued his papal encyclical *Humanae Vitae*, reiterating, in great detail, the traditional R.C. teaching on birth-control, that is, banning all artificial means of contraception. *Humanae Vita* caused uproar in Church circles, not least among students and me at the Anglican chaplaincy.

My chaplaincy job at an end, I then went to work at Church House, for ACCM the Advisory Council for the Church's Ministry which advised the bishops on the advisability of Ordination to the priesthood, those who had been to the Bishop believing that they were called to be priests.

It wasn't long before bereavement confronted me. I told ACCM I'd have to leave - I couldn't cope with both. Anyhow, I wasn't really enjoying my work at ACCM. By the very nature of the work, it was bureaucratic, and I missed the spirit and atmosphere of the chaplaincy.

A World Turned Upside Down

## Chapter 33

# FIRST WIDOWHOOD

*Does one kiss a dead body?*

My entrance into widowhood was the next upheaval, along with the drama that seems to surround my life at every turn.

Derek was in Farnborough Hospital having tests for his kidney disease, a form of Bright's, to see if they could find the cause. They knew what was happening: goodness was going out of his body and badness was staying in. They didn't know why, so the condition couldn't be treated.

After work one evening I visited Derek in hospital and found him sitting up in bed, looking flustered and flushed, red in the face. Obviously, something was wrong.

"What's the matter?" I asked, not a little perturbed at his unusual demeanour.

"Mother's been in – she's just gone! She gave me this bottle of Guinness."

His mother had been visiting and causing trouble, and he was drinking the contents of the bottle. He wasn't a drinker in the usual run of things and, so far as I was aware, he had never before had Guinness.

Derek then started to relate all the derogatory things his mother had been saying about me: I was this, I was that, I hadn't done this, I hadn't done that, etc., running me down. How dare she! She didn't know me.

And here was Derek tacitly accepting what his mother had said.

"But you know it's not true! You know what your mother's like," I declared indignantly.

What presumption to say *anything* about me, for good or ill? She had only met me twice, on the two frosty occasions described earlier. I don't pretend that my housewifery was perfect. I was out at work during the week and didn't get home until 6.30 pm or later; and what with my post op. depression and Derek's schizophrenic outbursts, life was hard. I can only say, I did my best in difficult circumstances.

Having listened to Derek relating his mother's disturbing soliloquy on Rosemary's "shortcomings", as can be imagined, I left his bedside terribly upset. I went round to my parents' house, not far from the hospital, crying my eyes out. They commiserated, being all too aware of Derek's mother's reputation: how she'd made life wretched for her next door neighbour, my mother's close friend, Sarah, and the dreadful lack of maternal care for her offspring.

Round at Sunnydale House that evening, we discussed the new miserable situation into which I'd been plunged. When we'd exhausted the subject at about nine o'clock, we concluded with the inevitable – there was nothing more to be said or done. My father took me home. I had a cup of coffee and retired to bed at about 10.15 pm. I'd hardly had time to settle, when at 10.30 pm the phone rang. It was Farnborough Hospital.

"I think you had better come. Your husband's not well," the nurse told me. "Right, I'll be there as soon as possible," I blithely replied, not knowing how on earth I'd get there.

"O dear! I wonder what's happened!" I muttered to myself. At the back of my mind I had a shrewd suspicion!

I phoned my father. Back he came to pick me up, and off we went back to Farnborough Hospital. I'd guessed right – Derek was dead. He couldn't face life any more. I understood. His troubles were legion and insoluble. He'd had enough.

Back in the ward for the second time that evening, this time sitting next to Derek's dead body. To kiss, or not to kiss? I wasn't sure if one kissed a dead body, or not.

I kissed Derek's cold, lifeless cheek. It was a strange moment - I'd never kissed a dead body before. The Lord had taken Derek to himself; death was sweet release for him (and for me!). At least I knew that he'd died a happier man than when I first met him, not that that was saying much. He'd told me that he had never been so happy. Derek was 35, leaving me a widow at 29; we'd been married eight-and-a-half years.

I started my married life with a disagreement with an R.C. priest – signing away any children I might have, to the Roman Church. I phoned the local R.C. priest to tell him what had happened, and so ensued disagreement with another R.C. priest, at the end of my married life - cremation. He was adamantly against it.

I consulted a certain Father P, a less traditional R.C. priest, to get his opinion. Some while back, when Derek was in desperate need of help, I'd hoped he would go to see Fr P. for help. He never did, he went to Fr Glaisyer instead.

Fr P's advice to me was that I should have Derek cremated if that is what I wanted and thought right. Derek was cremated and his ashes are buried in the churchyard of St George's Church, Bickley!

## I move from Leaves Green

Grateful though I was that my Sutherland grandmother's bungalow had become available just at the time when Derek and I were to be married, but for this city girl, Leaves Green was 'out in the sticks'. After a late concert or meeting in London it was always a matter of great concern that I might miss the train in London and so miss the last bus from Bromley to Leaves Green. Now that Derek had died, I decided to sell the bungalow and look for something closer to Bromley. I couldn't afford Blackheath!

My parents helped me to look for a suitable place. Having looked at two or three flats, I decided on a lovely ground floor flat in Shortlands, near Bromley called Fir Tree Court. The flat was one of eight flats built on the site of a large old house, with a beautiful mature garden. My parents helped me on my removal day.

---

On the night I'd come out of hospital after my brain operation, I'd felt called by God to dedicate my life wholly to Him, but a certain event not long after my move to the flat put paid to any idea of becoming a nun! I'd had a short talk with the Reverend Mother of the Wantage Sisters, to test the waters and see how I felt about the idea. Reverend Mother told me to go and think about it. I don't know why I chose Wantage. I'd met some of the Wantage Sisters and they had impressed me, and maybe it had something to do with my great grandmother, who I knew well, who had been born and bred in Wantage.

I liked to think I could live the life, but I knew in my heart of hearts that I wasn't fit enough, with my epileptic condition ever hovering in the background. I could never have kept the obligatory rising at 2 am for the night

Office and then up early every morning for daily Mass – before breakfast, of course.

Having finished all the business of winding up Derek's estate, then dealing with the sale of the bungalow and the purchase of the flat, I could relax at last, and enjoy my lovely new flat. It overlooked this spacious garden surrounded by beautiful trees, but living alone was a mixed blessing.

In the event, the decision I had to make was taken out of my hands. One morning I had a rude awakening, suddenly finding myself overwhelmed by an explosion of sexual desire. I'd never experienced anything like it before. It was torment. Sex had had a low priority in my marriage and by silent mutual agreement the matter was never discussed. In those days, the topic was hardly *ever* mentioned. After a tiring day's work and journey down from London we returned home, only to be weighed down by problems galore!

What cruel irony: I was now a widow! And here I was, with yet another problem, unexpected, unwanted and uncalled for. Certainly, it ruined any idea of becoming a nun. I, in *limbo*, endured torture, day after day, month after month, year after year. The Christian belief is that sex is for marriage and to this belief I remained steadfast. Temptations there were, but I was victorious.

---

I was working in a solicitor's office near to the Inner Temple. I enjoyed walking through the hushed legal world of the Inner Temple, along the little alleyways, through the ancient squares where members of the legal profession have their chambers, and past the Temple Church; one is taken back into history. The silence of this unspoiled area is profound. It is difficult to realise that the busy, traffic-filled bustle of Fleet Street is so closeby.

Back to my desperate situation, I felt I must go to church in my lunch hour and spend time with God. I decided to go to St Mary-le-Strand, situated in the middle of the Strand. I had passed it many times on the No. 11 bus, but never before had I been inside. I mounted the stone steps just as Father T, the Rector, was by the door, saying goodbye to members of the congregation after the mid-day Mass. I hadn't intended speaking to him or anyone else. I didn't know him, but felt moved to ask him if I could have a word.

We sat in the vestry and I tried, falteringly, and with downcast eyes, to convey my problem. Unaccustomed as I was to speak of such intimate things, I falteringly managed to convey my story, ending with "… and here I am, a widow!" He listened sympathetically to my distress. The upshot was his suggestion that I contact the Heather Jenner Marriage Bureau in Bond Street. I was taken aback by this unexpected advice - but was most grateful.

"Thank you very much for the suggestion. I'll think about it," I said sheepishly and with an embarrassed half-smile. "Now, I must get back to the office. This is my lunch hour." I left, determined to make the phone call.

His very suggestion was liberating! I took courage in both hands, and rang Miss Jenner. She invited me to go for an interview. I'd never embarked on anything like this before! Well, I thought, I might meet someone suitable, I might not… but, yes, I just *might*. Who could tell? The very possibility kept me going and gave me hope.

What would we do without hope? Hope is one of the theological virtues, along with faith and love.

Even when all is dark and desolate, there is always hope.

A World Turned Upside Down

## Chapter 34

# WIDOW MEETS WIDOWER

### *Overwhelmed by love*

Early in 1970, I received a phone call. A kindly-sounding gentleman on the other end of the line greeted me. His name was Stanley Pays. We spoke for a while on the 'phone and he suggested that we should meet. We agreed on an evening and that he should come to my Fir Tree Court flat.

Stan arrived, understandably a little nervous, not knowing who or what he was going to find on the other side. I, likewise, hesitatingly opened the door, not knowing whom *I* would find on the other side.

I welcomed my visitor in, introducing myself, and invited him into the living room. So commenced a fascinating conversation. What a lot we had in common!

We could have talked for hours. For a start, we both came from the same part of South-East London. In fact, he had grown up in Kitto Road, just round the corner from where I was born in Erlanger Road. Incredible! It transpired he had gone to Aske's Boys' School at the top of Jerningham Road; my mother had gone to Aske's Girls' School at the foot of the same road.

We shared a deep appreciation of classical music, a love that we had both found for ourselves in our teens. Most importantly, we bonded spiritually in our discipleship of Jesus Christ.

On learning of his love of classical music I put on a 45 rpm record of the two Papageno arias from Mozart's 'The Magic Flute'. I loved these two arias, and still do. I'd played them on several occasions when various friends came for coffee. Each time, I'd proudly informed the friend that the singer was the baritone, Dietrich Fischer-Diskau, assuming they'd be sure to know the name, he was so well known. Not one ever did! I had tired of this non-recognition of the singer, and not knowing how knowledgeable about music my visitor was, and not wishing to embarrass him, I put on the record and said nothing about the illustrious singer. To my utter surprise, Stan suddenly asked, "Is this Dietrich Fischer-Diskau?" Such was his knowledge of classical music! We *were* on the same wavelength, in yet another aspect of life.

There the similarity ended. Stan's learning was prodigious. He had attended the local primary school in Waller Road, Hatcham, the parallel road to the west of Erlanger Road. He was the first pupil from that ordinary State school to get a scholarship to Haberdashers' Aske's. Academically, Stan had excelled, especially at Maths and English Literature, not to mention chess. But he seemed to excel at almost everything else, too, – except sport, and, on his own admission, he didn't excel in the realm of the practical. Stan was a costs accountant by profession. His mother had taught him to play chess; he belonged to the Aske's chess club and taught many other pupils how to play chess. He should have gone to university but circumstances had not permitted it.

Our conversation that evening could have gone on and on, but time ran out. Stan was a widower with two little girls. He had to get back home to relieve the babysitter minding his two daughters, and he had to run the babysitter home. In one evening what we had in common was stunning. We agreed to meet again.

The first time I met his two daughters, Marian and Joanna, at their Orpington home was the day of Joanna's sixth birthday, in June, and she was having a party. The party over, I was introduced to Joan, Stan's cousin's daughter, who had courageously run the party for him and Joanna's ten-year-old sister, Marian. I seemed to take to them straightaway, and they to me. It was love at first sight, you could say.

I told Stan about St George's, Bickley, my spiritual home, where I went every Sunday morning to High Mass. He was otherwise committed on a Sunday morning, teaching in the Sunday school at the local Methodist church, and he had two little girls to consider.

Later, I said to Stan, "It's Ascension Day next Thursday. I shall be going to All Saints' Church, Margaret Street, for the evening Sung Mass. You're most welcome to join me, if you wish. All Saints', the other church that has significance for me. Father Glaisyer had been a curate at All Saints', Margaret Street, but now, as Vicar of St George's, Bickley, he wouldn't agree to having an evening Mass."

Stan was delighted by the idea of celebrating Ascension Day with me.

"Yes, I'd love to come with you," he assured me.

On his return home from work, off we went to London and to Margaret Street, near Oxford Circus.

Stan had been brought up at Rye Lane Baptist Church. With that and his present involvement with the Methodists, did make me wonder how he would react to worship at All Saints'. I need not have worried. He was so appreciative of Anglican liturgical worship: the music, the choir singing, the set parts in Latin, the ceremonial – even the incense. All of that was new to him but, praise the Lord, he felt at home and realised,

"The Liturgy will enable me to fulfil the contemplative side of my life, which, quite frankly, the Non-Conformist hymn and prayer sandwich services don't permit."

We passed through the gateway of All Saints' after the Mass and turned right into Margaret Street. I was in for a surprise. Stan turned to me and popped the question, "Will you marry me?"

I gasped silently! I wasn't expecting that. For a moment I was lost for words. I had to get my breath back as we walked along Margaret Street to the underground. We hadn't known each other that long.

"Yes!" I replied, a bit hastily. Still taken aback and not quite sure if I'd said the right thing. The realisation hit me: I'd be responsible for his two dear little girls! As a new mummy, what was I letting myself in for? Could I cope? Yet, deep down, I hoped I'd made the right decision. Stan was overjoyed.

During our courtship, and after, we frequently went back to Hatcham to visit Stan's mother.

"You are 200 per cent approved of by Mother," Stan told me.

This was welcome news for him. Stan told me how Susie, his late wife, had never gained his mother's approval. Stan couldn't explain why: "Susie did her level best to please her mother-in-law," he commented sadly, shaking his head. "However hard Susie tried, she never managed to do so."

He was so relieved that it was otherwise, with me. The relief was mutual. As may be imagined, to have the approval of my mother-in-law was welcome news for me, too, in view of *my* previous experience!

The two girls' spontaneous acceptance of me was almost embarrassing; it was only six months since the death of their natural mother. Stan, the two girls and I were a quartet of love in a most wonderful way – almost too good to be true. But it *was* true and it was wonderful!

On our various sorties in the car, I sat in the back seat with Marian and Joanna, an arm around each of them, and we sang hymns, psalms and spiritual songs, to quote the psalmist – and some of the old music hall songs as well!

Widow meets widower – it sounds ideal, and so it was. We were all *so happy*. Two little girls without a mother would have a new mummy to love and cherish them. Sounds providential, and I believe it was.

Stan was deliriously happy that we had met and fallen in love. He desperately wanted to marry me yet, understandably, he was still mindful of his recently deceased wife. I knew Stan was grateful that his daughters and I got on so well together, but I was aware of the conflict this must have created.

I went to see Father G, my spiritual mentor, about my decision to marry Stan, a widower, and to take on his two motherless little girls.

"Are you sure you can cope?" was almost his first reaction. He was only too well aware of my previous troubled life: epilepsy, brain operation, and emotional battering in my first marriage. I understood his concern. Obviously, one can't be 100 per cent sure, but I was as sure as I could be and I didn't waver. Stan and I had so much in common, even to the point of both having had a difficult first marriage.

We went ahead. The date was arranged: the 11$^{th}$ July 1970. This time I was to be married in *my* spiritual home, St George's, and this time, by *my* parish priest.

Our wedding day arrived and the church was packed full of invitees and other well-wishers. The marriage service was beautifully done, as was every service taken by Fr Glaisyer. Not a little overawed by the crowd of witnesses, here I was, going to the altar for the second time. I was all mixed up inside when the consequence of my decision to say, "Yes" in Margaret Street hit me.

What *was* I was taking on? Maybe Fr G. was right! *Was* I going to cope? Perhaps not! There was no easy answer, and anyhow, at that point, it was too late. These thoughts crowded in upon me, giving me a nasty churned up sensation inside.

Service over, promises made and register signed, I walked back down the aisle smiling appreciatively at all present. My churned up inside was churned up no more.

The reception was held in the garden of Sunnydale House. The sun shone gloriously upon us as Stan and I welcomed our guests. It was a supremely happy occasion, with everyone so glad for both of us. Love abounded. The heartfelt love showered upon me by Marian, by then ten, and Joanna, just six, was overwhelming. They threw their arms around me ecstatically and I gladly threw my arms around them. My love for them previously had been dangerously immediate, but I had held back a little bit of myself until I was married to their dear daddy. Suddenly, Marian and Jo realised they were free to call me "Mummy"! And everybody witnessed it. Normally, I am not one to enthuse greatly about children. I expect some were surprised by my closeness to the girls. This was different. The final barrier was removed and now we were now free to demonstrate fully our love for each other. It was all *so* wonderful.

My vocation was, and still is, to help suffering humanity. Marian and Joanna fell into that category, but my decision to marry their father was my first and foremost consideration, not *their* lack. Nevertheless, their need of a loving mummy was a very valid part of the picture.

Love in profusion was showered upon me and I wholeheartedly reciprocated. I was happy but emotionally drained. I'm not complaining – it was wonderful – but I was weary. I had been without positive emotion for three years or more, when suddenly I was giving out love to three people, and receiving their love in return. I was overwhelmed.

---

I introduced Stan and my two new daughters to Walsingham when they were little and they both loved it. We each had a room on the top floor of the ancient hospice; each room was given a name taken from the Litany of Loreto. The girls were most amused to find that their new mummy was given the room called 'Mystic Rose'.

I moved into Stan's house in Orpington. Another unforeseen problem. Susie's ideas were not to my taste. Inevitably, the house was full of things that weren't mine: the pictures, the curtains, the ornaments, the colour schemes.. I could never say it was *my* home. But I had to live with all these non-me things. I hadn't realised previously how this situation would *so* adversely affect me. I'd assumed I'd have sufficient detachment to enable me to cope.

Anyhow, Stan had agreed we'd have to move to make a new start to celebrate our new family set-up, so I pushed down my thoughts and feelings and didn't tell him how badly I was affected.

*Overwhelmed by love. Marian, Joanna and me at Walsingham*

My flat in Bromley sold, and the search for a larger house began. Just at that time, the property market seized up. It was a sellers' market, so few properties were being offered us. All estate agents were sending out particulars of the same house. A suitable property, at the right price, right accommodation, right location, etc. seemed to elude us; and even when a house did appear to suit, it was snapped up before we'd had a chance to look at it. First come, first served. To be first on the doorstep is easier said than done, especially for the non-car driver such as myself.

However, one fine day the breakthrough came. We received details that looked hopeful and, as ever, from several agents: a house was for sale in the Hastings Road on Bromley Common.

On this particular occasion, I was on a bus as soon as possible after breakfast. The No. 61 from Orpington passed the property, which was near Locksbottom. Post haste, I got off the bus and on this occasion was first on the doorstep! The house was just what we wanted. At last! After two long years of searching and waiting.

The next hurdle was of a different order and was not far off!

I went out to do some shopping one afternoon in the warm sun, and as I was walking down Court Road into Orpington I had an unexpected encounter with the living Lord. I was a little wary, because in the past an encounter such as this had so often pre-empted a crisis.

"Lord," I asked, "what is it this time? Surely, not another crisis!" I was a little concerned. That evening, it happened!

Stan became very ill. I dialled 999. The ambulance arrived and off we went to Orpington Hospital. Stan had a temperature of 104°. Colitis was diagnosed; in fact, it was Crohn's disease, a 'close cousin'.

Stan lay ill in his hospital bed; *so* ill that the possibility of his dying was not far from my mind.

"No, please Lord," I pleaded silently, "I can't go through all that again."

Stan didn't die, but he remained in hospital for a fortnight, too weak for words, almost literally. After a few days I had to approach him for his approval that we purchase the house on Bromley Common. Stan trusted me to do what was right. Weak though he was, he said, "If you consider it the right thing to do, we must go ahead with the purchase of the house."

The decision was mine. Quite a responsibility. Deep down, I felt convinced that No. 248 Hastings Road was just the house for us. Everything about it seemed so right. I dealt with the solicitor managing our sale and purchase.

Stan, in his hospital bed, shakily appended his signature to both conveyances.

He got better and was duly discharged from hospital, just strong enough to deal with the move. Only just! We were settling into our new home when, six months later, he caught pneumonia. The doctor said he had to be confined to bed for four weeks before returning to work. Relief all round. He was living on Complan.

## Chapter 35

# SHATTERED!

### *I had a big hole deep down inside me*

Stan was a costs accountant, and on only his second day back in the office after his bout of pneumonia, I was at home when the telephone rang. The woman the other end coldly informed me, "This is Orpington Hospital calling to tell you, your husband has been brought in dead! He died in the office, or it might have been in the ambulance bringing him in to the hospital," she added.

Imagine my horror! I could hardly believe my ears. Thoughts of his imminent death had receded in the previous weeks, yet Stan had died of a pulmonary thrombosis – a clot of blood going to the lung. He was 42. We'd been married just two-and-a-half years! Yet again, something good was given to me, only to have it taken away.

Alone in the house, I replaced the receiver, aghast, unable to take in the dreadful fact of the matter. What a good thing I am not one for fainting! I've never fainted in my life. But this mode of imparting such information was cruel. Couldn't the hospital have shown a little more compassion? Shouldn't a policeman have come to the house to break such dreadful news? Of course, the woman on the phone couldn't have known that this bereavement was second time round for me. My first had been only four years previously; its very closeness made this announcement extra cruel.

Fortunately, I had sufficient presence of mind to get on the phone straightaway to break the terrible news to my parents, to close friends, and to Alan McCabe, Vicar of Holy Trinity Church, where we had gone every Sunday for the six months we had lived on Bromley Common. Then came the simply awful task of breaking the devastating news to Marian and Joanna, then thirteen and eight. It was one of the most dreadful things I've ever had to do. Their utter sense of shock matched mine, as we tried to take in the fact that their darling daddy was dead: their second bereavement in four years, as well as mine. They loved their dear daddy and still do. He meant so much to them. Day after day, we three shed copious tears, as did many a visitor – *all* were stunned by the news.

Here I was again, my world turned upside down; I was fearful, left with sole responsibility for two children I had known for such a short time. Up to then, their father had taken the lead in many aspects of our family life. For the three of us left, our new circumstances were unbelievable. I don't think I managed too badly, in my dazed state, though I say it myself. Somehow, I managed to rise to the occasion. The girls have never lost their faith and all three of us were in church the Sunday after Stan died, and every Sunday after.

Alan McCabe, our local vicar, gave us tremendous support. He took me in his car to discuss the funeral arrangements with the local undertakers in Locksbottom. I found myself sitting in the same undertakers' office as I had sat four years before, making almost identical arrangements to the ones I'd made then. I was so overwhelmed by the stark familiarity of the proceedings, I burst into tears.

Alan took Stan's funeral service: it was a real celebration of Resurrection joy, the sure promise of Christ's victory over death, the victory in which Stan was now sharing. It was what I believe a Christian funeral should be, and it was just what Stan would have wanted, showing forth the very spirit we Christians should have in the shadow of death, Jesus being the gateway to eternal life. I have not been to such a joyful funeral service before or since. Ironically, Stan's over-80-year old mother was present.

Alan would drop in frequently during the coming months to see how we were faring. I was grateful to him for his concern for us.

My inner self had shattered and I had a big 'hole' deep down inside me, a partial breakdown, and a state I had to live with for what seemed an interminable length of time. I walked round the house or round Bromley in a stunned, dreamlike state, endeavouring to do the shopping and deal with all the business that had to be done – the mortgage, the house insurance, the sending off of death certificates to the various institutions that needed a copy, etc.

I could still pray after a fashion, though not in depth, for the deep part of me had shattered. I was in a state of utter bewilderment and desolation, hanging on to God by naked faith. In my weakness His grace prevailed, as I sustained Marian and Joanna in their faith and helped them come to terms with the inexplicable. We never missed our nightly prayer times. Both, always willingly and faithfully, came with me to the Sung Eucharist every Sunday morning ay Holy Trinity Church. Never did I have to cajole them. For them as for me, it was the most natural place to be on a Sunday.

The two girls have never lost their faith in Jesus Christ. Both continue to be involved in the life of the church where each now lives: one is a Reader, the other, a Priest.

Before Stan died, it had been realised that both he and Alan had been to Haberdashers' Aske's School, Hatcham, and that their time there had overlapped. Alan was younger than Stan and, so far as Alan was aware, their paths hadn't crossed.

Then, one day, when Alan and I were discussing Stan and Aske's, the penny dropped. Alan suddenly declared, "Of course, I remember Stan Pays! It's all coming back to me. He taught me to play chess!" Alan kicked himself for not having realised that, while Stan was alive.

What would I have done without the many friends who called to commiserate? Dear Joan Scott from Holy Trinity Church was a wonderful support and a frequent caller at the house, on her way back from shopping; and dear Joan and Teddy Wood, who lived at Lee, near Lewisham, who often called in. I thank God for their faithful, loving, prayerful support. Joan and Teddy and I had some truly inspiring prayer times together. These and many other friends and acquaintances dropped in to see us; their visits helped to keep me sane during this dreadful time.

I hung a little poem, author unknown, in the hall, to remind me that God loves me and cares for me, however I might feel, and He knows about the desolation I am going through in the midst of the latest tragedy of my life:

> *"God loves, He knows, He cares,*
> *Nothing that truth can dim.*
> *He gives the very best to those*
> *Who put their trust in Him."*

Alone in the house, I would recite it out loud to help restore my thoughts and feelings when they'd got out of perspective.

When people realised the cruel circumstances in which I found myself, some have shown surprise that I didn't ask, "Why me?" I think that is a fatuous question. My response is, "Why not me?"

The only thing that I can say about the mystery of suffering is, "God's ways are not our ways." I don't pretend to understand. He teaches us something through our sufferings. After all, see what His Son had to suffer - death on the Cross.

The queries in my heart and on my lips were:

"What's the big idea, Lord? What *is* it all about? What *are* you doing with me, Lord?"

Chapter 36

# MY THIRD MARRIAGE

*Blessed for a third time*

**The Lord speaks a word of encouragement**
One night, I felt impelled by the Spirit to submit myself to God in silent prayer. In my brokenness, as I knelt before the Lord, I heard Him say: "You're going to get married again!"

Well, this was a real word of encouragement. It's not often I've been told this sort of thing. I quite understand how such a claim can be easily dismissed when someone says that they have heard God speak. (I admit, the rational in me has done so myself, when someone has used the phrase.) Some will say it's self-delusion, others, wishful thinking.

To hear God speak is a strange occurrence that defies description; I believe that it really was a word from God. But what was to come was also strange.

**Two further prophetic words**
Margaret, a close Christian friend, was another great support during this dreadful time. She would often call in to see how I was getting on. I'd told her nothing about this word from the Lord, but shortly after it had been given to me, we were in the sitting room, having a coffee and discussing my plight, when suddenly she gave me a steadfast, knowing look and with an air of authority said, "You're going to get married again!" I was taken aback and I told her that these were the very words that God had used when He spoke to me! Coincidence, you may say. Perhaps. But for me it was confirmation.

Two weeks later, I was in a Bromley restaurant, deeply depressed. I was talking to the woman sitting opposite and I told her about the latest bereavement. Our conversation continued, when suddenly she looked at me purposefully, and said, "You're going to get married again." Exactly the same phrase – for the third time. Surely, this was confirmation of what the Lord had said, rewarding faith with hope. What encouragement these words of prophecy were, in my darkest moments.

---

Again my life was to be turned upside down when, within two years, God's word was fulfilled. I met Robert Radley, born and bred in Radlett in Hertfordshire.

Robert is a committed Anglican, a Reader in the Church of England. Providentially, we met at All Saints' Church, Margaret Street. He is a Chartered Mechanical Engineer, then working for a firm of Civil Engineers, responsible for constructing pumping stations, making dirty water clean.

We were married in the April of 1975 in Holy Trinity Church, Bromley Common. Robert was willing to take on Marian and Joanna; both he and his mother were most generous to them, in so many ways. Robert's father had died only a few years earlier, so we were both in a similar situation.

I was so grateful for Robert's support, and very relieved not to be a one-parent family any more.

Robert's car journey to and from his office in Epsom took him across Hayes Common and Keston Common. After two years, the traffic was getting heavier and heavier, and his journey became nigh impossible.

Another move was on the horizon, not just to make his journey to work easier but to make yet another new start. This move was, admittedly, a bit too soon after my previous move, but I understood Robert's difficulty.

However, I could not have foreseen what a providential move it would prove to be. But that is another chapter.

## Chapter 37

# THE YEARS RESTORED

***"I will restore to you the years which the swarming locust has eaten…" (Joel 2:25)***

We sold our spacious, well-built semi-detached house on Bromley Common and purchased a gracious detached house in Sanderstead, South Croydon. Engraved on the hopper at the top of one of the downpipes is the date "1901", so the house is definitely of late Victorian vintage.

When we decided to purchase, we knew nothing about the local Church of St Mary, Sanderstead, and the ministry of the vicar of the parish. Nor did we know that the date of our move, the 4th March, happened to be the vicar's birthday, not that that holds any real significance.

On the Saturday after we moved in the four of us went round to the vicarage to introduce ourselves, and we met Fr Victor Julian. We were in church on the Sunday. In more ways than one, I felt as if I had "come home". St Mary's seemed to be an updated St George's, Bickley, but without the incense, a that point!

Just a fortnight after our move to Sanderstead, I went to Fr Julian to make my confession to receive Absolution – a spiritual cleansing. I had been to confession many times before and had always found it liberating, but on this occasion the Lord blessed me with an unexpected liberation.

At the end of my confession I mentioned my shattered inner self and the big hole deep down inside me, not because it was in any way sinful, but to let the priest know of my spiritual state. Without a word, he immediately went to get the holy oil and he anointed me, making the sign of the cross with the oil on my forehead.

In a trice and on the spot, the Lord healed me. My shattered inner self and the big hole deep down inside me, suddenly and completely disappeared. After more than four years of inner brokenness my prayer had been answered, in God's good time. I was absolutely thrilled by this healing miracle and was full of thanksgiving to God, and to the priest for his faithful ministry.

The Lord had definitely wanted to get me to St Mary's Church, Sanderstead. I little knew when we moved in, how the ministry of the vicar of the parish would turn my world upside down in such a wonderful way. What joy was mine!

I had prayed for God's healing, of course, as had many another prayed for me, and now, to quote C.S. Lewis, I was "surprised by joy".

No way do I dismiss the prayer previously made for me when, apparently, "nothing happened". We should never say that. I believe that something *always* happens when prayer is offered up, even if it may appear otherwise. Prayer is a big subject, but suffice it to say, as I said earlier: "God's ways are not our ways." Maybe it was meant that I had to wait for this particular moment for the healing to take place in the ministry of this particular priest, for I believe my healing was a moment of affirmation and encouragement for him too.

Being in the right place at the right time is a facet of being in the will of God. So it was that, unbeknown to us, we had moved into a parish whose vicar was actively involved in the healing ministry. I learned from him how *his* world also had frequently been turned upside down. His circumstances were very different from mine, but I believe that his suffering enabled him, spiritually-speaking, to enter into mine.

Sitting at the feet of Father Victor Julian, I learn much, and it proved to be the start of a new chapter in the general healing of my wounded inner being, furthering my hope of inner transformation.

Discernment of spirits was another of Fr Julian's gifts: he knew where every person was, in the spiritual life. When members of the congregation became aware of their priest's gift of discernment, it was not a little disconcerting that he possibly knew more about us than we knew about ourselves!

## I want to get back to in-depth prayer

On my second visit to the vicarage, I said to Fr Julian,

"I have come to see you because I want to thank you again for the inner healing I received. It is wonderful to be without that shattered inner self and that big hole deep down inside me.

"I'd like to get back to in-depth prayer. My ability to pray hasn't completely gone, yet I feel stymied and I need to talk about it. Now, thanks to this miracle of inner healing, there is space for growth, so to speak."

Fr Julian then asked me, "How do you pray?"

It was a difficult question to answer. I'd never before been asked to articulate that. I did my best to convey something:

"I try to empty my mind of everything and endeavour to concentrate on God."

Fr Julian understood.

"Wonderful!" I thought to myself. Here was a priest, blessed with spiritual gifts and with a real empathy with my spiritual need.

## We speak of St Teresa of Avila

As we discussed my getting back to prayer, Fr Julian then spoke of the writings of St Teresa of Avila and St John of the Cross, the two great Spanish Carmelite Saints. I knew some of their writings and have found them helpful, even if I didn't understand everything! Now I was being led into further depths of life in the Spirit.

"I feel a certain affinity with St Teresa of Avila," I added. "The date of my Baptism is her Feast Day, 15$^{th}$ October, which seems significant to me.

"Do read the writings of E. Alison Peers, if you can get hold of his books on St Teresa and St John of the Cross," Fr Julian advised. "He's well worth your while reading. Unfortunately, most are out of print…" The name of E. Alison Peers was familiar. I'd read one book by him but I hadn't realised that he was an acknowledged expert on these two Carmelite Saints.

"I had a Second Conversion experience, as I walked down Victoria Street to the office," I told Fr Julian, only for him to inform me,

"St Teresa of Avila had a Second Conversion experience when she was around 30 years old." I hadn't realised that. Interesting!

## We make Pilgrimage to Avila

Recently, I have had the privilege of going on a pilgrimage to Avila, led by Father Norman Banks, formerly Vicar of St Mary's Church, Walsingham, and now a Bishop. He was very much in the spiritual tradition of the Carmelites. We were permitted to have our Mass in two of the most significant places connected with St Teresa: The Convent of the Incarnation, where Teresa started her life as a Carmelite nun, and St Joseph's Convent, the first of her many new Foundations.

It was a wonderful pilgrimage – something I had always wanted to do.

---

## "I seem to be on a treadmill of suffering"

As the conversation with Fr Julian progressed, I said to him,

"I seem to be on a treadmill of suffering, with the epilepsy and all the other trauma that has afflicted me, life has been terrible. I feel as if I have missed out."

He nodded understandingly and quoted a verse from the Book of Joel: "I will restore to you the years which the swarming locust has eaten…" (The Bible, Joel 2:25). That really spoke to me. Aptly, It goes on to say, "I will pour out my Spirit on all flesh" (Joel 2:28).

Later on, Fr Julian had rightly discerned another aspect that was holding me back: an unhealed little girl still running around inside me, in need of healing. I was aware of this. He told me, I aareed. he had been through similar.

Having understood my non-discursive way of praying Fr Julian suggested that I attend the 10 o'clock Mass on a Thursday morning, and stay on afterwards. I agreed.

I was a regular attender at this Mass and I duly stayed on in church afterwards to do business with the Lord, for a further two or three hours, with Fr Julian my encourager, from time to time.

The Lord took me deeper into the presence of God, and Fr Julian confirmed later, "I think the healing you've been praying for has been fulfilled." Somehow, he knew, such was his gift of discernment.

## The relevance of Our Lord's Incarnation

I came to see on a deeper level the relevance of the Incarnation of Jesus Christ for us, His disciples; and that through prayer, our human nature will gradually become more Spirit-filled, that each might become a little incarnation of Jesus Christ. I came to understand the stress some put on the centrality of the Incarnation, rather than the Crucifixion, though the former cannot be realised without embracing the Cross. Possibly, this was partially the message of Bishop John Robinson in his book, 'Honest to God' (see Addendum 7).

A paraphrase of what I gave my mother to read on this subject helps explain my beliefs about the Incarnation:

"Mary, the Mother of Jesus, was the first Spirit-filled Christian. Why was she Spirit-filled? That she might bring forth Jesus Christ into the world. Christians believe Jesus Christ to be fully human and fully divine, the two natures inextricably intermingled. Jesus took, His divine nature from the Holy Spirit and His human nature from Mary. Jesus, the Word of God made flesh, dwelt on earth, tempted as we are, but was without sin.

"We women and men fall short of the glory of God. We are in need of the grace of God, as found in Jesus Christ. He is merciful and forgiving and He can redeem all the ways in which we fall short of God's glory. He will assist us in our desire to be more like Him. We come to Jesus Christ through the Cross not only for His forgiveness and His healing, but to acquire greater self-knowledge and so deepen our relationship with Him.

"Let us open our heart to Jesus and invite Him into our life. When we are ready, He will show us the parts of our life in need of His redeeming Love. Our life is a sacramental journey. Slowly, but surely, by prayer and inner healing we shall come to incarnate more of the Spirit of God, that by His grace we become wholly Spirit-filled manifestations of His love to the world. Whatever our worldly work, office cleaner or managing director, we are to be a little incarnation of the Incarnate Lord, that is the Christian vocation."

## Inner Transformation

Sometimes when I came out of church on a Thursday morning, everything around me appeared to be tinged with glory, and I seemed to be part of it. I sensed the Lord's transforming power taking place within me, whilst realising that I still had a long way to go. Our spiritual pilgrimage never ends on this side of death.

I have Father Julian to thank for my inner transformation so far. Of course, the Holy Spirit was the Person who actually achieved this work in me, but it was our parish priest who accompanied and encouraged me along the way. However…

A few years later, Fr Julian fell sick. The demands of parish life were too much for him and his spiritual gifts atrophied. One Sunday morning, as I knelt in prayer during the Sung Eucharist, I looked up at the altar as he was praying the Prayer of Consecration and I "saw" our priest, as in a vision, "falling to bits". That, in fact, is how it turned out to be.

Father Julian died in 1987, aged just 67.

## Chapter 38

# WANTED YET NOT WANTED

*The little innocent's nine months in the womb*
*My reins are thine; thou hast covered me in my mother's womb.*
*(Psalm 139.12)*

When does a person's spiritual journey start? I believe it starts during the nine months in the womb. I say this from personal experience.

One fine spring day in 1989 I was walking round the house and garden, round Croydon, round London, or wherever, overwhelmed by a peculiar sense of being wanted yet unwanted, both at the same time. Prayer was nigh impossible: I felt spiritually stifled, overlooked, unacknowledged, and, yes, unwanted. I was at odds within myself, ill at ease in the depths of my being, and helpless to do anything about it.

I'd had this horrid sensation previously, on and off, over a span of time, but on this particular day I was consumed by it and it consumed me. Fortunately, I was at home. I was feeling *really* ill, so dire, that I was forced to go and lie on the bed, only to find myself wriggling where I lay, undergoing the physical process of 'being born'!

I had been re-living life in the womb and re-living my mother's feelings of frustration about the many problems that beset her: feelings that unwittingly, she was communicating to me. (See Chapter 2)

This strange reliving of what happened when the Second World War was looming large occurred exactly 50 years after the year of my birth.

Imagine the confusion experienced by the little innocent within her mother, the outside world completely beyond the innocent's ken. I'm not pointing a finger at my dear mother's reaction to all the frustrations and difficulties that engulfed her, but her infant, soon to be born, was picking up something disturbingly not nice. My mother wished I weren't around and dealt with the situation by leaving my presence unacknowledged and, overlooked. In her heart of hearts, I can quite understand, she wished I weren't there, with the second World War imminent!

Now, of course, the little innocent is not so innocent, now she knows what it was all about.

Not long before she died, my mother quite openly told me,

"I deferred having a baby in 1938 because of rumours of war, rumours that had come to nothing." And, she added *so* definitely, "You *were* wanted." Did it occur to her, I wonder, that I might think otherwise?

Her frankness and openness surprised me. She wasn't usually able to speak so openly of intimate matters; and, in view of what was to occur, it was most affirming. At the time, nothing adverse had surfaced, but I am so grateful that she should have given me this word of assurance.

## The following is what happened next - 50 years on:

A dreadful confusion reigned within me! As I say, I was feeling wanted yet not wanted both at the same time. This assailed me the whole time, as I walked round the house, as I walked round London or wherever.

This was not just a question of feeling "out of it", as at a party, though it very possibly contributed to that feeling. There were more profound consequences, when on at least three occasions the frustration experienced had made me feel *so ill*, it had resulted in a serious panic attack.

This was the start of yet another inner healing (I will explain how that happened in the following chapters). I didn't share with my mother this overwhelming sense of being wanted yet unwanted. Frankly, I wasn't sure she would understand, possibly she wouldn't *want* to know that her unborn baby had been picking up her negative thoughts and feelings. And I am almost certain that it wouldn't have occurred to her that it would all surface 50 years later!

Those three words, "You *were* wanted", hold such significance for me. Understandably, the only way for her to deal with the situation at the time was to overlook me and try not to acknowledge my presence. I expect it was sweet relief for her to be delivered of me 22 days after the Declaration of War. Doubtless, sweet relief for *me*, also!

## Chapter 39

# IN THE WOMB OF THE CONFERENCE

### *April 1989, overlooked and unacknowledged*

I attended our annual charismatic conference at High Leigh in the April of 1989, and at one point I was feeling *really ill*.

I was a founder member of our Pentecostal Mass in Bethnal Green, and the conference was a fruit of our Bethnal Green vision. In 1989 I was the only person present from our earliest days, who was still supporting the annual conference. Numbers attending had increased to well over a hundred. At this particular conference, the chairman stood up and made a special announcement to the assembled gathering:

"We are now going to hear how this conference started from its small beginnings in Bethnal Green in the East End of London."

With that, a certain priest was invited to address the conference - he had been our first celebrant and we hadn't seen him for years. He had just turned up in this particular year.

It was well known that I was the only supporter of the conference still attending from our Bethnal Green days. Every year the attendees showed me much love and appreciation, but evidently the man at the top and certain members of the committee viewed me differently. Presumably they considered me unfit for the task of relating our history, something I was quite capable of doing.

Here I was, "in the womb" of that conference, so to speak, significantly overlooked and unacknowledged. I'd been feeling spiritually stifled for seven months of the nine in the womb, on the receiving end of my mother's fears and frustrations. Fifty years on, and I was still feeling wanted yet unwanted, both at the same time! Wanted by the ordinary people, yet evidently unwanted and overlooked by the 'hierarchy', at least by the chairman. Yet again, I was feeling *really ill*, physically, spiritually and emotionally.

On the final morning, as we stood at the front door bidding farewell to friends old and new from many different parts of the country, one of the priests discerned my distressed state and concernedly asked,

"Rosemary, are you all right?"

"I'm just tired, thank you," I replied with a wan smile. I didn't like avoiding the truth, but that wasn't the moment to enlarge on the real issue causing my distress.

The London coach set off from High Leigh and the driver dropped off his passengers, as usual, in Portland Place, around midday. I said final farewells to friends from London and the South-East, trying not to let on about my inner confusion, and we all went our separate ways. I decided I must go to nearby All Saints', Margaret Street, where I knew a priest would be available to hear Confessions. I had to talk about my devastation. I couldn't go home feeling as I did.

I fell on my knees, confessed my sins, and then related my confusion and devastation, and the reason for feeling as I did. The priest gave me Absolution and advised me to find someone with whom I could discuss the problem. Easier said than done!

No priest came immediately to mind regarding this rather delicate intimate matter. Father Julian, locally, was no longer available.

It was four months later that I was prompted to phone a certain Father X.

Meanwhile, in late August of 1989 I was booked to go on retreat at Pleshey, near Chelmsford, Essex. I'd always wanted to go to Pleshey because of Evelyn Underhill's connection with that retreat house. Evelyn was Anglican mystic, spiritual director and writer of 'Mysticism' – a classic on the spiritual life. She made Pleshey her centre for retreat-giving in the early 20$^{th}$ century, and this was my first opportunity to go.

Spiritual frustration started whilst I was at Pleshey. The retreat wasn't exactly what I'd expected and again I was feeling overlooked and unacknowledged. After two days, I almost went home. Yet again, I didn't know what to do with myself, and another panic attack ensued. I screamed silently from the depths of my soul, "Lord, have mercy on me. Deliver me of this unbearable confusion and desolation."

Little did I know, deliverance was at hand. My prayer was soon to be answered.

## Chapter 40

# A CONVERSATION WITH FATHER X

### *Friday 1st September 1989*

As I mentioned in the last chapter, I had phoned Father X to make an appointment to see him. The only time convenient to both was Friday 1st September 1989 – the day I returned from Pleshey, not really the most convenient for me.

As I crossed London with my luggage I was feeling *most* peculiar and not a little silly. I knew Father X only cursorily and, obviously, didn't know how he would respond to my story. I'd not shared anything quite like this with him before.

"What a fatuous traipse," I thought, as I made my way across London. "Why on earth am I going to see Father X? As if he can do anything to help! Quite possibly he won't know how to deal with an experience so obscure and intimate."

I arrived at Father X's front door and rang the rectory bell. He welcomed me into his study.

"Now, tell me, what's the problem?" he asked.

Falteringly, 50 years after my birth, I started to relate the wanted/unwanted syndrome that was, I believed, "my life in the womb", I began to feel even sillier as I spoke. My story sounded too far-fetched for words, too strange for one such as he to understand.

What relief! Father X seemed to accept what I told him, at least on an intellectual level. But empathy at heart level? I wasn't sure. If the matter were beyond his, understandably, real empathy would not be possible. However, after a pause…..he took a big breath, and to my utter amazement proceeded to share with me his own very similar experience: how *his* mother had also been similarly affected by the War, and how *he* too had been affected in his adult life. He had understood only too well what I was trying to convey: his empathy was complete. I was overwhelmed – it was almost too good to be true. Unwittingly, I had been led to precisely the right person with whom to share my problem!

He spoke of situations he found difficult to cope with, that resonated with me and helped me to understand the cause of one or two of my hang-ups, with which I had never previously made a connection. My encounter with him was truly providential. I thanked him profusely, and departed feeling very humbled that he had seen fit to share his own story with me. I look upon that day as the day the Lord's healing really started.

It was only later that I realised that the date of our discussion, 1st September 1989, also had an element of the providential: it was exactly the 50th anniversary of the action that had started World War Two – Hitler's invasion of Poland – the very cause of our respective problems.

To some, the idea of an "in the womb" experience may seem too fantastic to be credible.

William Johnston S.J, has written about it in his book, 'Mirror Mind'. He tells us that the mystics can also experience the moment of their conception! The mind boggles. I haven't been made aware of that – yet!

## A final word

I was visiting my dear Mama in her little flat in Hildenborough, near Tonbridge, shortly before she died. Quite unexpectedly, she commented favourably about my healed and restored being:

"Oh, I have seen a difference in you. You're so much better now; you're confident and self-assured; you're a different person."

With a slight, on-going nod of the head and an appreciative smiling look in my eyes, I gratefully received her perception of my enhanced demeanour. She had discerned the outward and visible sign of my inner, invisible transformation by grace.

"It's through prayer it's happened," I told her. I don't know if she understood the connection. With quick thinking, I added, "I happen to have one of my articles I wrote for the leaflets I produce for our Days of Renewal. I've got it with me. Perhaps you'd like to read it."

Hesitantly, I passed her the article, entitled 'Mary, the First Spirit-Filled Christian'. It wasn't the sort of topic I would normally think of showing her. It just happened to be the only one I had on me at the time. She read the article and looked up at me steadfastly and knowingly, and opined,

"I think we have underestimated you!"

I cannot tell you what that little remark meant to me, and *still* does. It was as if a little reconciliation had occurred. She was admitting her lack of understanding of me over the years. Yes, she *had* underestimated me. She now accepted the fact that I wasn't the incompetent dolt she had assumed me to be.

For some years now, I have not only been writing my autobiography but have also been researching my family tree.

The unexpected encounters that follow came about not through any pre-arrangement. They made the relevant parts of my family history come alive.

## Chapter 41

# THE NEW MILLENNIUM

## *The Queen lights the Millennium Candle*

It was New Year's Eve at the end of the second Christian Millennium. The year 2000 about to break. I had a ticket for a seat in Southwark Cathedral for the service in the presence of Her Majesty Queen Elizabeth II, who was to light a candle and formally start the official celebrations. I wanted to join the festivities up in London, but not knowing what was before me I was getting "cold feet".

The cathedral ticket strengthened my resolve to go, yet courage was ebbing low. I managed to gather myself up and I ventured forth! At Sanderstead Station, our local station, I was heartened when, quite unexpectedly, I met Quentin and Jane Spurring, our next-door-but-three neighbours, also bound for the Millennium celebrations in central London. I told them how I'd been in two minds about going and was still a little wary. Quentin and Jane were a great encouragement and, true to their name, they were spurring me on!

When the train arrived in London it slowed down, awaiting the signal to enter London Bridge Station. That gave me time to glance across to see The Tower Bridge as we passed by its southern end, and I delighted to see yet again that spectacular edifice designed by Horace Jones.

The Tower Bridge has emotional significance for me: both grandmothers were present at its official opening in 1894 by the then Prince of Wales, the future King Edward VII. Seeing The Tower Bridge go up still thrills me.

## The buzz of London

There was a tremendous atmosphere in London that night: the vast, milling mass of humanity was assembling to see in the start of the new millennium, and the crowds were growing. I bade farewell to my Spurring neighbours. I never saw them again that night.

I was alone, but there was no cause for concern, for the southern end of London Bridge was familiar territory to me. I made my way eastwards through the crowds and managed to find a space on the bank of the Thames, near The Tower Bridge. From there I watched the most spectacular firework display. I'm not a great firework enthusiast, but this display was fantastic.

After the fireworks, I wended my way back through the crowds to Southwark Cathedral where I joined the throng of assembled worshippers. I was ushered to a seat in the south transept to await the arrival of Her Majesty Queen Elizabeth II and the dawning of the third Christian Millennium. The sense of anticipation in the cathedral that night was tangible. Her Majesty arrived and she was seated quite close to me! It was a wonderful service and I had a good view of the Queen all the way through.

The climax came, of course, when the cathedral clock struck midnight and the Queen lit the Millennium Candle officially, to welcome in the Year 2000, celebrating 2,000 years of Christianity.

The service over, I left the cathedral and returned to the celebratory crowds outside: the hour was one o'clock in the morning! As with all good things, the celebrations had to come to an end. I managed to squeeze my way across Borough High Street, again encompassed by a mass of humanity all aiming for London Bridge Station. It was a very controlled, good-humoured crowd, as had been the case all evening: I witnessed no bad behaviour or vandalism and, to everyone's credit, there was no inordinate pushing and shoving.

I had been caught up in dense crowds in London before. There was the occasion when I and many others couldn't get into Cannon Street Station because of a fire in the Cannon Street signal box; then there was the Lewisham rail crash, as a result of which again commuters couldn't get into Cannon Street Station; and, lastly, there was the snow of 1963 that had settled unusually deep in the City, and remained so for several weeks after the snow had fallen. All these had prevented trains from running in and out of London, and dense crowds of commuters formed, hoping to get into the station to catch the train home. But these were as nothing compared to the numbers and the crush on the New Millennium night.

I edged my way forward inch by inch. We seemed to be making progress, yet the density of the crush around me seemed to remain the same. People inside London Bridge Station must have dispersed; at last, I managed to get on to the station concourse. There was no sign of where to go for a train. I wasn't even certain that trains were running, when an announcement came over the tannoy loud and clear:

"A train for East Croydon is due in on Platform 5." That was good to know.

Now I had to negotiate my way through the crowd-filled concourse and onto the nearest platform. Slowly, but surely, and some way along the platform I'd got to, I then had to make my way to the foot of the stairs; I managed to get up the crowded stairs, across the crowded bridge, and down further crowded stairs onto Platform 5.

I couldn't afford to miss that train.

With much difficulty I reached Platform 5 just as the East Croydon train rumbled in. It came to a standstill and I *just* managed to squeeze myself onto the train – it *was* a squeeze, too! Breathe in – tight! The carriage was bulging, seemingly to bursting point. No doubt every other carriage was similarly 'bulging'. Very gingerly, the train edged its way out of London Bridge Station, heaving under the weight; the carriage swayed and felt not a little dangerous! Presumably, it was deemed safe. No use thinking about it, one had to trust the driver and the good Lord!

I'm glad to say, we arrived safely! Hundreds of celebrators, exhilarated yet weary, descended at East Croydon Station, grateful and relieved to have made it.

The next hurdle was to manoeuvre my way through crowds of people hoping to get to the taxi rank – where I encountered yet more crowds! High was the demand for taxis that night/morning and high were the fares! I got in the queue, and as I waited I took the liberty of asking around me, "Anyone going to South Croydon, who'd like to share a taxi?"

Providentially, a young chap nearby chirped up, "Yes, I'm going to South Croydon!" We got together and agreed to share a taxi and, of course, the fare, not that we knew how much that would be.

When my new acquaintance and I got to the front of the queue, at last, a taxi drew up and in we got, trying to give the driver the impression that we were old friends. In fact, neither even knew the name of the other! The taxi driver dropped my acquaintance off in St Augustine's Avenue, and as he said goodbye he pushed a £5 note into my hand. The taxi driver delivered me at my house on the other side of the Brighton Road, and I paid the driver the £10 he charged. I never saw my young acquaintance again to thank him for joining me, and to tell him that his financial contribution had been exactly right.

Arrival time home? 2.30 am! What a memorable night it had been!

# FINALE

## An unexpected answer to prayer

I now attend St Mary's Church, Bourne Street, near Sloane Square, Westminster. There was to be an unexpected answer to a prayer of yesteryear, when a small group from the parish went on a retreat at Ascot Priory. I asked the priest leading the retreat if he would anoint me for the healing of my painful legs and back – I had difficulty standing – and for the depression it was causing me. He happily agreed, and at our final Mass he invited me up to the altar, where he anointed me with holy oil and prayer, making the sign of the cross, on my forehead.

I returned to my place, wonderfully immersed in the Holy Spirit - the depression had gone, and, I was silently speaking in tongues with a fluency that I had not experienced before. This brought me further inner release, and was an unexpected answer to prayer, made 40 years previously. Later that day, I happened to meet the priest and I told him, in whispering tones, what was happening to me. He seemed rather unimpressed! This fluency of praise to God in a new tongue continued throughout the day and for many days after. I thanked the Lord for bestowing the gift afresh on me, now with greater fluency.

However, in the train on our way back to London, the priest revealed his disapproval. He told me that speaking in tongues wasn't "traditional Anglican spirituality", implying that it shouldn't have happened to one such as me, - but it had! It hadn't occurred to me to pray for it when he had anointed me. I hope that my testimony of the experience might have helped him to reconsider his inflexible view on the subject; for, not only was I an Anglican who took the spiritual life seriously, it was he who had been responsible for the anointing. I might add, it was done very prayerfully in the Name of Jesus Christ our Lord.

I trust you have found my memories interesting. It was difficult to embrace every aspect of my life and to mention all the interesting people I have met over the years. I have not been able to include everything and everyone. I apologise if anybody feels left out.

I have to admit that many aspects of my spiritual pilgrimage have been difficult to write about - to do so has often been costly: a painful and saddening exercise. Fortunately, there are two sides to every coin.

The Russian monk, St Seraphim of Sarov declares that, "The aim of our Christian life is the acquisition of the Holy Spirit." To this end, I trust I have related something that has inspired you to deepen your faith in Jesus Christ, especially if suffering has been your lot.

## A Beautiful Flower

*Come unto the Lord,*
*Receive his embrace,*
*Lift up your heart*
*To the source of all grace.*
*When you stand in his Presence*
*In the quiet of the hour,*
*Pray that your soul*
*May unfold like a flower.*

*Abandon your self*
*To God's every demand:*
*His Will, it is sovereign,*
*His Word is command.*
*When humbled before him*
*Beseech him to shower*
*Your soul with his grace,*
*As a dew-sprinkled flower.*

*You are God's glory,*
*His glory is yours,*
*All spiritual gifts*
*He gladly outpours.*
*When your heart is surrendered*
*To his sanctifying power*
*Your soul will unfold*
*Like a beautiful flower.*

**Rosemary Radley**

# Addendum 1

# UNEXPECTED ENCOUNTER AT THE OLD BAILEY

*"When we lived in Marsala Road…"*

I have had several encounters that can only be described as "providential." There was my meeting up with Marion Syms in Ethiopia; the next one was meeting Josephine; then with Bishop Joseph Dadson; then with Father Patrick Phelan in the 'Pret à Manger' restaurant.

What follows was my first providential encounter.

As I was growing up I would frequently hear Grandmother Anderson say to my mother, "When we lived in Marsala Road…", adding some interesting and obviously memorable incident that had occurred. So it was that the name Marsala Road, Ladywell, was very familiar to me, but it was just a name. In those days I didn't even know exactly where Ladywell was. "Somewhere in the vicinity of Lewisham," I was told. If only I'd been a little older I would have been more able to appreciate the significance of my Grandmother's memories of life in Marsala Road in the early 20$^{th}$ century. I have since discovered the exact whereabouts of Marsala Road, not that far from Ladywell Station.

It was in 1903 that my Great-grandparents, Alfred Ernest Stevens and his wife, Caroline Maria (known in the family as Gramp and Gran), moved from Queen Elizabeth Street, Horselydown. With their son, Norman, and daughter, Alice Kate, my grandmother, they relocated to the 'fairer climes' of the Village of Ladywell, situated between Lewisham and Brockley, close to the Hillyfields, in South-East London.

Ladywell is so-called because it was once the place of Our Lady's Well. Sadly, the site of the Well was lost with the coming of the railway.

When my Great-grandparents were looking for a long term place to live they rented No. 104 Marsala Road, a three-bedroom Victorian terraced house.

Next-door-but-one, at No. 108, lived my 2 x Great-aunt Lizzie, my Great-grandmother's sister, both of whom I knew. I never met Great-aunt Lizzie's husband, 2 x Great-uncle David - he had died before I was born. Their surname was Price. They had two daughters, Elizabeth Ellen and Florence. They were known in the family as Aunt Bet, who was a teacher, and Aunt Flo. I had more to do with Aunt Bet, the elder of the two aunts, because she was godmother to both my mother and me.

I first met 2 x Great-aunt Lizzie and Aunts Bet and Flo and Aunt Bet's headmaster husband, Uncle Alec (whose surname was Mayer), not at Marsala Road but much later. By then they had moved to the little Essex village of Layer Breton, near Colchester. I was only a small girl; but I remember them well. To me, they all seemed to be in their dotage. 2 x Great-aunt Lizzie certainly was; Great-aunt Lizzie's daughters, were not quite in that category.

My reason for relating the above in such detail will soon become apparent.

## Visit to the Old Bailey with the Friends of Southwark Cathedral

In 1982, the Friends of Southwark Cathedral were booked for a guided tour of the Old Bailey. I was standing by the door to the Central Criminal Court, awaiting the arrival of the rest of the group. Also waiting was a certain gracious elderly gentleman, Mr Hills. (Fear not, neither he nor I were due to be in the dock!) I knew Mr Hills, by sight, but had never before spoken with him. As we waited we struck up a conversation:

"Where are you from in the Diocese?" I enquired, always an easy starting point among Friends of Southwark Cathedral.

"Ladywell", he told me, adding, "near Lewisham", in case I'd not heard of Ladywell.

"Oh!" I interjected, "My mother was born in Ladywell."

Mr Hills then told me that he lived in Marsala Road!

"Really?" I exclaimed, "My grandparents and Great-grandparents lived in Marsala Road when they moved to Ladywell."

"So what?" You might ask.

Mr Hills showed obvious surprise that I should know of Marsala Road and it prompted him to start reminiscing. He stood there, volunteering his memories of yesteryear, especially those of the family that lived next-door-but-one to his family.

"The old lady at No.108 would sit at the front room window, twitching the net curtains, watching out for all the passers-by. She knew all goings-on in the road!" he added, laughingly. "Their name was Price." My ears started to prick up.

Casting his mind back, Mr Hills continued,

"The old lady's daughter was a teacher," he recalled. "I think she married a man who was also a teacher. His name was Mayer: M-A-Y-E-R." Mr Hills spelt out the name very slowly, as if to make sure I'd heard it properly. My ears pricked up further! His detailed memories were getting intriguingly familiar -

"But that was pre-First World War," he added. "I mustn't bore you with all this ancient history, of no interest to you!"

Of *no* interest to *me*? I queried silently to myself. I could hardly believe my ears. His reminiscing was by no means boring. With every sentence Mr Hills' reminiscences were getting more and more interesting! I was incredulous to hear his story, as he mentioned familiar name after familiar name, familiar fact after familiar fact, all of which tied in with what I knew of the family. Everything was falling into place. With ears fully pricked, I let out an exclamation,

"But, *that's* my aunt – and my 2 x Great-aunt! *Their* surname was Price! I knew them both!" I replied excitedly. Everything was falling into place.

"The old lady next-door-but-one was my 2 x Great-aunt Lizzie, sister of my Great-grandmother, Caroline Maria, both of whom I met. I never met 2 x Great aunt Lizzie's husband, 2 x Great uncle David, he had died before I was born.

Indeed, Aunt Bet was a teacher, who became Mrs Mayer after her marriage to Uncle Alec, a headmaster. Aunt Bet was godmother to my mother and me."

Mr Hills then told me, "I was born at 104 Marsala Road in 1910 and I've lived in that house all my life!"

"Your house," I exclaimed excitedly, "is the very house where my Great-grandparents, Alfred Ernest and Caroline Maria Stevens, lived." 2 x Great-aunt Lizzie, twitcher of the lace curtains, of whom Mr Hills spoke, lived at No. 108. What a tremendous coincidence!

As a result of this providential encounter I made enquiries of Lewisham Council to find out details of the Stevens/Hills' tenancies. I spoke to a very helpful lady, who said she would look into the matter. She rang me back and informed me that Alfred Ernest Stevens and family had moved into No.104 Marsala Road in 1903 and had left at the end of December 1906. Mr Hills' parents had almost certainly taken over the tenancy from my Great-grand-parents in the February of 1907, two months after my Great-grandparents had moved out to a larger house, 53 Ermine Road, a lovely house near the Hillyfields, at a time when my Great-grandfather's business, as a Master Carter, was at its height. My mother was born in 1909 in No. 53 Ermine Road.

Mr Hills' unexpected recollections brought my family's past vividly into the present for me in a most surprising way and in a most surprising place – the Central Criminal Court of The Old Bailey!

Addendum 2 relates another of my providential 'coincidences'…

## Marjorie Alice Anderson is born in Ladywell

On 9th June 1909 my mother, Marjorie Alice Anderson, was born at 53 Ermine Road, Ladywell, near the Hillyfields. Her first memory was when she was 2½ years old (exactly the same age as my first memory). "I remember looking over the side of the pram," she told me.

I have a photo taken of her when she was 3 years old, dressed in her gorgeous Edwardian finery: she had a simply beautiful wide-brimmed hat trimmed with white ribbons, her long curly hair tied with bows, flowing out from under her hat. Her coat was trimmed with a fantastic large white lace collar and white-laced cuffs. Sunday best isn't the word for it!

The respective mothers of my parents were old friends when they lived in Horselydown. I was most amused when my mother told me how she recalled seeing her husband-to-be.

"My earliest memory of seeing Daddy was when *he* was 3½! I was 5½!"

---

I mention her birth in Ladywell, an area of South-East London. so-called because Our Lady's Well was there. My mother had no pretensions to be identified with Our Lady, St Mary. It is a strange coincidence that she was to give birth to me, at a place known as New Cross! An apt description of my life - the 'n' and the 'c' in lower case, of course! Only recently, has this occurred to me.

## Addendum 2

# COFFEE AT THE GRAND HOTEL, FRASERBURGH

My husband Robert and I were staying near Fraserburgh, researching my family history, when I had yet another providential encounter.

Robert, knowing my predilection for a mid-morning cup of coffee, dropped me off at the Grand Hotel, Fraserburgh, and left me sipping a cup of coffee whilst he did a reconnoitre of the town. Sitting in the coffee lounge in an armchair opposite me was a gentleman also with a coffee. A businessman, I'd assumed. We got talking:

"What brings you to Fraserburgh?" He asked

"My husband and I have been up to Orkney to see if we could find out more information on my Sutherland forebears, who came from Stromness," I explained. "I was a Sutherland before I married, and, of course, I still am a Sutherland!

My mother is an Anderson, and the Andersons came from Phingask. On our way back home from Orkney, we thought we would take the opportunity to stop off in Fraserburgh to see if we could find something more about my Anderson forebears."

I told him about our red book, as it is known in the family, entitled 'The Andersons of Phingask and Their Descendants', of which I am one! (Phingask is a village near Fraserburgh.)

"The red book was compiled in 1910 by an illustrious solicitor, who had had it published privately. My Great-aunt Gertrude Anderson had bought a copy, and she gave it to my mother years ago. It's a mine of information; we are fortunate to have a copy. I can't imagine how the compiler was able to find out so many facts and figures about the family history of the Andersons of Phingask and collate them so admirably and in such detail."

The gentleman in the Grand Hotel was interested to learn the reason for our coming to Fraserburgh. He would find himself even more interested in a few days time.

Our conversation continued, and he decided he should reveal his hand:

"I'm an Anglican priest, Rector of St Peter's Episcopal Church in Fraserburgh! I often come up here to have a cup of coffee. It's a good place to meet people," he went on to explain.."

I was aghast and surprised to learn that he was an Anglican priest in 'mufti' (plain clothes) – not a businessman after all.

"Oh really!" I exclaimed, "My husband and I are committed Anglicans. Perhaps we could come to your Sung Eucharist next Sunday?"

"Yes, of course, do come and join us on Sunday. It's a Confirmation Service too, so you will meet the Bishop!"

"Thank you, we'd like to come," I assured him.

The hotel certainly was a good place to meet the local Rector. On Robert's return from his reconnoitre of Fraserburgh I introduced him to my fellow coffee drinker, Rector of St Peter's Church, Fraserburgh.

I could understand why he went to the Grand Hotel to meet people; there seemed to be so few around in Fraserburgh town.

Robert and I returned to our B & B place and we studied the Anderson red book more closely. We found mention of St Peter's Episcopal Church, Fraserburgh, whose Rector we had just met, and it was clear that this was in fact the church where George and Mary Ann Anderson, my great uncle and great aunt, had worshipped when they lived in Fraserburgh in the 19th century. Later, George Anderson was to become Treasurer of the Bank of Scotland, for which he received a knighthood.

That evening, we studied the red book again to find out if this was the St Peter's Church to which Sir George had donated a window in memory of his father; and to which his wife, Lady Mary Ann, had donated the bishop's chair and the credence table. I had known previously about their gifts and was now assured that this was the right church.

Next Sunday, Robert and I were duly present at the Sung Eucharist at St Peter's. At the end of the Service, we went over to inspect the bishop's chair. The Rector came over with the Bishop to join us and I was duly introduced to the Bishop, as a descendant of Lady Mary Ann Anderson who had donated the bishop's chair.

The Bishop was absolutely delighted to meet me and shook my hand with great fervour.

"I am *so* pleased to meet you. Before I became a Bishop. I was Rector of

St Peter's, so I've known that chair for *many* years. Now a Bishop, I've sat on that chair so many times. But I've never before met anyone connected with it.

"Yes, my mother is an Anderson," I told the Bishop, as I pointed to the name 'Lady Mary Ann Anderson' inscribed on the Bishop's chair. "Lady Mary Ann was my Great-aunt. And she it was that also donated the credence table."

I went on to tell the Bishop, "Sir George Anderson, her husband, became Treasurer of the Bank of Scotland, when he was knighted. He donated a window in the church in memory of his father, who was a faithful worshipper in this church."

"I am so glad to have met you. Please, give your mother my kind regards," The Bishop added. He appeared to be over the moon at meeting me, and I too was over he moon by his welcome. We bade the Bishop and the Rector farewell, which involved another emotional handshake with the Bishop. I was overwhelmed, received like royalty.

All this because of a providential encounter over a cup of coffee at the Grand Hotel.

---

Of course, one of the first things I did on our return home was to phone my mother to tell her of all that had happened in Fraserburgh, especially the Bishop's delight at meeting a descendant of Sir George Anderson. Mother, of course, was delighted and similarly overwhelmed to hear my news.

Not long after the above encounter, I was to learn of another, but different, connection with my Great-uncle George Anderson and Great-aunt Mary Ann Anderson. I obtained their marriage certificate, which informed me that they were married in St Mary's Church, Queensbridge Road, Haggerson, East London. [George and Mary Ann were cousins. Mary Ann already had the surname, Anderson, so she didn't have to change her surname on marriage.]

St Mary's Church? – it was a new one on me. I thought I would enquire of the Sisters of St Margaret at The Priory to see if they knew the church. I'd never heard of it.

I duly phoned and spoke to Sister Elizabeth, who I knew well.

"Hallo, Sister, Rosemary Radley speaking. I'm phoning to see if you know of St Mary's Church, Haggerston?"

To my great surprise she informed me,

"Yes, certainly," she replied, "St Mary's used to be our parish church, just up the road from here. The church was destroyed by a direct hit in the Second World War. Why do you ask?"

"Well, I have just found out that my Great-uncle George Anderson and Great-aunt Mary Ann Anderson were married at St Mary's Church, Haggerston, in the County of Middlesex. I'd never heard of it, and certainly had never imagined that it might have been The Priory's parish church."

"There are only two Sisters still in the Community, Sister Beatrice and Sister Frances, who were here during the War," Sister Elizabeth continued. "Do come along one day. I'm sure they would be very happy to tell you all that they remember of St Mary's."

I knew both Sisters, cursorily. A date was arranged for me to see them and hear about St Mary's and the Sisters' work in the parish. The two Sisters were intrigued to learn of my family connection with their once parish church, and a most interesting conversation ensued over lunch. What the two Sisters had to relate was news to other sisters who had joined the Community after WW2.

"St Mary's Church was a very large church and very beautiful – it was a tremendously large building, and the Community was very involved in the parish." they said.

"The Sisters did a great deal of pastoral work in the parish, visiting the sick and the house-bound, running clubs for the elderly, mothers and babies, the young people etc." Sister Beatrice told me.

After lunch, Sister Frances very kindly took me to the square in which St Mary's Church had been, before it was bombed. She and I stood where the bride and groom, George Anderson and Mary Ann Anderson, would have stood in October 1870 before walking down the aisle to be married. Sister Frances and I stood next to the font, the base of which was still apparent, where the bride and groom would have stood, and Sister gave a short, imaginary commentary on how it was at George's and Mary Ann's wedding. It was a very moving short reconstruction of the ceremony.

## Addendum 3

# THE NURSING SISTERS OF ST JOHN THE DIVINE

The Community of the Nursing Sisters of Saint John the Divine is of great interest in the history of both the Church and medicine, for it was the first Anglican sisterhood to be founded with full episcopal sanction and support. It was also the first Anglican nursing sisterhood – involved with King's College Hospital and St Thomas's Hospital in the training of mid-wives.

In 1848 the state of hospital nursing was abysmally low. The women recruited were almost entirely untrained and were from the lowest stratum of society, often drunk and immoral. In their hands, the hospital wards housed patients drawn from slums of inconceivable squalor, with a reputation for filth, alcoholism and vice. As the wards were so filthy, no respectable woman would enter them. The problem seemed insoluble.

After the opening of King's College Hospital in Denmark Hill in 1840, the founder, Professor Todd, tried to improve the working conditions but failed because of the type of women employed. He came to the conclusion that reform could only be attained by religious discipline. But Todd was an Irish Protestant, who did not approve of any practice smelling of Roman Catholicism, and the very idea of a dedicated community was repugnant.

In his dilemma, he approached Bishop Blomfield of London, who informed Dr Todd that free religious associations of women dedicated to service had existed since the Reformation. Although faintly smelling of Romanism, Dr Todd invited the Nursing Sisters of St John the Divine to train young women as nurses. The Bishop of London became a co-founder and was their first chairman.

On the 13th of July 1848, the inaugural meeting took place at Hanover Square Rooms. Among those present were the Bishops of Norwich, Salisbury, Manchester and London, and Dr Todd's outline scheme was approved. The Bishop of London then set out a formula: "An Institution of Sisters, but there would be no vows, no poverty, no monastic obedience, no celibacy, no cloistered seclusion, no tyranny exercised over the will or conscience, but a full, free and willing devotion to the cause of Christian charity." The Bishop of London had enabled a Community to be founded within the establishment of the Anglican Church.

Sisters were received on six months' probation and were engaged for a term of two years, unpaid; indeed, they were expected to subscribe at least £50 a year to general funds. Nurses were to be respectable women of good character, willing to engage themselves for a term of five years. They would be paid £1 a month, after the two years' term was up.

It was laid down that no one should be admitted as a member of the Institution without a certificate of Baptism, as well as a certificate from the clergyman of the last parish in which she had resided. This had to state her to be, to the best of his belief, a person of good moral and religious character, a member of the Church of England, and a regular communicant.

It is little known that the nurses of St John's nearly succeeded in reaching the Crimea before Florence Nightingale in 1854. Fourteen Sisters and nurses had been trained. Florence Nightingale interviewed six nurses, and she accepted all six – a remarkable tribute to the improvement in nursing standards already effected by the St John's system.

For the first year back home from Crimea, and the Sisters joined those that had been left behind and were so busily employed in bringing order, decency and cleanliness into the wards that they had no time to oversee probationers, who were sent from the Middlesex and Westminster to gain experience. From 1857 onwards, St John's House regularly maintained a training school for probationer nurses at King's College Hospital. There has been no break in the history of that school, which is therefore the oldest nurses' training school in Britain, even older than Florence Nightingale's foundation at St Thomas's (by some four years).

During the 1860s the association with St John's brought great renown to King's College Hospital – parties came from all over the world to study the nursing arrangements. A deputation was sent from Russia. Czar Alexander II was so impressed with their report that he decreed the formation of nursing sisterhoods under the aegis of the Russian Orthodox Church.

Around 1859 a regular uniform was adopted by St John's: a purple and white check gingham dress, and black outdoor cloak and bonnet for the nurses, while the Sisters wore a full robe of blue, covered by a bib and apron.

The nurses' cap was intricately pleated and ruffled; that of the Sisters was plain, with bands tied in a wide bow. All dresses had a short train, the purpose of which was to prevent any unseemly show of ankles when the wearer stooped over a bed. Whenever the House accepted a nurse for employment she was awarded a bronze badge, and the Sisters wore a silver cross, both of which bore the Eagle of St John.

The discipline was strict, the work hard, the hours long, and the food scanty. Day nurses remained on duty from 8 am until 8.30 pm, and they were not permitted to sit down while on the wards. At midday, they had a dinner break of half-an-hour and were allowed a quarter-of-an-hour for tea at some convenient time in the afternoon. Breakfast of bread and butter and one cup of tea or coffee was taken at 6.30 am, and at supper one slice of meat or one slice of pudding, but not both, at 9 pm.

All the nurses attended the daily morning and evening services held in either the hospital chapel or the chapel of St John's House. Sisters read prayers in the wards.

The nurses cared for patients who suffered from typhus, cholera, typhoid and tuberculosis, often falling victim themselves.

In 1878, the 30th anniversary of their foundation, St John's was flourishing. But the Sisterhood then undertook a quite different type of work, when in 1880 their chaplain, the Bishop of Bedford, called attention to the need for help in the slum areas of Poplar, where later the Mother House was opened.

Today, the Community continues, albeit diminished in size and significance.

## 'Call the Midwife'

The Mother House of the Nursing Sisters of John the Divine was in Poplar, East London, with a Daughter House in Deptford, until the move to Birmingham.

Previous to the 'Call the Midwife' series recently shown on BBC television, The Community was almost unknown. Even in church circles. I would mention the Community to people, and hardly anyone had heard of it. Now, thanks to the successful TV series, most people know of it.

'Call the Midwife', first shown in 2012, is based on the life and work of the Sisters in Poplar. As a result of this series, the Community has been unexpectedly pitched into the realm of 'stardom'. The popularity of the series took the BBC by surprise; it was highly spoken of by so many viewers.

I wasn't aware of the first series until it had almost ended. In 2012 I visited the Community at their Birmingham Mother House, and the subject of the TV series came up:

"Our sudden rise to fame has taken us by surprise," Sister Margaret Angela told me. "We have been inundated with letters, e-mails and telephone calls from people all over the world, for whose delivery the Community was responsible. One man even wrote to say that now he too felt famous!"

I think I know what that man meant. When I went to see the sisters I described myself as "one of theirs". I feel part of their history and they are part of mine.

It so happened that my visit coincided with the final episode of 'Call the Midwife' series, when it was broadcast the first time round. It was strange to watch it in the company of the Sisters, and interesting to hear their comments on what we were watching, not that much was said.

*Nursing Sisters of the Community of St John the Divine in the habit they wore before deciding to dress in mufti.*
My thanks to the community for permitting me to reproduce this photo.

# Addendum 4

# ADVENTURES IN LANGUAGE

Since my school days, there have been several small opportunities to converse in French in England and sometimes abroad. I sometimes encounter French people in London with limited or no English. They are glad to meet someone able to speak French and who can explain how to get to Buckingham Palace, or wherever. I'm able to assist them in their own language, and am frequently complimented on my French. Some even assume that I am French, or that I must have lived in France - which I haven't.

My father always took the trouble to learn some basic words of the language of the country he was visiting. I find myself doing likewise.

I started German when I went to secretarial college and then at an evening class at the Regent Street Poly. Later, I learnt basic Italian at evening class.

In the late Sixties I was booked to go to Czechoslovakia and hoped to find someone to teach me some Czech. Providentially, I met a Czech Jesuit priest who introduced me to a Slovak lady, Mrs Felzmannova, who, very conveniently, lived in Bromley. She kindly gave up her time to teach me basic Czech. That has held me in good stead when I've visited Prague, Pilsen and Karlovy Vary, a spa town in Sudetenland.

Karlovy Vary is a beautiful spa town. *Not one* Czech person did I meet who was able to speak English – a very challenging situation. I don't know how I would have fared without my fairly good German and my very basic Czech.

On a recent visit to Germany I felt greatly affirmed when our German host asked me, "Where did you get your fluent German from?"

"*Nacht Schule,*" I told him. I couldn't say "Bromley High School," could I?

## I learn basic Albanian at the Koha restaurant

A few years ago I came across the Koha, Albanian for hearth, a restaurant run by Kosovans in St Martin's Court, near Leicester Square Underground Station. The waiters helped me to acquire some basic Albanian. Not only was that interesting in itself, it was invaluable when my lovely cleaning lady cum cook, Hasime Krasniqi, a Kosovan, first came to help me with the housework

She and her family had only just arrived in England when I met them in about 1993 at the day centre run by Croydon Baptist Church to help immigrants settling into life in England. I got in with a group of Kosovans, and one day a young chap came over to me and asked in perfect English, "Do you know anyone who needs help with housework?" This was Fidan Krasniqi, only 16, asking on behalf of his mother.

"Well, *I* need someone," I replied. "Who is it that's wanting to do housework?"

"My mother, Hasime, she's sitting over there," Fidan said, pointing to his mother on the other side of the table.

Hasime and Fidan came to the house to discuss the matter, and so started a wonderful partnership. Once a week, I was glad to have her come to do some housework for me and she was glad to earn some money and have the opportunity to speak English. When she first came, Hasime couldn't speak a *word* of English! My smattering of Albanian and an Albanian dictionary helped her to settle in and helped our communication problem. However, Hasime's English has progressed in leaps and bounds! What started as a smattering is now fluency itself. She is incredible!

She is a tremendous help around the house, in all sorts of ways other than cleaning – she's happy to do cooking and ironing, and even starting or unpacking the washing machine. She goes the second mile. What should I do without Hasime?

I help her financially, of course, and sometimes in kind, and I've helped her with her English. I call Hasime my wonder woman, not only because of her wonderful help in the house but because of her wonderful command of English, now *so* fluent and colloquial; her vocabulary continues to increase.

But, poor soul, her lifestyle is stymied because she cannot read or write - Albanian, let alone English. Her father wouldn't permit her to go to school because, being Muslim, he was of the opinion that 'girls don't need to be educated'! What a travesty! Now, the highly intelligent Hasime suffers terribly from her inability to read and write.

We get on so well, Christian and Muslim, we may be. We sometimes discuss an aspect of our respective beliefs. We don't let any disparity get in the way of our together-ness. I am not afraid to tell her what I believe. I have to leave it to the Holy Spirit of God to do the rest. By my love she will know Him.

A World Turned Upside Down

# Addendum 5

# SAINT TERESA OF AVILA

Teresa of Avila, a 17th century Spanish Carmelite nun, Saint and mystic, and, fairly recently, declared a Doctor of the Church for her writings on the spiritual life.

I was baptised on the 15th October 1939, which happens to be the Feast Day of St Teresa of Avila, though my parents were quite unaware of this fact. So, it was under her patronage that I was unwittingly received into the Kingdom of God. I have a certain affinity with Teresa of Avila, in spite of her very different circumstances: a Roman Catholic nun, living through the time of the Reformation and what came to be known as the counter Reformation.

The Carmelite Rule of Life, at that time, had become slack and worldly. Teresa endured many difficulties by members of her own Order, who would have nothing to do with her Reform. And she always had the strictures of the Inquisition to consider. The nuns and friars of the Carmelite Reform became known as the Discalced, i.e. unshod; and those who didn't embrace the Reform were known as the Calced.

In his book, "St Teresa of Jesus, Foundress" (P. 91) E. Alison Peers, an Anglican expert on St Teresa and St John of the Cross, relates Teresa's mention of flowers: that she speaks of carnations and thistles, of roses and the dry twigs of rosemary - I like to think she is not unmindful of this dry twig of that name!!

As stated above, Teresa of Jesus, as she was known in the Religious life, was intent on renewal of the spiritual life of the Carmelite Order. In a lesser way and in a very different state of life and circumstances, I too have prayed and worked for spiritual renewal of the Church in our own day. E. Alison Peers tells us (Chap l Life XL (CWSTJ, I, 289) "that one of the things Teresa thought about most was the spiritual progress of Christ's children, and this she thought about until it became 'the aim of all her desires'".

## Who does she think she is?

I share Teresa's desire, but do not presume to compare her depth of holiness and her deeds of faith and love, her spiritual gifts and her vision, with my paltry life; and, to be sure, I am no Doctor of the Church! But, as a founder member of a group involved in holding Days of Renewal in London and Renewal conferences at Walsingham, I too have prayed and worked for a spiritually-renewed Church. See Holy Spirit Renewal I & II, Chapters 30 & 31.

But, some might think, "Who does she think she is?" and consider me presumptuous to identify with this Christian woman acknowledged a Great Saint. It is, in all humility that I dare to declare a certain empathy with St Teresa of Avila, a woman who had mystical experiences, whose writings on mystical theology, have inspired me and many another. And it has also to be remembered that during her sojourn on earth, Teresa had to wrestle with sin and suffering just as we do?

Far greater presumption is that millions down the years to the present day have claimed identity with Jesus the Christ, the perfect Son of the Living God, in the hope of attaining to his perfection. "Be ye therefore perfect, even as Christ is perfect" (Matt. 5.48). The lives of the Saints encourage us on our way. They now belong to that part of the Body of Christ we call the Church triumphant. But even the Great Saints frequently found themselves on the losing side in life, yet their steadfastness led them to victory and into the nearer Presence of God. I cannot but believe that the perfected ones in heaven, having been this way themselves, now have prayerful concern for those of us in the Church militant, as we continue the struggle here on earth.

We are all sinners called to be saints. Union with God through his divine Son in the power of his Spirit is what St Teresa encourages the Christian believer to do. This should be our aim. At Baptism, we are given an especial Christian name that identifies us with Jesus Christ.

The instruction to be perfect, in St Matthew's Gospel, is understood with difficulty and few believers seem to take it seriously. It means, of course, that we must put prayer first. St Teresa reminds us that those who have no desire to grow in the Spirit, shrivel!

Such was Teresa's suffering, when after one particularly hazardous journey in her rickety coach, on the badly kept-up road between two of her convent foundations, she exclaimed, "Lord, if this is the way you treat your friends, no wonder you have so few!"

---

## Retreat to Advance

I am a firm advocate of silent retreats to further spiritual renewal. I have belonged to the Association for Promoting Retreat, the APR, ever since I made my first retreat in 1961 at the House of the Anglican Sisters of Bethany in Lloyd Square (since closed), near King's Cross.

A pamphlet published some while back was aptly entitled, "Retreat to Advance", a title that perfectly encapsulates the reason for making a retreat: to achieve inner silence and so deepen our knowledge of God and self. Silence is a valid and fruitful means of encouraging growth in the spiritual life. When on retreat we have to do our bit, but by the grace of God, our life will be transformed.

## Addendum 6

# POPE JOHN XXIII AND THE SECOND VATICAN COUNCIL

Soon after Derek and I were married, Giovanni Roncalli, Patriarch of Venice, was elected Pope. He took the name, John XXIII. He was almost ninety and, in view of his advanced age, was considered, rather dismissively, a 'caretaker' Pope. He was a humble, holy man of peasant stock, and he became known as dear old Pope John.

Ironically, although Pope John XXIII was an old man when elected Pope, he was no mere caretaker, but a man of vision whom many considered a Saint. He was concerned about much that had become anachronistic and irrelevant in the Roman Catholic Church. In 1962 he convened the Second Vatican Council, opening the windows of the Vatican, metaphorically-speaking to let in the Holy Spirit. It was called a Second Pentecost.

*Aggiornamento (Latin,* Bringing up to date*)* was the purpose of Vatican II, to bring the Roman Catholic Church into the modern world, renewing the Liturgy and reforming much that had become fossilised, especially in the life of monks and nuns. Generally, these changes have been most welcome. Renewal of the legalistic mind-set has taken longer to achieve, though that too has almost changed.

As partners in a 'mixed' marriage, Derek and I were grateful to have lived through the improved relationship between our two Churches, as a result of the ecumenical utterances made by the RC bishops at Vatican II. We Anglicans and other Christians were no longer heretics; we were now to be known as 'separated brethren'.

We have dear old Pope John XXIII to thank for the change in attitude of the Roman Catholic Church

A World Turned Upside Down

# Addendum 7

# WARTIME RATIONING

Shortage of food was a grave problem after the War, so rationing continued. It was generally assumed that the end of War would herald the end of rationing. That was far from the case! Between 1945 and 1951, not only did basic food rations *not* increase, it came as a real shock when, in some instances, the amount was *decreased*.

Increases and decreases in rations made headline news on the wireless; we listened intently to find out if the ration of such-and-such a commodity was to be increased or, better still, taken off ration altogether. The possibility that rations could be decreased didn't occur to people at that point. It came as a horrid surprise. I don't pretend to have understood everything, but I certainly knew if the news was good or bad by my parents' smile of delight or their woeful sigh of despair. Obviously, an increase in rations gave the grown-ups a great morale boost and their relief was communicable. It could be bad news and the parents' mood swung from hope to despondency: "O dear, things don't look too good, do they?" was the sort of remark my mother and grandmother would make.

Of course, I was too young to remember details of the rationing, but having recently come across the following, I thought its inclusion might be of interest:

"The Government announced on 22nd December 1943, just in time for Christmas, that there were only enough turkeys for one family in ten! A month later, 22nd January 1944, it was announced that lemons would be available for Shrove Tuesday at 6½d (*c.* 2p). On 15th November 1946, the Government said that food controls were to be relaxed, but bread would remain on ration. On 24th June 1947 the milk allowance was cut to 2½ pints per week. On 17th March 1948, the cheese ration was cut from 2 to 1½ oz per week."

Spirits were raised when, on 15th April 1948, the milk ration went up to 3½ pints per week. On 5th December 1948 jam rationing ended. Big deal!

On 6th May 1948, twelve extra clothing coupons were made available. Rationing of footwear and furnishing fabrics came to an end on 9th September 1948.

Then it was announced that the bacon ration was to be increased; and later, better still, taken off ration altogether – a cause for considerable delight. Rationing ended in 1951.

Needless to say, the post-war daily diet was monotonous. Corned beef was on the domestic 'menu' ad nauseam. I have an abiding memory of corned beef, corned beef and yet more corned beef. Mummy served it up in different guises, trying to make it more interesting.

Bananas were not to be seen during the War. Even when the War was over they were very scarce; they had to be imported – an expense the country could ill-afford. When bananas came into the shops they were quickly snapped up and only sold on children's ration books. [The first post-war consignment of bananas arrived in Britain on 1st January 1946.]

Bason's, the greengrocers at the top of Westcombe Hill, whose regular customers we were, would tell us in a low tone of voice when they thought the next delivery was due, and they would keep some for us "under the counter".

Compared with the tedious fare of corned beef, to me Spam was delicious. After a delivery, customers had to be at the shop smartly, otherwise word got round and the shelves soon emptied.

*On the beach. Can you spot which is me?*